BUDAPEST

BUDAPEST

A CULTURAL HISTORY

Bob Dent

UNIVERSITY PRESS

2007

OXFORD
UNIVERSITY PRESS

Oxford University Press, Inc., publishes works that further
Oxford University's objective of excellence
in research, scholarship, and education.

Oxford   New York
Auckland   Cape Town   Dar es Salaam   Hong Kong   Karachi
Kuala Lumpur   Madrid   Melbourne   Mexico City   Nairobi
New Delhi   Shanghai   Taipei   Toronto

With offices in
Argentina   Austria   Brazil   Chile   Czech Republic   France   Greece
Guatemala   Hungary   Italy   Japan   Poland   Portugal   Singapore
South Korea   Switzerland   Thailand   Turkey   Ukraine   Vietnam

Copyright © 2007 by Bob Dent

Foreword © 2007 by George Szirtes

Published by Oxford University Press, Inc.
198 Madison Avenue, New York, New York 10016

www.oup.com

Oxford is a registered trademark of Oxford University Press

Co-published in Great Britain by Signal Books

Library of Congress Cataloging-in-Publication Data
Dent, Bob.
Budapest : a cultural history / Bob Dent.
p. cm.
Includes bibliographical references and index.
ISBN 978-0-19-531494-6 ; 978-0-19-531495-3 (pbk.)
1. Budapest (Hungary)—Description and travel. 2. Budapest (Hungary)—
Civilization. I. Title.
DB984.4 D46 2007
943.9'12—dc 22   2007060033

9 8 7 6 5 4 3 2 1

Printed in the United States of America
on acid-free paper

Foreword

The stranger visiting Budapest for the first time in 2006 will experience quite a different city from one visiting pre-1989. Budapest is now what it set out to be: a major Western metropolis set on a picturesque stretch of the Danube, charming, beautiful in a gaunt, lived-in way that persuades the visitor of its validity as a proper city of the imagination. And so it is, though the beauty, the gauntness, and the lived-in quality would have registered quite differently in the last years of the old regime.

Budapest then was a city full of scars, its walls often ragged with bullet holes, its stucco dropping away, its statues missing arms or heads, its colours grimed, its elevations laced over with wooden scaffolding. Groups of ten to twenty men would be casually digging in the street or mending a roof. The shops you see now would not have been the shops you saw then. The cars in the street would have been Trabants and Skodas and Zastavas, not BMWs and Volvos. There would have been far fewer foreign restaurants and more home cooking in cheap but reasonable establishments. The history that still haunts the place would not have been dressed in hussar uniform, wearing a shako, but a beret, a cheap suit, its hair slicked back, looking somewhat cavernous.

Both histories are real, of course, only one is dressed for the carnival, the other is eternally in working clothes. Every city should be judged more by what you see above the shops than by what is in them, and the walls of Budapest are history's furious scribbling and overwriting. The walls are mad with activity: friezes, heads, garlands, the conventional forms of a myriad of architectural languages. Every building is its own monument. There is little restraint, little self-effacement. Instead there is a continual talking, as there is in Hungarian society, which is given to monologues and flourishes. It is a small country making big gestures, if only to create some elbow-room within its isolated language and shrunken borders.

When I was a seven-year-old child I knew little directly but for our street, the nearby major roads, the City Park, the trams, and the peculiar, overwhelming boskiness and precipitousness of the far side of the river.

We lived in Pest, a slowly rising plain covered in streets echoing Milan, Paris, Berlin, Vienna—not that I knew that then, though now I do. Those streets were natural landscape to me as they were to most of the inhabitants. Life was straight and perpendicular, rising like enormous theatrical curtains on either side of us. We could duck into courtyards and sense the silence of an interior world that seemed to be holding its breath, then gently opening onto creaks of doors, distant radios, someone shaking out a tablecloth on the third floor, and a perfectly neat square of sky—one the lodgers there considered their own—clamped over it like a breathing, transparent lid. It is more difficult to enter courtyards now; combination locks and swipe-cards speak of insurance brokers and burglaries.

Buda, on the other side of the river, consisted—and still does—of thick foliage, cobbles, steps and vast, utterly fantastical villas. Old Hungarian stories tell of the spinning castle set on a vast duck's foot, replete with fabulous wealth, leisure, parties, whispers and intrigues. These opulent nineteenth- and early twentieth-century villas that were privately owned before communism were subdivided into apartments after 1948. A good friend now lives in an apartment in a smaller, humbler villa in Buda, the potted history of the house being illustrative of Hungarian life at ground-level.

It was built in the 1920s for a well-known poet and journalist, a short Jewish man who kept a diary. He married an actress and they took on the minimal staff of a housekeeper and an odd-job man/gardener, both of peasant background up from villages. In the latter days of the war a detachment of fascist militia broke into the house, robbed the couple, made the poet dig his own grave in the garden and shot him. After the war, when the house was split into three apartments, the widow took one of them, along with the housekeeper and the gardener. When she died the place passed to the housekeeper who allowed the gardener to stay on in a small room. We met them both in the mid-eighties, she a sturdy woman still respectful of gentlefolk, and he a wizened tiny figure full of smiles and curses, his closest friend an ailing elderly dog. He'd sleep in the garden in the heat of August, having trimmed the edges with a tiny pair of secateurs. The dog died, and so did he. The old woman sold the apartment by an arrangement that allowed her to live in it until she herself died (a not uncommon arrangement in Hungary) and still enjoy the profits of the sale. She bought a lot of jewellery and a colour television. Never having watched television before she assumed the people on it were there in her room, and that a late night newsreader had fallen in love with her, so she put on lipstick, garnished herself with jewels and communed with him. When she died the apartment was bought by a small foreign business who established an office there, while maintaining a bedroom and some domestic comforts. Then the business moved away, and then... and then. *And then* is the story, the longest part of it inhabited by the old servants.

Meanwhile, back in Pest in the 1980s there was samizdat literature, liberal thinking within tight cultural frames, and elements of old turn-of-the-century Pest being revived and conserved and made a point of pride. Old lamp-posts were relocated, wooden cobbles relaid, the great tenements repainted (though turning grimy again in a couple of years because of the pollution from all those Trabants and Zastavas.) It was as if the country were waiting for something to happen that never would.

And then it did happen. In 1988 Jánor Kádár, who had run the place since the failed revolution of 1956, was removed from office. Gorbachev had proclaimed *glasnost* and *perestroika* and everything was strangely and uncertainly up for grabs. All through 1989 there were articles, associations, proclamations, arguments, interviews and marches following on each other's heels at a dizzying pace. Then a minister used the word "revolution" rather than "counter-revolution" to describe 1956, almost in passing, and there was no turning back. Within less than a year Hungary, like most of its fellow members of the Warsaw Pact, had popped out and wouldn't be back.

It is well worth remembering this when walking around Budapest. It is still, at the time of writing, a city in post-traumatic condition, half elated, half terrified. The houses are wearing their new clothes of paint, the statues and friezes have recovered lost limbs and heads, the battle against grime is making progress, but this is all skin, skin and apparel. History is written on individual bones, and it is those bones that hold together the nervous system that produces the houses, streets and parks, the trams, buses and metros that constitute the physical landscape. Everything is interim here and always has been.

And yet it is beautiful, quite ravishingly, humanly, slightly overweeningly beautiful, as human beings can be; an overweeningness humbled by time and the ferocious moods history sometimes gets itself into. But humility is not its natural key. It doesn't play at prettiness, it prefers grandeur, faded, beaten about grandeur. That is its great glory.

George Szirtes

Preface

The chapters in this book are mainly focused on locations—streets, squares and areas in Budapest—and the stories they tell about the city, its history and culture. A number of intermediary chapters are thematic, notably those on the city's cafés, its baths, its food and its folk/jazz/gypsy music. The chapters can be read in any order.

In line with the aim of the series, this book introduces Budapest's present-day identity and its links with the past. The historical parts accordingly concentrate on the past two centuries, since it is the events and developments of the past two hundred years which have most firmly contributed to the city's character. Indeed, Budapest as a unified capital city emerged only as recently as 1873. Nevertheless, earlier historical periods have not been ignored, for example the Roman era of two millennia ago, the high point of Hungarian medieval culture during the fifteenth-century era of King Matthias, and the period of Ottoman domination from the mid-sixteenth to the late-seventeenth century.

Certain relatively recent key dates, turning points and significant periods are often referred to in the text. The following is a brief outline of these twists and turns in the history of Hungary and of Budapest

In Brief

The second quarter of the nineteenth century in Hungary is known as the Reform Period. It was an age of national and cultural revival. In March 1848, reflecting revolts against absolutism elsewhere in Europe, there was a rebellion against Habsburg domination of Hungary, which spilled over into a War of Independence. The Hungarians were defeated and the following years were marked by severe repression. In 1867, however, there occurred the so-called Compromise, whereby Hungary gained a large degree of autonomy within the Habsburg Empire, the name of which, reflecting the new realities, was officially changed to Austro-Hungarian Dual Monarchy.

1873 saw the administrative unification of the formerly separate townships of Pest, on the left bank of the Danube, Buda across the river, and Óbuda, or Old Buda, an area on the right bank to the north of Buda. Thus was born Budapest.

At the end of the First World War, the Dual Monarchy collapsed, there was a democratic revolution in Budapest and Hungary became independent. On 21 March 1919 a communist-dominated, Bolshevik-style Council Republic was established, which lasted 133 days. This was quickly followed by a right-wing counter-revolution under the leadership of Miklós Horthy, who remained the titular head of Hungary for the next quarter century. The inter-war period is thus often referred to as the Horthy era.

One of the main characteristics of the Horthy era was irredentism (the term originated in nineteenth-century Italy), the demand for a revision of the 1920 Treaty of Trianon, which was part of the post-1918 Versailles peace settlement. Under the terms of the treaty Hungary, as a defeated nation, was forced to accept the loss of two-thirds of its pre-war territory and half of its former citizens, though the majority of these were non-Hungarians: Slovaks, Serbs, Romanians and others.

Hungary joined the Second World War as an ally of Germany following the latter's invasion of the Soviet Union in June 1941. In March 1944 Hitler sent troops to occupy Hungary, fearing that his unreliable ally might change sides. Seven months later, in mid-October, Horthy was overthrown by the Arrow Cross, the Hungarian fascists. The Soviet army finally cleared Budapest of German forces and their Hungarian allies in February 1945. A period of coalition government was followed in 1948–9 by the establishment of a one-party, Stalinist police state, which lasted in its intensity until the death of Stalin in 1953.

All the major events of the 1956 Hungarian uprising took place in Budapest. Following its suppression the country was headed by János Kádár, who turned out to be one of the longest-serving political rulers of Eastern Europe, losing office only in 1988. His period, which witnessed a process leading from initial repression to eventual liberalization, is often referred to as the Kádár era.

Hungary's political changes of 1989 were peaceful, the most symbolic event of that year being the re-burial ceremony in Budapest of Imre Nagy, the prime minister during the 1956 uprising who was subsequently executed. 1990 witnessed a general election under a multiparty system, the first for many years. On the economic front the 1990s witnessed an acceleration of market reforms already underway in the previous decade and a relatively speedy process of privatization.

A Cautionary Note

Hungary is a very centralized country, Budapest being not only the political but also the economic and cultural capital. At the same time, about eighty per cent of Hungary's citizens live outside the capital in villages and towns, the largest of which is only just over one-tenth the size of Budapest, in terms of population. If only for this reason, provincial Hungary is a world somewhat different from metropolitan Hungary, and while that difference is certainly being reduced there still remains a certain tension (sometimes generated by politicians for their own purposes) between the provinces and the capital. At times the differences have been reflected in literature and intellectual debate, generating schools of "populists" and "urbanists". It should be borne in mind, therefore, that this book is essentially about Budapest, rather than about Hungary.

Names and Terminology

In Hungarian surnames come first (thus Kovács János, the equivalent of Smith John in English). In the text the English order is used, though not in the case of names of streets and squares, which are often named after a person. With a handful of exceptions, the Hungarian terminology found on maps and street-name plaques is used (utca = street, út = road, tér = square).

The word "Magyar" is Hungarian for "Hungarian". The term "the Magyars" is often employed to refer to the ancient Hungarians who, migrating from the east, settled in the Carpathian Basin towards the end of the ninth century. It is also sometimes used to designate ethnic Hungarians, as opposed to other Hungarian citizens of non-Hungarian ethnicity.

For Kati—without whom it wouldn't have happened

Contents

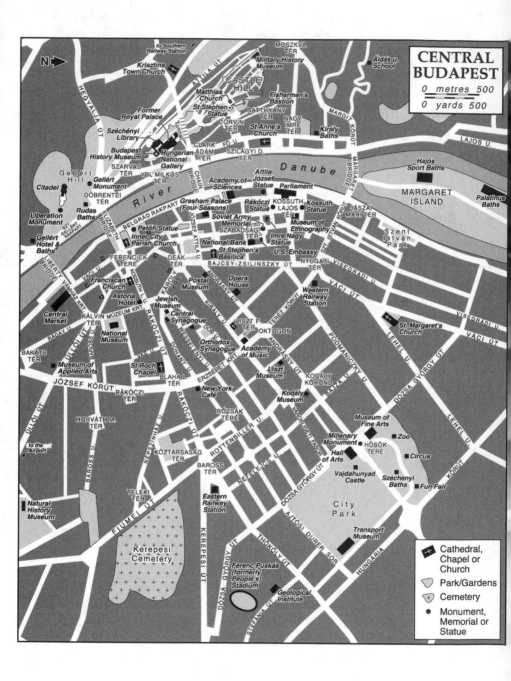

CENTRAL BUDAPEST

0 metres 500
0 yards 500

N

to Southern Railway Station

MOSZKVA TÉR
Military History Museum
Áldás u. School

Krisztina Town Church
CASTLE HILL
Matthias Church
St Stephen Statue
Fishermen's Bastion
BATTHYÁNY TÉR
CORVIN TÉR
St Anne's Church
NAGY IMRE TÉR
Király Baths
MARGIT KÖRÚT
LAJOS U.

Former Royal Palace
Széchényi Library
Budapest History Museum
Hungarian National Gallery
CLARK ÁDÁM TÉR
FŐ U.
SZILÁGYI D. TÉR
SZARVAS TÉR
YBL MILKÓS TÉR
Hajós Sport Baths
MARGARET ISLAND
Palatinus Baths

Gellért Hill
Gellért Monument
DÖBRENTEI TÉR
Danube
Attila József Statue
Parliament
MARGARET BRIDGE

Citadel
Rudas Baths
CHAIN BRIDGE
Academy of Sciences
Rákóczi Statue
KOSSUTH LAJOS TÉR
Kossuth Statue
JÁSZAI MARI TÉR
Szent István Park

Liberation Monument
River
Gresham Palace (Four Seasons)
Soviet Army Memorial
SZABADSÁG TÉR
Museum of Ethnography

Gellért Hotel & Baths
ELIZABETH BRIDGE
BELGRÁD RAKPART
JÓZSEF ATTILA U.
Petőfi Statue
Inner City Parish Church
National Bank
St Stephen's Basilica
Imre Nagy Statue
U.S. Embassy
NYUGATI VISEGRÁDI U.

LIBERTY BRIDGE
VÁMHÁZ KRT.
FERENCIEK TÉRE
DEÁK TÉR
BAJCSY-ZSILINSZKY ÚT
VÁCI ÚT
VISEGRÁDI U.

Central Market
KOSSUTH L. U.
Franciscan Church
KÁROLY KRT.
Postal Museum
Opera House
Western Railway Station
VÁCI ÚT

BAKÁTS TÉR
KÁLVIN MÚZEUM KRT. TÉR
Astoria Hotel
Jewish Museum
Central Synagogue
LISZT F. TÉR
OKTOGON
TERÉZ KÖRÚT
St. Margaret's Church
VISEGRÁDI U.
VÁCI ÚT

RADAY U.
National Museum
RÁKÓCZI ÚT
VAS U.
DOHÁNY U.
Orthodox Synagogue
Academy of Music
ANDRÁSSY ÚT
PODMANICZKY U.
LEHEL U.

ÜLLŐI ÚT
BAROSS U.
Museum of Applied Arts
St Roch Chapel
BLAHA L. TÉR
ERZSÉBET KRT.
Liszt Museum
KODÁLY KÖRÖND
BAJZA U.
DÓZSA GYÖRGY ÚT

JÓZSEF KÖRÚT
RÁKÓCZI TÉR
New York Café
Kodály Museum
VÁCSIGET FASOR

HORVÁTH M. TÉR
NÉPSZÍNHÁZ U.
RÁKÓCZI ÚT
RÓZSÁK TERE
ROTTENBILLER U.
Museum of Fine Arts
Millenary Monument
HŐSÖK TERE
Zoo
LEHEL U.
KÖRÚT

to the Airport
BAROSS U.
KÖZTÁRSASÁG TÉR
BAROSS TÉR
NEFELEJCS U.
Hall of Arts
Circus

FIUMEI ÚT
TELEKI TÉR
Eastern Railway Station
DÓZSA GYÖRGY ÚT
AJTÓSI DÜRER SOR
Vajdahunyad Castle
Széchenyi Baths
Fun Fair

Natural History Museum
KEREPESI ÚT
City Park
Transport Museum
HUNGARIA

Kerepesi Cemetery
DÓZSA GYÖRGY ÚT
KEREPESI ÚT
THÖKÖLY ÚT
STEFÁNIA U.

Ferenc Puskás (formerly People's) Stadium
Geological Institute

Cathedral, Chapel or Church

Park/Gardens

Cemetery

Monument, Memorial or Statue

BUDAPEST

chapter one
BY THE DANUBE

"...the Danube, whose gentle waves embrace past, present and future."

Attila József

"Wise, turbulent and great"
The section of the River Danube flowing through Budapest represents less than one per cent of its total length of 1,770 miles. Yet it is an extremely significant section, since it defines an essential aspect of one of the major cities through which the great river flows.

Of the four European capitals located on the Danube—Vienna, Bratislava, Budapest and Belgrade—Budapest is the only one where the river clearly dissects the city in two, running directly through its centre, and is thus an inescapable and central part of the metropolis itself. Add to that the facts that the Buda Hills on the right bank reach right down to the riverside, that Pest on the left bank, in contrast, is flat, and that a series of impressive bridges, each with its own history, span the river, and you arrive at the almost inescapable conclusion that Budapest's Danube panorama constitutes one of the most striking city-centres in Europe, if not in the world.

"Budapest is the loveliest city on the Danube," wrote Claudio Magris in his celebrated history-cum-travelogue *Danube* (1986). He is not alone in his view. In December 1987 Castle Hill and the entire Danube panorama from Liberty Bridge to Margaret Bridge were added to UNESCO'S World Heritage list, alongside such places as the Acropolis in Athens and London's Westminster. First-time visitors to Budapest never fail to comment on having been quite unprepared for the magnificent view which unfolds before them by the Danube in Budapest. From whatever vantage point you choose—the Pest embankment, the Fishermen's Bastion behind the Matthias Church on Castle Hill, or the Citadel at the top of Gellért Hill—the riverside view is breathtaking.

If one view can be said to eclipse all others, perhaps it has to be the one looking south from the middle of Margaret Bridge. Hungary's impressive neo-Gothic parliament is to the left, right by the riverside,

Castle Hill with the Matthias Church and the former Royal Palace to the right, while Gellért Hill is straight ahead, towering above the broad sweep of the Danube with the Chain Bridge in the centre. Yet this is not a picture you often see reproduced, the south-facing view towards the sun presumably making it awkward even for the most professional of photographers.

Is the Danube really blue? That is a question that intrigues visitors, being familiar, as most are, with Johann Strauss the Younger's famous waltz *The Blue Danube*. The familiarity of the music has been enforced countless times by its use in influential films such as Stanley Kubrick's *2001: A Space Odyssey*. Yet on this score (to employ a rather lame pun) there is potential for disappointment. The river may look blue on occasions, particularly if you have your back to the sun and there is a clear blue sky above, but generally the colour of the Danube is too often more of a murky grey.

Yet this prosaic reality has not stopped the river providing inspiration over the centuries for numerous writers and poets. Attila József, one of the most widely read twentieth-century Hungarian poets, composed his *By the Danube* in 1936. A seated statue of József can be found by the river at the southern end of parliament, and nearby on the ground are a couple of lines from his poem, in which he describes the Danube "as if it flowed from my own heart in a spate... wise was the Danube, turbulent and great."

Can a river be wise? Presumably the anthropomorphic allusion is to the fact that the river rolls on through the city, generation after generation, observing all its traits and characteristics, absorbing and preserving them like an old sage. In that sense the river is also great, greater than any individual. It is also great in the sense of large (the everyday Hungarian word József employs—*nagy*—has this dual meaning) and clearly the Danube in Budapest is indeed large, spanning over 1,600 feet at some points in the city's central area.

Turbulent? Certainly the Danube in Budapest has witnessed some turbulent times throughout history, but there is also a literal meaning that can be applied. Until the 1860s when the city stretch of the river was finally and fully regulated and the present-day embankments were constructed, the turbulent Danube would frequently break its banks and flood each side, causing havoc and destruction. The most devastating flood, up to then Pest's most serious natural disaster, occurred in 1838. On the night of 13-14 March that year, the Danube burst its banks and caused a huge flood which lasted several days. Over 150 people died and thousands were made homeless. The extent of the flood can be gauged from a number of plaques around the city showing the height the water reached. There is one on the façade of the Rókus

3

Church on Rákóczi út, almost a mile from the river. (The plaques usually show a pointing finger with the word *vízállás*.)

Another reminder is the large relief on the side of the Franciscan Church overlooking Kossuth Lajos utca in central Pest depicting the heroic deeds of Baron Wesselényi, who personally rescued many citizens in his boat. It seems, however, that not all boat operators were as selfless as the baron. A British traveller, Julia Pardoe, was in Hungary at the time and recorded some eyewitness accounts that told of boatmen striking at drowning wretches whose remnants of property were insufficient compensation, while they "hurried off to rescue some wealthy sufferer who could pay them every inch in gold." Wesselényi's own story did not have a happy ending. He was one of the leaders of the anti-Habsburg opposition in the Hungarian and Transylvanian Diets and his heroism during the flood was soon forgotten by the authorities. In 1839 he was accused of treason and imprisoned because of his political activities.

The construction of the embankments in the 1860s led to the creation of one of Europe's most striking promenades, at least in terms of the view it offers. The Pest-side upper embankment between the Chain Bridge and Elizabeth Bridge is known as the Corso and for over a century has been a popular place for strolling, for taking the air, for seeing and being seen. Its heyday was in the inter-war period, the atmosphere of which was captured by the writer Sándor Márai in an article published in 1935. "What is the Danube promenade?" he asks.

Let's say that it is a dozen cafés with music, pretty women, a cosmopolitan public and terraces all in a beautiful setting with the view of the Castle, Gellért Hill and the bridges. And yet there is something beyond all this, something nowhere else to be found in the world in this combination of elements. This show window of Pest, glittering and floating, as if on the very surface of the Danube, is metropolis and lido, salon and pier, St. Mark's Square and the Levant all in one. The place, elegant in its very vulgarity, surprising and charming, never before seen and instantly enchanting, has indeed no match in the whole wide world.

What generated a certain elite atmosphere in the pre-Second World War era was a string of hotels along and near the embankment. These elegant establishments bore equally elegant names such as the Grand Hotel Hungária, the Grand Hotel Ritz, the Carlton and the Bristol. Their guests would come from all over the world.

Strolling on the Pest embankment today and taking in the marvellous view, it is difficult to imagine the scene here in the winter of 1944-5, towards the end of the Second World War. At that time, as the city was surrounded by the Soviet Army and the Germans were eventually holed up on Castle Hill and Gellért Hill, a tremendous battle raged, during which the Pest embankment was almost completely destroyed and with it the hotel row. It was not until late 1969 that the Hotel Duna-Intercontinental (today called the Budapest Marriott), newly designed by József Finta, opened its doors and a certain semblance of the old times began to reappear.

The international guests started to return and some certainly did their best in reviving the old times. One of the liveliest occasions must surely have been Elizabeth Taylor's fortieth birthday party at the Duna-Intercontinental in February 1972 while Richard Burton was filming *Bluebeard* in Budapest. Two hundred invitations brought celebrities from around the globe, including Ringo Starr, Princess Grace and Stephen Spender. "Little Mickey Caine had flown from LA," wrote Burton in his diary. The world's press also attended and recorded the lavish display, though Burton also donated the equivalent cost of the party ($45,000) to a good cause. (Always a rebel, despite his wealth, while in Budapest Burton insulted two ambassadors and their wives at a British Embassy party, swore at his hosts, condemned all privilege and walked out. At least that is the story as related by his biographer, Melvyn Bragg.)

In 1981 the Duna-Intercontinental was joined by the Forum Hotel (today, somewhat confusingly, called the Inter-Continental), also Finta's design, and in the same year by Lajos Zalavári's neighbouring Atrium-Hyatt Hotel (today the Sofitel Atrium).

A Bridge to the Future

These days crossing the Danube in Budapest is an everyday occurrence, though it can be a rather frustrating experience for car drivers and their passengers. There are currently seven road bridges spanning the Danube in Budapest within a river stretch of less than seven miles, which amounts to quite a lot of bridges. From the traffic point of view, however, the bridges act as funnels for all the vehicles aiming to cross the Danube. Given that the wealthier residential areas are on the Buda side of the river and that the main commercial, diplomatic, political, business and related establishments are, by and large, on the Pest side, the result is that the morning rush-hour often sees the bridges blocked with cars in the Buda-to-Pest direction, and vice-versa during the afternoon rush-hour.

"Rush-hour" might need some explanation. Traditionally, Hungarians are "early to bed, early to rise" (not that that makes them, in the words of the English saying, "healthy, wealthy and wise") but it does mean that rush-hours are slightly earlier than might be expected. In Budapest the traffic is extremely busy from soon after 7 am to around 9 am. The afternoon peak starts around 3.30 pm and can last until after 6 pm. Friday afternoon is special, with the "rush-hour" sometimes beginning even around 2.30 pm, at least in the summer months, the general understanding being that "everyone" is leaving the city for their Lake Balaton weekend cottages, sixty miles to the south-west.

In previous times crossing the river was always a problem. Until the middle of the nineteenth century there were only temporary means of making the crossing. From spring to autumn small boats would be lashed together and planks laid across them to allow pedestrians and horse-driven carriages to cross. The problem was that the boats had to be untied and separated whenever river traffic wanted to move along the Danube. Occasionally, however, the level of the water was so low that it was possible to cross by coach or even on foot, in the manner of crossing a ford. Then in winter there was an ingenious solution: an "ice bridge". In the very cold weather from December to February the Danube used to freeze to such an extent, in terms of both depth and solidity, that it was possible to establish a form of ice bridge, which was strong enough to carry both people and horses. The local authorities used to check the viability of crossing points, reinforce these with extra ice and cover them with straw. Needless to say, citizens had to pay a fee for the "bridge". The ice was solid enough not only for crossing purposes but also even for balls and fairs. All that finally came to an end with a tragedy in 1883 when the ice broke during a ball being held on the frozen river in front of the Greek Orthodox Church near Petőfi tér. The frozen "dance floor" collapsed and dozens of people drowned in the freezing water.

All the earlier uncertainty about crossing disappeared with the completion in 1849 of the Chain Bridge, invariably described as the first permanent bridge over the Danube in Budapest. (That the Romans had wooden bridges here centuries before is usually conveniently forgotten in terms of that designation.) The Chain Bridge, with its twin towering stone piers echoing neo-Classical triumphal arches, has become one of the symbols of Budapest and its image has been reproduced countless times, in etchings, paintings, photographs and on postcards. Yet there are essential background and emotional reasons for this, apart from the aesthetic appeal of its appearance.

The Széchenyi Chain Bridge, to give it its full title, was the brainchild of Count István Széchenyi (1791-1860), the most prominent Hungarian reformer of the first half of the nineteenth century. Széchenyi came from one of the wealthiest land-owning families. He was, according to a variety of sources, a relatively conservative type, but at the same time he was intent on dragging Hungary from its ancient feudal condition into the realities of the developed nineteenth-century world. In 1820 bad weather had forced him to wait eight days before he could cross the river by ferry to attend his father's funeral. Allegedly this was the reason which spurred him on to establish a proper bridge across the Danube in Budapest. With this in mind Széchenyi visited England on a number of occasions to learn from the then most technologically advanced society. Today he might even be called an industrial spy, since he spent much time visiting a variety of specialists to discuss in detail the latest inventions, and he even imported, underhand, machinery from England. The most famous result of his endeavours is undoubtedly the Chain Bridge, in some ways still the pride of not only "postcard", but also real Budapest.

"It was under the soaring vaults of the Chain Bridge that old Hungary marched into new Hungary," the novelist and newspaper contributor Gyula Krúdy once wrote. Through its arches, he said, obsolete slogans and ideas were thrown, and over the bridge the wind spread the seeds of freedom and rejuvenation. Is that not rather exaggerated, in relation to a mere bridge?

Bridges are means of getting from one place to another, across an otherwise apparently difficult divide. Széchenyi's view (which came to be accepted) was that the creation of a new, permanent bridge would not only be of practical use, but would also be of symbolic, almost ideological value. This would be the bridge, he argued, that would not only definitely unite Pest and Buda for the first time, but also the whole country. Furthermore, as a feat of engineering it would show that Hungary was in line with the then most developed nations. One of those nations was Great Britain, often portrayed as the industrial power-house of the nineteenth century and internationally renowned for its feats of engineering. Perhaps it is not surprising, therefore, that Széchenyi commissioned an Englishman, William Tierney Clark, to design the bridge. Tierney Clark must have been a smart operator in terms of getting paid more than once for the same job. His design adopted for Budapest was virtually a copy of his 1832 (still standing) bridge at Marlow, which spans the Thames, and closely resembled London's original Hammersmith Bridge, also his work.

The Scotsman Adam Clark (no relation) was employed to supervise the project as chief engineer. Adam Clark stayed on in Hungary, married a Hungarian and was involved in a number of other projects, notably the creation of the tunnel under Castle Hill, which runs west from the Chain Bridge. He died in 1866 and is buried in the Kerepesi Cemetery in Pest. The square on the Buda side of the bridge is named after him.

In May 1849, during Hungary's War of Independence, the Austrians planned to blow up the not-yet-completed bridge. Adam Clark thwarted their plans by having the anchoring chambers flooded with water. When it was finally inaugurated, on 21 November 1849, the Chain Bridge, at nearly 1,250 feet, was one of the largest suspension bridges of the time. When it opened, a controversial toll was levied on all who used it, thus breaching the privileges of the nobility who had previously been exempt from such taxes. This was another of Széchenyi's ideas—in the new bourgeois democracy all citizens would be equal in terms of taxation, with the exemptions of the privileged being abolished. In practice tolls ceased in 1918, though they were not legally abolished for a further two years.

The bridge was reconstructed at the time of the First World War, since when it has officially been called the Széchenyi Chain Bridge. Destroyed by the Germans in January 1945 during the siege of Budapest, it was rebuilt and reopened on 21 November 1949, the centenary of its original inauguration.

Painters and writers were attracted to the themes the bridge represented right from the start. One of Hungary's most famous historical paintings, Miklós Barabás' *Laying the Foundation Stone of the Chain Bridge*, proudly hangs in the Hungarian National Museum. The large oil painting, measuring thirteen by nine feet, was executed in 1864, though the event it portrays took place in 1842. Interestingly, in that earlier year Barabás had produced a watercolour depicting exactly the same theme and with exactly the same title. They make an interesting comparison. The top two-thirds of the earlier, much smaller, version show the interior of the massive wooden struts and beams which had been created to dam the river and create space for the work to proceed. Below, the foundation stone appears to have just been, or is in the process of being, placed. It is surrounded by a massive crowd of barely distinguishable onlookers, their attention primarily engaged by the central event of the foundation stone being laid. The later version, produced a full twenty-two years after the event, also shows the wooden beams and struts in perfect perspective, but now the figures surrounding the foundation stone, which is clearly in the process of being laid, are given more space and are portrayed in much greater detail. Indeed, they are recognizable historical characters, who, furthermore, are all directing their gaze not at the central event, but at the viewer, as if the painter had captured them with a modern wide-angle-lens camera for a group photograph.

The explanation for this intriguing difference may well be that the 1864 oil painting was a work undertaken on commission for Count Simon Sina, a banker, aristocrat and landowner of Greek origin, and one of the wealthiest men of his day. His father, George Sina, had been a chief financier backing the construction of the Chain Bridge. Barabás was among the first Hungarian painters who managed to live by means of art, which was largely due to his exceptional skill at portrait painting. Presumably the count wished to see his father among the dignitaries and nobles of the Hungarian elite. So there he is, George Sina, right in the centre of the oil painting, not dirtying his hands with the physical work, but, like the others, gazing at the painter/camera. Maybe he was there in reality. In any case, the painting wants to tell us that. In the picture, Sina is flanked by a crowd which includes prominent figures of mid-nineteenth-century Hungary, such as István Széchenyi, the political leader Lajos Kossuth and the poet Sándor Petőfi, irrespective of

9

whether they were present there in reality or not, though as the chief initiator of the bridge, Széchenyi, at least, was surely there. The fascination with the bridge and its symbolism continued into the twentieth century. The writer József Lengyel chose the theme of Széchenyi and the bridge for his 1971 documentary novel *Hídépítők* (published in English as *The Bridgebuilders* in 1979). It is a work devoted to the story of the Chain Bridge and its three main creators— Széchenyi and the two Clarks.

The members of Hungary's centre-right government of 1998-2004 were also fond of the name Széchenyi, employing it for a variety of their projects. They even funded a film called *The Bridgeman* (2002) about the initiator of the Chain Bridge. At the time it was the most expensive Hungarian film produced to date. It was also rather controversial, bringing into question the accepted view that Széchenyi ended his life by committing suicide while in a mental hospital in Döbling near Vienna. Such an end does not seem compatible with Széchenyi's rich and varied life as a reformer, writer and propagandist, whose practical enterprises characterized Hungary's so-called Reform Period of the second quarter of the nineteenth century.

"The greatest Hungarian"
Born into an old aristocratic Hungarian family in 1791, Széchenyi was brought up in the spirit of national service and national renewal. His father Ferenc Széchényi (they spelt their names slightly differently) was instrumental in founding the Hungarian National Museum in Pest and the National Library, which latter today bears his name and is located at the rear of the former Royal Palace complex on Castle Hill.

At the time an army career was not only *de rigueur* but also seen as a way of advancement for the sons of noble families. István Széchenyi duly signed up and as an officer he travelled extensively in Europe, seeing action in fighting against Napoleon I. The modern conditions he found in France and particularly in England had a great impact on him, and he resolved to do his utmost to change the backward and feudal conditions still prevailing in his native Hungary.

One of his most celebrated gestures took place in 1825 at the Diet (estates' assembly) in Pozsony (today Bratislava, Slovakia). Széchenyi, speaking in broken Hungarian, itself a drama given that German or Latin was the official *lingua franca*, theatrically offered a year's income towards the establishment of a Learned Society for the development of Hungarian arts, science, language and literature—a body which eventually became the Hungarian Academy of Sciences. Széchenyi's other practical initiatives during his life included the regulation of the Danube for navigation purposes and the introduction of steam shipping, the establishment of English-style thoroughbred horse studs and horse racing, and, according to some sources, he is even attributed with the introduction into Hungary of the English-style gas light and flush lavatory, which latter even today is still often called *angol* (English) *WC*.

Széchenyi's writings also had a great impact. *Hitel* (Credit, 1830), *Világ* (Light, 1831) and *Stadium* (1833) argued for economic advancement and a modern financial and banking system. No wonder his fellow nobles often resented his efforts, since essentially he was trying to shake them out of their backward, albeit comfortable complacency. Many pointed the finger at the person, rather than his ideas. Despite his arguments for economic thrift on the societal level, he himself often lived a lavish lifestyle and he was a noted womanizer to boot.

His contemporary, and in some ways political rival, Lajos Kossuth called him "the greatest Hungarian", a description quoted endless times but rarely explained from Kossuth's point of view. Unlike Kossuth, the political revolutionary, Széchenyi was essentially a reformer, believing that economic progress would lead to political changes, without necessarily disturbing Habsburg hegemony. The Vienna court, however, and Metternich in particular, viewed Széchenyi with great suspicion, as a character with dangerous ideas.

The tensions between the tendencies of reform, revolution and resistance from above eventually resulted in the social explosion of March 1848 and Hungary's subsequent War of Independence against Habsburg rule. Although Széchenyi joined the first independent cabinet under Lajos Batthyány, the tensions proved too strong for him and he ended up in an asylum where he spent the last years of his life. Not that they were entirely inactive years; he managed, for example, to have articles published anonymously in the London *Times*. Thus his continuing influence in the cause of Hungary kept him in the eye of the Vienna authorities. Following one police raid a relapse occurred and on 8 April 1860 he put a bullet through his head.

His funeral deeply moved the whole country. His body was brought by train to Sopron in western Hungary and from there his coffin was carried on people's shoulders to his estate at Nagycenk. The Viennese police ordered the funeral to be held on 11 April, a day earlier than planned. Nevertheless, about 6,000 people attended the ceremony, and on the following day thousands more mourners arrived. In three days as many as 50,000 people paid their respects.

Above the portal of the parish church in Nagycenk village there is the Széchenyi family motto: "Si Deus pro nobis, quis contra nos" (If God is with us, who can be against us). The nearby statue of István Széchenyi bears an inscription of Széchenyi's famous saying "Magyarország nem volt, hanem lesz" (Hungary did not exist—but it will). The combined sentiment of those two sayings helps explain Széchenyi's reputation for Hungarians, yet it is a reputation which also spread abroad. Even Charles Dickens wrote a eulogy about him a whole decade after his death.

The prime Budapest statue of István Széchenyi stands, appropriately, near his major creation, in the square at the Pest end of the Chain Bridge. The four secondary figures of the statue represent Széchenyi's varied fields of activity: Minerva (trade), Neptune (navigation), Vulcan (industry) and Ceres (agriculture). Behind the statue stands the neo-Renaissance building of the Hungarian Academy of Sciences. On the right side of the building, facing Akadémia utca, is a large, detailed, bronze relief of the famous scene at Pozsony in 1825. In the foreground, dressed in Hussar officer's uniform, stands Széchenyi as he offers his income for a year to help establish the Academy.

At first the Academy had no permanent home. Then in 1859 a committee was established to organize the building of one. A closed tender was offered to three architects, Imre Henszlmann, an Academy associate, Heinrich Ferstel, designer of Vienna's Votive Church, and Miklós Ybl, who was later to design the Budapest Opera House. Two other architects were bold enough to submit plans without invitation. However, the committee, dissatisfied with all proposals, invited further contributions from Leo von Klenze of Munich and Friedrich August Stüler, the architect of Berlin's National Gallery and Stockholm's National Museum.

Stüler's design was accepted, but the decision generated great controversy. Some were dismayed that a foreigner had been chosen to design a building regarded as being of national significance. Others argued as to whether neo-Renaissance or neo-Gothic was a more appropriate style for a Hungarian national institution, although, ironically, neither style bore any relation to indigenous Hungarian traditions. Despite the controversy, Stüler's design was put into effect and the Academy building was formally inaugurated in December 1865.

The Enchanted Garden

After the Chain Bridge almost three decades had to pass before a second bridge was built in Budapest. Almost 2,000 feet long, Margaret Bridge was designed by French engineer Ernest Gouin following an international competition and built in 1872–6 by the Société de Construction des Batignolles company of France. Among the completed plans submitted there were some grandiose schemes. One included a 200-foot lookout tower in the middle of the bridge, another a pantheon of statues symbolizing the counties of Hungary. The committee awarding the contract rather went for a more delicate "Parisian" approach. Margaret Bridge was a welcome addition to the city from the practical aspect but it could not match the symbolism of its predecessor, the Chain Bridge, even though the great epic poet János Arany penned a twenty-verse ballad to commemorate its inauguration.

Interestingly, the bridge is "bent", its two arms meeting in the middle at an angle of 30 degrees such that each is at right angles with the current of the river, which flows south on either side of Margaret Island, the "playground" of Budapest. Regarded by many as the city's finest park, Margaret Island has been referred to as "the pearl of the Danube", "an enchanted garden" and "an earthly Paradise". These are excessive descriptions but they aim to capture something about the island's atmosphere and in particular its exceptional location. There are plenty of parks in Budapest, but this is both park and island, right in the middle of a river, at the same time constituting a central element of the city.

In his *Budapesti kalauz Marslakók számára* (A Martian's Guide to Budapest), published in 1935, the noted essayist and literary historian Antal Szerb wrote: "In the narrow park, to the left as well as the right, you can occasionally see the shimmer of the Danube, between the almost too pretty flower beds… where it is our custom to be children and to grow old." Margaret Island is indeed a favourite of young and old, locals and visitors. Here you can find not only open spaces, peaceful walkways (cars are banned from most of the island), trees, old ruins, springs and fountains, but also two large swimming pool complexes, tennis courts, bicycle paths, children's' playgrounds and an open-air theatre. In short, Margaret Island is a place of relaxation for all.

It was not always like that. For most of its history the island has been private property, closed to the general public. In medieval times it was known as the Island of Hares, suggesting that the place was used as a hunting ground, apparently owned by the royal court. This is reinforced by the fact that in the late twelfth century the island was also used as a royal residence. In addition, the island was home for a number of ecclesiastical bodies. In the thirteenth century King Béla IV had a convent built on the island for Dominican nuns and for a while under his patronage the nuns became the largest ecclesiastical landowners in the country.

The island and the bridge are named after Béla's daughter, Margaret. According to tradition, Béla vowed during the disastrous Mongol invasion of 1242–4 that if Hungary were victorious his daughter would be brought up as a nun. History has not recorded what she thought of that at the time. Nevertheless in 1252, when she was aged ten, Margaret was brought to the island where she lived an apparently ultra-pious and ascetic life until her death in 1271.

After the victory of the Ottomans over the Hungarians at the battle of Mohács in 1526, the island became depopulated and during the Turkish occupation many of its buildings were destroyed. After the Ottoman period the island became the home of the St. Clare nuns, but when the order was suppressed it passed into the hands of Archduke Palatine Alexander. Palatine Joseph took over the island in 1795 and in line with his zeal for renewal had vines and rare trees planted. Many European dignitaries participated in vintage festivals here in the first half of the nineteenth century.

Towards the end of that century Margaret Island gained in popularity as a bathing and holiday resort, first with the gentry and aristocracy, later with writers, scientists and scholars, and then with the better-off members of the bourgeoisie. Besides resident guests (staying at hotels and villas on the island), a large number of visitors came to the island for just a day or evening to take a walk, a bath, or have a drink at the well, a meal at a restaurant, to enjoy the gypsy music or listen to the play of a military band, perhaps to classical music, or maybe to take part in one of the balls and banquets. The "society" columns of the newspapers listed the notables and celebrities who put in an appearance on the island. In 1893, in a multi-volume publication called *The Austro-Hungarian Monarchy in Words and Pictures*, the renowned Hungarian writer Mór Jókai wrote that Margaret Island was

> *the enchanted garden of Budapest... the favourite entertainment complex of the Budapest public... Steamboats arrive every half-hour, carrying visitors intent on having a good time, enjoying a holiday, or being cured of an ailment [at the island's medicinal baths]... In the very middle of the Danube, the island is far away from the noisy streets of the city; its air is untainted by dust, its apartments are both well-decorated and comfortable; its shady esplanades are broad and clean; the fresh green of the lush vegetation is a sight for sore eyes...*

The most famous of the writers frequently staying on the island was János Arany, who spent the last summers of his life here and who wrote many of his poems about or on Margaret Island, including his epic *Toldi szerelme* (Toldi's Love), part of a trilogy set in the fourteenth century and relating the adventures of a youth with great strength. One of his best-known poems commemorates the grove, sitting in whose shade he liked to spend some time: "Under these oaks I like to tarry; Far from noisy big-town flurry."

The city bought the island in 1908 and placed it under the management of the Budapest Council of Public Works. Visitors were charged an entrance fee, which doubled on Sundays and holidays. This rather exclusive system lasted, apart from the brief period of the 1919 Council Republic, until 1945 when the island was declared a free public park for all citizens.

Gloomy Sunday

Following Margaret Bridge the time which elapsed before another bridge was constructed was reduced to about twenty years, and then two new bridges appeared in fairly rapid succession. Liberty Bridge, the

city's shortest, was ceremonially opened on 4 October 1896 by Emperor Francis Joseph, who symbolically struck into place a silver rivet bearing his initials. The bridge bore his name until 1945.

The elegant, three-part steel structure of Liberty Bridge has some tragic connections. Over the decades a large number of people have climbed to the top to commit, or threaten to commit suicide by jumping off. When the Chain Bridge was built it, too, was used as a jumping-off platform for would-be suicides. Margaret Bridge fulfilled a similar function after its construction. Yet in this connection, it is Liberty Bridge which has been the most "popular", perhaps because its structure is relatively easy to climb.

Suicide has long been a rather morbid, albeit significant, element of Hungarian social reality. For very many years, right from the beginning of official registration, Hungary had the highest suicide rate in Europe and one of the highest in the world. In recent times it has fallen somewhat in the international "league table", but at the end of the 1990s Hungary was still in sixth place in terms of the annual rate of male suicides per 100,000: 49.2, compared with 19.3 for the USA and just 11 for the UK. Hungary's rate for female suicides (15.6) put it in second place (USA: 4.4; UK: 3.2).

Why the rate of suicide has been so high in Hungary is a question which has vexed medical specialists and social commentators for decades. There is no generally accepted explanation. Some point to the alienation, atomization and lack of real social solidarity during the so-called communist decades. But was Hungary any different in this respect from neighbouring countries? And why is the suicide rate still very high? Others look back further into the country's history and point to the centuries of foreign domination—under the Ottomans, the Habsburgs and the Soviets—inducing a culture of "unfreedom" and despair. Yet others highlight the perceived loneliness of Hungary's existence, caught between its "Eastern" roots and its striving to be "Western", resulting in a lack of firm identity. Social historians and sociologists note the "acceptance" of suicide as a means of resolving serious problems, an attitude somehow strengthened by the fact that many prominent and creative Hungarians, from Count István Széchenyi in the nineteenth century to the poet József Attila in the twentieth, have chosen the path of suicide, generating a certain heroic status for this form of death.

All the explanations may contain some truth, but all are unsatisfactory overall. Nevertheless, gloom and pessimism are widely seen as being part and parcel of Hungarian culture. The nation's solitariness, hope against hopelessness and a melancholic search for identity are reoccurring themes of Hungarian literature. There is even a popular melody associated with depression and suicide. *Gloomy Sunday* was composed in the 1930s by pianist Rezső Seress and the words were added by László Jávor. The moody tune eventually became known world-wide, thanks to a version being recorded by Billy Holiday. It included the lines:

> *Little white flowers won't waken you;*
> *not where the black coach of sorrow has taken you.*
> *Angels have no thought of ever returning you.*
> *Would they be angry if I thought of joining you?*

Interestingly, this is a much more individualized and arguably commercialized lyric than the original Hungarian, which has no reference to white flowers, angels or anyone joining anyone. Instead, it is somewhat more about society, even political.

> *People are heartless, greedy and wicked... Love has died!*
> *The world has come to its end, hope has ceased to have a meaning.*
> *Cities are being wiped out, shrapnel is making music...*

Either way, the legend grew, both in Hungary and abroad, that the tune was associated with, even directly responsible for the suicides of countless people. Newspapers abounded with stories of suicides found dead clutching copies of the lyrics or with the music playing endlessly on a gramophone. One thing is certain: Rezső Seress himself committed suicide in 1968. Perhaps he was depressed at not having been able to benefit from the royalties due to him in view of the massive success of his creation in the West. Today there is a plaque in memory of Seress inside the Kulacs restaurant at the corner of Dohány utca and Orsvát utca in Pest. The Kulacs was one of the venues where he used to play.

Reflecting on the intensity of the Hungarians' existence and the "loneliness factor", Budapest-born Arthur Koestler once even asserted that "to be a Hungarian is a collective neurosis." If that is true, perhaps an answer ought to be sought as to why there are not more suicides in Hungary!

As the potential suicides climb the structure of Liberty Bridge they approach one of four eagle-like figures at the top. These are representations of the mythical "Turul" bird, the legendary totemic ancestor of the Magyars. (*Magyar* is Hungarian for "Hungarian", and the term is widely used in English when referring to the ancient or "original" Hungarians.) As the legend has it, Emese, a consort of a Scythian king, dreamed that a *turul* impregnated her by divine command, announcing the historic mission of her son-to-be, who would conquer distant lands. The son was named Álmos (derived from the Hungarian for "dream", *álom*), but it was his son, Árpád, who eventually led the Magyar tribes in their conquest of the Carpathian Basin.

There is another, much larger and more impressive Turul sculpture overlooking the Danube from the heights of Castle Hill above the Buda end of the Chain Bridge. Pointedly, this, the largest bird statue in Europe, and the Liberty Bridge turuls, appeared in 1896, the year of the bombastic celebrations in Budapest to mark the 1000th anniversary of the Magyar Conquest. How a nation descended from a giant bird ties in with the Hungarians' often proclaimed post-Conquest conversion to and defence over the centuries of Christianity has never fully been explained.

A Friend of Hungary?

1903 saw the completion of Budapest's next bridge, Elizabeth Bridge, which linked the foot of Gellért Hill and the square by one of the city's oldest churches, the Inner City Parish Church. At the time, and up to 1926, this was Europe's largest single-span bridge. Its construction involved considerable urban redevelopment on the Pest side, resulting in what we more or less still see today around Ferenciek tere. The bridge standing today, however, is different from the original. All the city's bridges were destroyed during the Second World War and all were rebuilt as they used to look, with the exception of Elizabeth Bridge, which was given a more modern, slim-line appearance. It was not until 1964, however, that the new bridge opened, which indicates how long it took for some post-war reconstruction to be effected.

The bridge is named after Elizabeth, the strikingly beautiful and slightly dissident wife of Francis Joseph. She was the subject of a cult following in Hungary, both during her life and, perhaps even more so, following her assassination by an Italian anarchist in 1898. Elizabeth has been dubbed the "Diana of central Europe", a designation easy to comprehend.

The popularity in Hungary of Sisy, as she was and still is commonly known, stems from the perception of her as a "friend of the Hungarians", as someone who was, behind the scenes, instrumental in bringing about the Compromise of 1867, whereby Hungary gained a large degree of autonomy within the Empire, and as someone who preferred to be in Hungary, even learning the language, rather than at the Vienna court. What is true is that she did befriend a number of Hungarian politicians, notably Ferenc Deák, and pleaded with her husband to give them a sympathetic ear. She could speak some Hungarian (though so could Francis Joseph) and through conversations with Miksa Falk, a noted journalist, she gained extensive knowledge about Hungary and its history.

In 1867, the year of the coronation of Francis Joseph and Elizabeth as king and queen of Hungary, the Hungarian state offered as a gift to the royal couple the former Grassalkovich Mansion at Gödöllő some 19 miles north-east of the capital. The queen spent much time here (prior to 1867 she had spent relatively few days in Hungary) and today the mansion, which is in the process of long-term, splendid restoration, is to an extent a museum devoted to the cult of Elizabeth. Many Hungarians believe(d) that this was her favourite estate because it was in Hungary. Her comment to the writer Mór Jókai in 1873 is often quoted: "One feels eternally free (in Hungary)." It may have been, however, that she was simply glad to be away from the Vienna court, for as she wrote to her mother from Gödöllő: "Here no one disturbs me, as if I were living in a village where I can come and go as I please."

Different historians and commentators offer slightly different emphasis regarding the extent to which Elizabeth really did or could exert influence on behalf of Hungary. But all agree that there was and still is among Hungarians a widespread *belief* that she played a prominent role as an ally and benefactor of Hungary. Historian András Gerő has paid particular attention to what he regards as the political and psychological roots of this belief. He points to the paradox of trying to reconcile respect for, even adulation of, the Habsburg connection with the political desire for national independence. Pointing to the "common knowledge", albeit based on anecdote and rumour, that Elizabeth did not get on well with her mother-in-law, Sophia, who was "not exactly a favourite with the Hungarian people", he asserts that this made Elizabeth even more popular among Hungarians. Furthermore, in terms of political psychology, the general affection for Elizabeth "was also enhanced by the fact that it provided public opinion with a vehicle in terms of which it could demonstrate its dislike for Francis Joseph while maintaining the appearance of loyalty to the dynasty."

That the emperor was detested is understandable, given the anti-Hungarian repression he oversaw following the defeat of the Hungarians in 1848-9, yet, fascinatingly, Gerő's view is that if "Francis Joseph not been hated so much, Elizabeth would probably have received far less attention... Elizabeth was the only person within the Habsburg dynasty who could possibly play the role of 'patron of the Hungarian people'—at least for those committed to the idea of combining loyalty to the Habsburgs with the pursuit of national interests. So a myth of Elizabeth was gradually created which gathered momentum in the first half of the 1860s," and which acted as a backcloth to developments leading to the Compromise of 1867.

As mentioned, the myth or cult of Elizabeth continued after her death. Just inside the entrance to the Hungarian Academy of Sciences, by the Danube, you can find a large relief depicting Elizabeth by the catafalque of Ferenc Deák, the Hungarian politician most closely association with the Compromise. The work of Barnabás Holló, it dates from 1914. By the Buda end of Elizabeth Bridge (which retained its name of royal connection throughout the so-called communist era) there is a large, attractive seated statue of Sisy, which first appeared in 1932, paid for by public subscription. So much money was collected after Elizabeth's death to set up a statue that there were recurring competitions for the design. One submitted by György Zala finally won the fifth competition in 1919, but it took another 13 years before the statue was eventually erected. Originally it stood in today's Marcius 15. tér, by the bridge on the Pest side of the river. It was taken away in 1953, but reappeared, restored, in its present location in 1986, interestingly three years prior to the political changes. The Elizabeth cult even went through a revival following the political changes of

1989-90. This was accompanied by the re-emergence of a certain nostalgia for the late-Habsburg era.

The People's Poet

Not far from the Pest end of Elizabeth Bridge, in Petőfi tér, which is at the southern end of the Corso, there stands a dramatic statue of the radical poet Sándor Petőfi (1823-49), one of the most celebrated characters in Hungarian history and perhaps the closest there is to being Hungary's "national poet", notwithstanding that he was of Slav descent and his real name was Alexander Petrovich. Nevertheless, Petőfi thoroughly identified himself as a Hungarian, albeit a rebellious one. His popularity stemmed both from his (often criticized) use of everyday language and from his political involvement.

Love and liberty were Petőfi's great themes and in pursuit of the latter he became one of the leaders of the youthful rebellion in Pest which sparked off the Hungarian revolt against Austrian rule in 1848. His moving "National Song" (*Nemzeti Dal*) captured the feel of the times with rousing lines such as "Rise up Hungarians... your homeland calls... it's now or never... Hungarians will be slaves no more!" Petőfi took up arms during the subsequent War of Independence and was killed in battle. His memory lived on, however, and indeed still lives on. His verses are used for teaching from an early age in Hungarian schools and in hundreds of towns and villages throughout the land his memory is recalled by countless street names, statues, busts and wall plaques.

Originally not belonging to the metropolitan literary scene, Petőfi roamed the countryside as a soldier and itinerant actor, but in 1846 he helped found the urban-based Society of Ten, a radical youthful group, eager for change. Liberty for all was one of his watchwords; "Freedom for the world" is a line of one poem (i.e. not just for Hungary). In the upsurge of the 1848-9 events he was actually rejected by his native constituency for the Diet (national parliament) because he was thought too radical. He was one of the few to regret that the "social revolution" of 1848 became a "war of national defence".

Petőfi's critical social stance is reflected in many of his poems. One of 1845, *A Magyar Nemes* (A Magyar Nobleman) is characteristic. A rusty, long-unused, bloodstained sword hangs on the wall of the "gentleman". He does not study, is always in debt and does not pay tax. Food and drink are his only "science".

Nought but idleness is life
I'm idle, therefore I'm alive
Peasants work until they die
A Magyar nobleman am I!

Just as Attila József in the following century would encapsulate in verse popular sentiments in relation to the urban, metropolitan environment, in his day Petőfi connected with an arguably over-romanticized, though genuinely felt feeling for the vast expanses of the Hungarian countryside stretching to the east of the Danube. As he wrote in *Az Alföld* (The Great Plain) in 1844:

Down on the sea-flat country of the great wide plain;
that's where I'm at home; that's my domain.
From its prison doth my eagle soul fly,
when the infinite plain unfolds before my eye.

The statue of Petőfi by the Danube shows him with a scroll in one hand and with the other raised as if proclaiming his "National Song". Given Petőfi's central role in the March revolution of 1848, the fact that it was erected in 1882, still in the Habsburg period, indicates that its appearance was a political statement in itself. In the decades following the 1848-9 war the Vienna authorities were obviously not keen. The renowned violinist Ede Remény was a prime mover and raised enormous amounts of money for the project on his European tours.

The patriotic mood and its central location help explain why the statue has often been chosen as the site for political demonstrations. A large, albeit illegal, anti-fascist rally assembled here in 1942. The date chosen was 15 March, the anniversary of the 1848 rebellion. During the Kádár era, in the period prior to the 1989 changes, unofficial demonstrations were often organized by oppositionists in front of the statue on 15 March.

In 1956 the statue was one of the initial rallying points for students on the first day of the uprising. At the time Elizabeth Bridge had not been reconstructed, which meant that the young demonstrators, in order to head for Bem tér on the Buda side and thus link up with students demonstrating on that side of the Danube, had to initially head away from the river, along Kossuth Lajos utca and then north towards the Western Railway Station, crossing later by Margaret Bridge. This enforced diversion necessitated the march passing through dense sections of central Pest, during which time many more people—residents, office and factory workers—joined and swelled the movement, making its impact greater than it might have been.

In contrast with Budapest's "historic" city-centre bridges (the Chain Bridge, Margaret Bridge, Liberty Bridge and Elizabeth Bridge), the later bridges have more of a "workaday" nature and a simpler design. Petőfi Bridge, connecting Buda with the southern end of the Great Boulevard was completed in 1937. Prior to 1945 the bridge bore the name of Miklós Horthy, Hungary's inter-war, ultra-conservative ruler. Árpád Bridge, named after the ninth-century Magyar chieftain, cuts across the north end of Margaret Island. Construction began in 1939 with a view to facilitating the crossing of workers from Óbuda to factories in the Angyalföld district on the Pest side. The work was held up by the war, however, and the bridge was not finally completed until 1950. Unsurprisingly for the times, it was named Stalin Bridge and was officially inaugurated on 7 November, the anniversary of the Bolshevik revolution. It kept the name until shortly after the 1956 uprising.

Budapest's newest and least attractive bridge, Lágymányos Bridge, was opened in 1995. It does not even have a "proper" name like its counterparts, its title simply referring to the area on the Buda side of the bridge. Lágymányos Bridge links Buda with the outer ring-road of Pest and the idea was to divert heavy vehicles away from the central areas, increasingly jammed with traffic. That has succeeded to an extent, but now the outer ring itself is no stranger to queues and jams.

The National Theatre

Near the Pest end of Lágymányos Bridge stands the part post-modern, part traditional building of the new National Theatre, which was officially inaugurated in 2002 on 15 March—note the patriotic date, the anniversary of the start of the 1848 revolt in Pest. Much controversy surrounded the building since the architect who won its design competition, Ferenc Bán, was not awarded the commission. That went to another architect, Mária Siklós, amidst widespread speculation about political favouritism surrounding the then government. Nevertheless, the building is a conspicuous and eye-catching addition to Budapest's Danube panorama and is strikingly lit at night.

The inaugural performance at the new National Theatre was a version of one of Hungary's most often performed dramas, *The Tragedy of Man* by Imre Madách. It is also one of the most controversial, both in terms of its meaning and in relation to its nature, some critics regarding it more of a dramatic poem than a play. The only work of Madách (1824-64) to achieve great success in Hungary, it has been translated into many languages and, in contrast to other noted Hungarian plays, has received critical acclaim abroad. This may well be because, unlike many other nineteenth-century Hungarian dramas, it does not focus exclusively, or even primarily, on issues of national concern, but is much more universal in its scope.

Its universality of theme, however, is partly at the root of its problematic nature. The drama consists of fifteen somewhat disjointed scenes in which God, Lucifer, Adam and Eve, in various dreams and guises, appear in settings as far apart as Paradise, Egypt, ancient Rome, the world of the crusades, the French revolution, commercial London and a utopian socialist community governed by science. That rich concoction could well end up as a nightmare for any director, but most have seemed to enjoy the challenge, even relishing the variety of potential possibilities of presentation.

The arguments are really over what it is all about. On the surface, and even at a deeper level, Madách appears to be presenting a history of mankind as a series of aspirations dashed by reality and human failure, in short an ultimately pessimistic view of the human condition. *The Tragedy of Man* was first published in 1860, a more than usually pessimistic time in the chronology of Hungarian consciousness, it being only eleven years after the defeat of the Hungarians in their struggle for independence from Habsburg rule, which was followed by years of harsh repression. Yet from the few comments about his drama which Madách has left, it seems his clear intention was to stress not pessimism, but rather hope and tragedy combined with the necessity of struggle, with hope still holding its place. The final line of the drama has the Lord saying to Adam: "...strive on, trust, have faith!"

Not that the text is a simple religious tract. Church leaders have criticised Madách for not really demonstrating the power of God and of faith, while at the same time materialist, Marxist critics have commented negatively on Madách's apparent belief in the incapability of mass humanity to liberate itself.

Constant struggle, constant defeat and yet with progress somehow emerging out of the ashes is almost a summary of Hungarian history, which is presumably the reason for the paradoxical title of Paul Lendvai's marvellous work, *The Hungarians—A Thousand Years of Victory in Defeat*, perhaps the best introduction there is to the complicated story of Hungary and its inhabitants.

A part of that story involves the history of the National Theatre as an institution and the various buildings it has occupied. The very notion of a national theatre, focussing largely on national themes and employing the national language was, inevitably, part of the nation-building process of the late eighteenth and early nineteenth centuries in Hungary. The National Theatre was first established in 1840 in the former Pest Hungarian Theatre, which stood on the site of the East-West Trade Centre, at the corner of today's Rákóczi út and Múzeum körút. The original theatre building was demolished in 1913.

The next home for the National Theatre was the former People's Theatre, which stood in the middle of today's Blaha Lujza tér. That building was pulled down amidst much controversy in 1964, allegedly because of the planned construction of the underground metro line. Following this, for over three decades the National Theatre had no permanent building of its own, which many regarded as a scandal. There were huge public appeals and various plans for construction of a new building in various locations, but all came to nought.

The political changes of 1989-90 resulted in new life being blown into the project and plans appeared to take on more concrete forms, in all senses of the term. As indicated above, the project involved a degree of controversy about the design, but there were also disputes about the location, fuelled by the fact that in the 1990s, while the Budapest municipal authority was consistently liberal/left-centre in its political composition, the national government changed political colouring three times after three elections, which led to a lack of administrative consistency and, especially in the period 1998-2002, to political antagonism.

The municipality and its mayor, Gábor Demszky, hoped to see the new National Theatre constructed in Erzsébet tér, in the city centre. Digging was started and foundation work undertaken. But the government, headed by Prime Minister Viktor Orbán, favoured the site by Lágymános Bridge, which is where the theatre was actually built.

With typical Budapest humour, the abandoned site in Erzsébet tér was known for some time as the "National Hole". Today the only drama which possibly occurs there is an occasional accident in the underground car park, which was eventually constructed instead of a theatre.

Hence there was much pomp and circumstance when the new National Theatre was inaugurated in spring 2002, party due to its long-awaited appearance, but also because the building was conveniently completed just two months prior to a scheduled general election. Yet that did not stop the government of the day being thrown out of office.

Directly behind the National Theatre stands a huge, concrete and glass, rectangular box-like structure, which, from a distance, looks like it could be a gigantic car showroom. This is the city's newest cultural centre, the grandiosely named Palace of Arts, which was officially opened in 2005 on the eve, predictably, of 15 March. While the building's external appearance does not please everyone, virtually all agree that the technical equipment inside is excellent and that the acoustics in its main auditorium, the National Concert Hall, and in its smaller Festival Theatre are superb. The organ of the concert hall is a masterpiece. It has five manuals, 92 stops and 6,815 pipes, ranging from a quarter inch to 33 feet in length. Built jointly by Hungary's Pécs Organ Construction Company and Germany's Mühleisen Company, it was inaugurated with much fanfare in April 2006.

Since its opening the Palace of Arts has managed to establish itself as one the prime live performance venues in the city, part of its attraction being that its programme is very broad-ranging, covering classical, jazz, folk, gypsy and light music, as well as dance, opera and operetta performances, with artists coming from both Hungary and abroad. As an additional attraction, the Palace of Arts also houses the Ludwig Museum of Contemporary Art. There have been plans, too, to construct further cultural institutions in this neighbourhood, the hope being that this newly developing part of the city by the Danube will in the future come to be recognized as a truly "European citadel of culture".

chapter two

AVENUE OF DREAMS

Budapest's Champs-Elysées

In the last quarter of the nineteenth century Budapest was one of the fastest growing cities in Europe, matched only by Berlin. From just over 300,000 in 1873, the year of the unification of Buda, Óbuda and Pest, by 1914 the population of the Hungarian capital had increased to reach almost one million. That growth in numbers was both reflected and generated by a massive programme of urban construction and reconstruction, which to a large extent determined the characteristic features of the central Pest area, giving the city on the left bank an appearance it has maintained to this day.

In 1870, three years before unification, a Metropolitan Board of Public Works was established, based on the model of London's similarly named body. One of its first projects involved the construction of a grand avenue, in the manner of the Champs-Elysées in Paris, which would sweep from the city centre out to the City Park, at the time on the outskirts of the main urban area. Work started in 1872 and after a dozen years most of it was complete.

Like many other streets in Budapest, the avenue has had a variety of names, which have changed depending on the political climate. It was originally called Sugár út (Radial Avenue) then in 1885, the year of its official inauguration, it was renamed after the post-1867 Hungarian Prime Minister and later Foreign Minister of the Austro–Hungarian Monarchy, Count Gyula Andrássy. A sign of how the times had changed by then is that Andrássy had once been hanged in effigy for his activities during the 1848-9 anti-Habsburg rebellion and had been forced to spend many years in exile. For a number of years after the Second World War the avenue was called Stalin Avenue, then for a brief period during the 1956 uprising it was designated the Avenue of Revolutionary Youth. In 1957 it acquired the title of Avenue of the People's Republic, a name it kept until 1990, when Andrássy út reappeared on the street signs.

The avenue, which extends in a straight line for nearly a mile and a half, was the most ambitious single project in the history of nineteenth-century Hungarian town planning. It is divided into three sections by two geometrically regular spaces, an octagon and a circle. The former, at the junction of the avenue and the Great Boulevard, which rings central Pest and is itself another construct of the late nineteenth century, is simply called Oktogon, though it, too, has had other names. From 1945 to 1990 it was known as November 7th Square, recalling the date of the Bolshevik revolution in Russia in 1917. For nine years prior to 1945, in contrast, it was named after Benito Mussolini, Italy's fascist dictator. Mussolini himself visited Budapest in 1936, the year the location was named after him. The other, circular junction, or Körönd, is today called Kodály körönd, since the great musician Zoltán Kodály used to live here.

As the avenue progresses each section becomes broader and the buildings on each side become smaller. The innermost section is flanked by apartment blocks of up to five storeys, with shops on the ground floor. The middle section has mainly apartment houses and some large mansion-type buildings. Here there are side pavements and secondary roads. Finally the third section, leading up to the City Park, has large houses and villas with gardens. These were originally occupied by wealthy families, though today they house a variety of offices, embassies, galleries and other bodies. Where renovation has taken place and these buildings are restored to their early glory, you certainly get an unmistakeable feel of the wealth which existed for some in pre-1914 Budapest.

Interestingly, in contrast with the exclusivity of the villas at the top end of the avenue, the apartment blocks in the first section were built to house both rich and poor, although there was clear segregation and differentiation in that the wealthy owners usually occupied large, lavish, multi-room, first-floor apartments overlooking the avenue, reached by elegant stairways. Poorer occupants were relegated to the sides or rear of the inner courtyards, and often had to make do with just a single room, sharing a toilet and other facilities, and were obliged to use a simple rear staircase.

It is possible to get a glimpse of one of the old apartments for the wealthy, or at least experience its size, since the first floor of no. 3 in the avenue today houses a Postal Museum. The neo-Renaissance building was constructed in 1884-6 for the wealthy Saxlehner family. Decorating the front staircase of the building is some impressive work by Károly Lotz, the country's most famous fresco master of the time, which includes pictorial allusions to the family's source of income, the commercial exploitation of one of Hungary's many mineral water sources. The museum is situated in what was the Saxlehners' seven-room apartment. Approaching the museum's entrance allows for a view of the inner courtyard and the rear of the building, though, as elsewhere, many of the original tiny rooms have been knocked through to make larger flats or even offices. This particular courtyard is not especially noteworthy, but there are many such inner yards in the city which are quite spectacular. No. 83-85 on the avenue, for example, has a very impressive, albeit run-down, double courtyard with loggia, well worth viewing if the gate is not locked.

The façades on Andrássy út, as elsewhere in the city, are often detailed and attractively decorated. (It is always worth looking at the façades in Budapest.) No. 7 on the avenue has huge atlantes, for example, while at no. 23 there is a pair of very attractive caryatids. The latter, the work of master sculptor Alajos Stróbl, depict Flora, the Roman goddess of flowers and spring. The building itself was constructed in 1885 for Mór Wahrmann, a prominent personality of the Pest commercial elite and, from 1869, Hungary's first Jewish member of parliament.

Many different architects were involved in the construction of Andrássy út, but there was a certain tendency to adopt neo-Renaissance styles, and even to make mini-copies of some well-known Italian buildings. The building at no. 69, today housing the Academy of Fine Arts, with its full-length balcony and Corinthian pilasters, is loosely modelled on Verona's Palazzo Bevilaqua. The Pallavicini Mansion at no. 98 has a loggia echoing the courtyard façade of the Palazzo Marino in Milan, and just off the avenue, near Oktogon, at 13 Teréz körút, is a small replica of the Strozzi Palace in Florence.

Architecture historian József Sisa highlights the view that in nineteenth-century Hungary (and German-speaking countries) "the neo-Renaissance style, because it connoted freedom, bourgeois society, and a scientific and enlightened attitude, was universally embraced as the stylistic equivalent of liberal political and laissez-faire economic philosophies." Thus the style suited the dream of constructing a major thoroughfare befitting a modern metropolis.

The Opera House

The most prominent neo-Renaissance building on the avenue, indeed its most prominent building of any style, is that of the Hungarian State Opera House, which stands on the north side of Andrássy út in its first section. The opera house is not only one of the most sumptuous buildings in Budapest, but one of the grandest buildings in Hungary. The interior, with its ornamental marble stairway and frescoes by Hungarian artists Bertalan Székely and Mór Than, is one of the richest in Budapest. The auditorium is among the most beautiful in Europe. Its large, round ceiling fresco, the work of Károly Lotz, depicts Olympus. With a seat on the top balcony you really are "in the gods"! Apart from attending a performance, one way of viewing the rich interior of the Opera House is to participate in one of the regular English-language tours of the building.

The Opera House was designed by Miklós Ybl, one of Hungary's most prolific and successful architects of the nineteenth century. Construction began in 1875 but was not completed for nine years due to financial problems, even though much of the funding came from Habsburg Emperor Francis Joseph. Cash limitations meant that Ybl had to produce ten different sketches for the façade.

In December 1881, during construction, there was a serious fire at Vienna's Ring Theatre, in which over 400 people lost their lives. It was one of the most serious fire accidents which plagued theatres in those days and it prompted the incorporation in the Budapest Opera of the latest safety designs involving all-metal, hydraulic stage machinery, making it the most modern concert hall in the world at the time. The hydraulic equipment lasted for nearly a century. All the materials for the original building were Hungarian except the huge chandelier in the main auditorium, which was made in Mainz.

The Opera opened in September 1884. Ferenc Liszt had been commissioned to write a work for the opening, but it was not performed because it included elements of the *Rákóczi March*, a Hungarian rebel melody referring to the early eighteenth-century anti-Habsburg revolt led by Prince Ferenc Rákóczi II.

Over the years the Budapest Opera became established among Europe's greatest opera houses. Gustav Mahler was its music director at one time, as was Otto Klemperer later. During the siege of Budapest in 1944-5 thousands found shelter in the huge cellars of the building, which amazingly suffered relatively little damage. The Opera was therefore able to open very quickly after the war, in spring 1945.

In the post-1945 decades the state granted the opera enormous subsidies, both for prestige and to facilitate access for everyone via low prices. All that has changed, but the tickets are still relatively inexpensive by Western standards. This is partly the reason why it can be difficult to attend the opera, unless advance booking is made in good time, though it is also because of the high quality of the performances and the international nature of much of the programme, particularly at the time of the annual Budapest Spring Festival in March and the "BudaFest" Summer Opera and Ballet Festival in August.

The façade of the Opera is richly adorned with much sculptural decoration. There are statues of Monteverdi, Scarlatti, Gluck, Mozart, Beethoven, Mussorgsky, Tchaikovsky, Moniusko and Smetana. In corner niches are Terpsichore, Erato, Thalia and Melpomene, representing dance, love poetry, comedy and tragedy. On one side of the entrance stands a large statue of the first musical director of the Opera House, Ferenc Erkel.

Erkel (1810-93) was the creator of several operas with Hungarian national themes. He was born into a musical family, his great-grandfather, his grandfather and his father all being musicians. The family organized concerts in which the young Ferenc participated and quickly learned to play music, such that by the age of ten he could substitute for his father on the organ. A year later he was already giving public performances. In 1844 Erkel wrote the music for what was to become Hungary's national anthem, the *Himnusz*. In line with its dour words written by Ferenc Kölcsey (the last verse begins: "Pity, God, the Magyar, then"), the music sounds to many outsiders rather morose and dreary, which has prompted one blunt Englishman to remark that with a national anthem like that it is no wonder that Hungary has traditionally had one of the highest suicide rates in the world.

Erkel was also the composer of one of Hungary's most frequently performed historical operas, *Bánk bán*. The opera is based on a drama by József Katona (1791-1830), the son of a provincial weaver. *Bánk bán* had been written in 1814 for a competition, though it failed even to get a mention from the jury. It was revised a few years later but performances were banned by the censor. Finally published in 1820 it received little attention and was never performed in the dramatist's lifetime.

The theme of *Bánk bán* is based on real events of thirteenth-century Hungary involving the rebellion of the potentate Bánk against foreign, mainly German, influence in the court and the murder of Queen Gertrude, who was German, while King Andrew II was away at war. The historical tragedy, although in a medieval setting, was seen as having very relevant contemporary national themes and this accounted for its later success. It was first performed in the 1830s and was regularly presented during the 1848-9 War of Independence, following which it was banned for a decade. Erkel's opera version of the drama was first performed in 1861 and has been a regular feature of Hungarian repertoires ever since.

Forever Smiling?

Another large, neo-Renaissance building stands opposite and complements the Opera House. This is the former Drechsler Mansion, which was constructed as an apartment building in 1883. At the time of writing it is in a dilapidated condition and is due for renovation as a hotel. A century ago there used to be a popular café, the Drechsler (sometimes known as the Reitter), on the ground floor. Nowadays it is difficult to visualize the original atmosphere of the avenue, constructed as it was in the era of the horse and carriage. Nevertheless, despite today's traffic and pollution, you can almost imagine the well-dressed citizens sipping their coffee on the terrace under the arches of the Drechsler, observing the elite arriving for the opera in their carriages. Our imaginations are helped by a few lines of Gyula Krudy, that keen observer of the metropolitan scene:

> *Real Andrássy Boulevard is where the asphalt is always immaculate, the parquet that is the carriageway is sprinkled with dust-repellent oil, the constable's frock coat is always pressed and his gloves white, the carriage wheels are red and have noiseless tyres, the cafés are bustling with life, in the restaurants they are constantly cooking, eating, the people are forever smiling...*

Whether the forever smiling people were an observable reality or a flight of fancy, Krudy seems convinced that the avenue was where "every gentlewoman in Pest who could boast an impeccable toilette, had the opportunity to present herself" and that "every burgher without any hope of entering either the Magyar nobility or baronage was eager to obtain the rank that can be obtained on one's own strength—a landlordship on Andrássy Boulevard."

For some the very existence of the avenue was like a dream come true. Adding to the excellence and glamour was the construction, in 1896, of the first underground railway to appear on the continent of Europe. Now Budapest was not catching up with, but ahead of Vienna, Paris and Berlin. The metro still runs the length of Andrássy út, just below its surface. Its stations have become mini-galleries, with photographic images of pre-1914 Budapest.

A Hungarian by Choice: Liszt

There is another statue flanking the entrance to the Opera House, depicting the great composer and pianist Liszt. For many people "Franz" Liszt is German or Austrian. For Hungarians he is "Ferenc", and definitely Magyar.

Liszt (1811-86) was born in the small village of Doborján on the Esterházy estate in western Hungary (today the place is called Raiding and is part of Austria). At the age of nine he dazzled an audience at a prestigious gentlemen's club in the nearby town of Sopron with a virtuoso piano recital and several improvisations. Three year later, at the age of twelve, he was already performing in Pest at the Inn of the Seven

Electors, a gathering place noted for its magnificent balls. His career took off and he later travelled widely throughout Europe giving countless performances to rapturous audiences, astonishing them with his technique.

The destruction caused by the great Pest flood of 1838 (see Chapter One) stirred his conscience. "Through this innermost tumult and feeling," he wrote to the *Gazette Musicale*, "I learned the meaning of the word 'my fatherland'... Oh my wild and distant country! Oh my unknown friends! Oh my great far-spreading family! Your cry of pain has brought me back to you. Touched to the depths, I bow my head, ashamed that I have forgotten you for so long ..." Following a series of benefit concerts he then was never far from Hungary, either in body or spirit. He would become, in the words of Paul Lendvai, the most famous "Hungarian by choice".

His presence in Budapest could draw adoring crowds, even on the street. In her memoirs, the English traveller Julia Pardoe wrote at length about his impact on the Hungarian public. Even the great romantic poet Mihály Vörösmarty composed an 84-line verse in his honour. Entitled simply "To Ferencz Liszt", it was both a eulogy to the man and a back-handed comment on a prodigal son.

Sing out a song in their deepest graves
our ancestors are compelled to stir,
so each immortal soul awaking proves
new life to descendants, made aware
of blessings in their Magyar fatherland.
They know that traitor sons are shamed and banned.

The adulation afforded Liszt in Budapest was not specifically a Hungarian phenomenon, though it was a good example of something broader. As Norman Lebrecht has argued in his biting critique of music as business, *When the Music Stops*, Ferenc Liszt, the piano maestro, following closely in the footsteps of Paganini, the virtuoso violinist, was one of the first performers to become a concert star, surrounded by hype and whipped-up emotion.

He was rather controversial in his personal life, too, generating many scandals. Despite being a novice for the priesthood and often wearing clerical garb, he was a great womanizer and fathered illegitimate children with, according to some sources, a number of married women. Yet, in the view of Lebrecht, that could add to the attraction. "Sinner or saint, his triple personation of the musical, the erotic and the sacerdotal inflamed the public imagination."

Despite his avowed love for his homeland and the reception he received in Budapest, Liszt never fully learned Hungarian. Lendvai says he had started to learn the language as early as 1829, but gave up after five lessons on encountering the word for unshakability: *tántorithatatlanság*. (Could anyone blame him?) Nevertheless, as he once wrote: "...notwithstanding my lamentable ignorance of the Hungarian language, I am and shall remain until my end a Magyar heart and soul." But what about after his end? Liszt's ashes are interred not in Budapest, but, in accordance with his will, in Bayreuth.

Other paradoxes concerned his writings on Hungarian traditional music and his compositions, such as his famous *Hungarian Rhapsodies*, twenty pieces in which there appears a tendency to mix up Hungarian folk themes with traditional gypsy music. It was an approach which rattled Magyar chauvinists as well as disturbing serious music scholars such as Béla Bartók, who once wrote: "The Hungarian Rhapsodies, which should say the most to us, are his least successful works (perhaps that is why they are so generally known and admired). Alongside strokes of genius we find altogether too conventional ideas—gypsy music, sometimes mixed with Italianisms (No. 6), sometimes in complete formal confusion (No. 12)." Even a head of government stepped into the fray. In 1886 Hungarian Prime Minister Kálmán Tisza declared, perhaps displaying a degree of prejudice: "At the very time when Hungary had lost almost everything but her music, Liszt chose to proclaim to the world that it was not Magyar music at all, but gypsy music." A distinction between the two can certainly be made on musicological grounds, but cannot gypsies simultaneously be Hungarians? This type of question has plagued Hungarian history for many years, and not only in relation to gypsies.

Andrássy út has a direct connection with Ferenc Liszt in that it was at no. 67 where he lived, on and off, for the last five years of his life. Today his former first-floor apartment is a memorial museum displaying a number of his pianos and other personal memorabilia. Free concerts are held here on most Saturday mornings. That, in a small way, continues a tradition established at the time of Liszt's residence, in that the building was the centre of Hungarian musical life in the late nineteenth century, as it then housed the Hungarian Academy of Music, of which Liszt himself was a key founder, its first president and one of its early piano teachers. Of this the Hungarians are very proud.

Yet, according to one of his biographers, Ronald Taylor, Liszt's view of the Budapest music scene was not unequivocally positive. Taylor quotes a letter Liszt once wrote to Ödön Mihalovich, one of his leading successors at the Academy. "If you were not chained to Budapest, your career as a composer would develop more freely. You can be certain that in a few years' time no Hungarian composer will make his mark anywhere but in his own country, where progress only proceeds by fits and starts."

In this, Ferenc Liszt has proved to be wrong, or at least only half right. There are a number of Hungarian composers who have certainly made an impact on the international scene—Béla Bartók, Zoltán Kodály, György Ligeti and György Kurtág, to name just four, though to what extent, if at all, they were "chained to Budapest" is an intriguing issue, as is the question of what is, for these and other Hungarian musicians, essentially "Hungarian" about their differing works. For Kodály and Bartók we can point to the folk music connections or origins (see below). For others the answer can be more intriguing.

Ligeti, who was born in Transylvania in 1923, who studied and later taught at the Academy of Music after the Second World War, and who left Hungary in 1956, was asked on the occasion of his 75th birthday whether it was possible to say that his music was Hungarian. This is part of what he had to say.

> *I am an Austrian citizen living in Hamburg and Vienna; as a child I held Romanian, as a young man Hungarian citizenship. Wherever I live I am a Hungarian Jew from Transylvania... My ideal was Bartók. The rhythm of my music stems from the rhythm of the Hungarian language; since I think in that language, it also indirectly determines my musical thinking.*

Since 1907 the Academy, officially called the Ferenc Liszt Academy of Music, has occupied an Art Nouveau building in the square named after Liszt, which runs off the first section of Andrássy út. For decades this has been the centre of concert life in Budapest. Not only the greatest Hungarian, but also the world's top composers, instrumentalists and singers have trodden, and continue to tread, the boards of its main concert hall. Budapest is undoubtedly a music-lover's city, and almost inevitably the visitor in search of top-class classical music will be drawn to the Academy.

The Academy's concert hall has one of the most ornate Art Nouveau interiors in Budapest, well worth viewing. Inside, too, are works by the artist Aladár Körösfői Kriesch (1863-1920), one of the leaders of the Hungarian Pre-Raphaelites, known as the Gödöllő School. English Pre-Raphaelite influence is clearly visible in his *Hungarian Wedding Procession in the 14th Century* along the walls and above the entrances to the main auditorium, and in *The Fountain of Art*, a large wall painting on the first floor. Both date from 1907.

"An instrument accessible to all": Zoltán Kodály

As with Ferenc Liszt, Andrássy út also has a direct connection with Zoltán Kodály. From 1924 until his death in 1967, Kodály had an apartment at no. 1 on the "körönd", the circular junction which divides the second and third sections of the avenue. Today the flat is a museum devoted to his memory and is decorated with many textiles, ceramics and other folk items he acquired over the years. The junction has borne Kodály's name since 1971 (Kodály körönd). Before that it was mostly nameless, though from 1939 to 1945 it was actually called Hitler Square.

Together with Béla Bartók, Zoltán Kodály established the study of Hungarian folk songs and folk music on a systematic basis. They travelled around the country recording songs for later analysis, their seminal work, *Hungarian Folk Songs for Voice with Piano Accompaniment*, appearing in December 1906. Yet as well as being a musicologist, Kodály (pronounced "code-aye") was also a composer and a pioneer of music education. He was a great advocate of the vocal chords. "An instrument is the privilege of the few," he wrote in 1941. "The human voice, an instrument accessible to all, free and still the most beautiful, can be the only soil where a general music culture may grow." The so-called "Kodály method", which places great emphasis on choral singing and the enjoyment of song, the linking of song with movement, the appreciation of the musical mother tongue, sight-seeing and scoring, improvisatory ability and the elimination of musical illiteracy as the basis of cultural education in general, has been both applauded and applied world-wide.

Surprisingly, perhaps, for a man who is deemed to have created a specifically Hungarian approach to music, Kodály acknowledged that he learned much from his visits to England. "The high level of English choral singing," he once wrote, "was for us a stimulating example." He drew on English music practice and in music teaching applied John Curwen's Tonic Sol-Fa method. He visited and conducted in Britain several times and had a close relationship with the English musicologist, Edward J. Dent (who, for the curious, is no relation of the present author, as far as he knows).

The intensely proud adoption of Kodály's approach in his homeland helps explain why music has played a major role in Hungarian educational practice. That continues today, though, to the disappointment of many, to a lesser extent; more "modern", "technologically-oriented" and "potentially commercially rewarding" subjects having been given a greener light in terms of state support and promotion since the 1989-90 political changes. At the same time, there are some who question the "method" itself, or at least the tendency for it to be applied in a routine, textbook way. There is also the conceptual challenge of the electronic aspects and the mechanical creation and reproduction of modern music. "Is it possible," asked István Balázs in the early 1990s, "to elaborate, on the basis of the Kodály approach, a method of musical education which remains open to contemporary musical culture and yet is able to incorporate in it traditional values, including folk music?" His own response is that while safeguarding Kodály's conception is kept on the agenda in Hungary, it should go hand in hand with a search for alternative solutions.

Given his view of the "democratic" nature of the human voice and his desire to bring (or rather give back) musical culture to the broad mass of people, it is understandable how Kodály could survive and even be promoted in Hungary's difficult post-1945 Stalinist era, since at that time there was, on the surface at least, the goal of at last making culture available to all. Kodály's views could fit into that political atmosphere, but they were not simply "for the moment". Well before that era, in 1934, Kodály had noted that the "Academy of Music came too early: there were not enough suitable students. The opera also came too early: it was brought into life not by the nation's desire, but by the desire for luxury of a thin select stratum; it could not get close to the heart of the nation… because nothing was done to make general musical education approach the level of the opera… A wide gap was formed, from a musical point of view, too, between the handful of elite people and the majority of the nation."

In the 1950s Kodály, using his relatively secure position, was able to protect or help a number of musicians who found themselves, for whatever reason, at odds with the politico-cultural establishment. On the eve of the 1956 uprising, a packed audience at the Academy gave a 15-minute ovation to Zoltán Kodály after a rendering of his unaccompanied choral work *Zrínyi-Szózat* (Zrínyi's Plea), which he had written the previous year. Zrínyi was a commander in the sixteenth-century wars against the Turks. The applause, according to British journalist Dora Scarlett who wrote about the incident in her memoirs, was accompanied by chants of the line *Ne Bántsd a Magyart*—Leave the Hungarians Alone!

Today Kodály is internationally renowned, not only for his writings on folk music and music education, but also for his many compositions produced during his long career, such as his 1923 *Psalmus Hungaricus*, written to celebrate the 50th anniversary of the union of Buda, Óbuda and Pest, and his *Symphony in C Major*, written nearly forty years later.

His background might not have necessarily pointed in the direction of fame, but is arguably a proof of the value of his own theories about a musical upbringing. Kodály was born in 1882 in Kecskemét, a medium-size town some fifty miles south-east of Budapest. His place of birth was the local railway station, though that was not because his mother unexpectedly went into labour while travelling—the family lived there as his father worked for the railways. Maybe it was the sound of train whistles which turned the young Kodály towards music, though more likely it was because his father played the violin, while his mother, Paulina Jaloveczky, one of six children of a poor inn-keeper, sang and played the piano.

As cultural historian László Kósa has pointed out, in the era of Kodály's birth employment on the Hungarian railways was an attractive position, with its guaranteed pension, working clothes, travel concessions, its insurance and hospital facilities and even its own housing estates. "Officials who worked for the railway, particularly station masters, were highly respected and cultured members of local bourgeois society." So perhaps Kodály's background was not quite as poor as might be assumed.

The wealth and standing of the Hungarian railways and their late-nineteenth-century institutions is well reflected in some of the largest buildings on Andrássy út. Diagonally across the Körönd from Kodály's former apartment, at no. 88-89, stands an attractive, large neo-Renaissance mansion, which was built for the Railways Pensions Administration in the early 1880s At the time of writing the building certainly needs some restoration, yet it is noteworthy not only for its size and proportions, but also for the attractive sgraffiti on its exterior and for its magnificent gate made by wrought-iron master Gyula Jungfer. Nearby, at no. 73-73, is a large building constructed in 1876 for the Hungarian Railways Administration, which is still based here. There are large reliefs at each end of the main façade. One is to the memory of railway workers who fell in the First World War, while the other was placed there to mark the centenary of the first Hungarian railway. In the hand of the figure is a model of the first Hungarian railway engine, which ran in 1846 from Pest to Vác, a town twenty-two miles to the north.

Even here we cannot escape music. The MÁV (Hungarian Railways) Symphony Orchestra, which was founded in 1945 partly to take "rolling music" around the country, is still one of Hungary's most prominent orchestras and regularly plays abroad. For 26 years from 1951 its conductor was Miklós Lukács, a former director of the Opera House and a noted conductor of Wagner's music.

There is even a Hungarian railway composer, the chief engineer Gyula Beliczay, a gifted spare-time composer who was rediscovered in the mid-1990s. Beliczay was born in 1835 and showed a talent for music from an early age. Yet his father persuaded him to follow what he considered to be a more secure profession and so he took up a career as a railway engineer, although he never abandoned his musical studies. His aptitude on the piano generated admiration from both Ferenc Liszt and Anton Rubinstein. Beliczay retired at the age of 51 and devoted himself to music. In 1888 he was even appointed professor of composition at the Academy, but he died five years later, perhaps leaving his potential unfulfilled. Nevertheless, his Symphony in D minor, his Mass in F minor and his serenade are still included in various repertoires.

Bartók and his Times

Much better known, of course, is the name of Béla Bartók, a contemporary, friend and colleague of Kodály. The pair worked together in their early years, researching the roots of folk song, though later their paths diverged somewhat. Before Kodály moved to Andrássy út in 1924, he lived for fourteen years in Áldás utca, in the then fashionable Rose Hill district on the Buda side. His apartment there, on the second floor of no. 11, became a cultural meeting place, Bartók and other musicians being regular visitors. Curiously there is no plaque on the wall commemorating this fourteen-year period in Kodály's life, which is rather surprising in view of the degree of Budapest's local patriotism and its municipal mania for erecting historical tablets. On the wall of 23 Nádor utca in Pest, for example, there is a large plaque informing the passer-by that Ferenc Liszt lived there in the early 1870s for a mere two years.

Béla Bartók was born in 1881 in Nagyszentmiklós, which is today in Romania. From 1894 he studied in Pozsony (today Bratislava, the capital of Slovakia) under Ferenc Erkel's son, László. From 1899 to 1903 he attended the Academy of Music on Andrássy út in Budapest and for a time he had lodgings on the avenue. It was in the concert hall of the Academy, on 31 March 1900, that he gave his first public performance in the city, playing Beethoven's Piano Concerto in C minor. After his studies he gave concerts in Germany and England, and in the course of his life he would appear as a pianist across the length and breadth of Europe.

Bartók became involved with folk music research in 1904-06, when he provided notations for many songs collected on phonograph cylinders by Béla Vikár. In cooperation with Kodály, he himself travelled miles across the country recording, collecting and analysing thousands of folk songs, which were then still a vibrant part of peasant cultural traditions. "I discovered that what we had known as Hungarian folk songs till then were more or less trivial songs by popular composers and did not contain much that was valuable," he would later write. "I felt an urge to go deeper into this question and set out in 1905 to collect and study Hungarian peasant music unknown until then. It was my great good luck to find a helpmate for this work in Zoltán Kodály, who, owing to his deep insight and sound judgement in all spheres of music, could give me many a hint and much advice that proved of immense value."

Bartók's interest encompassed not only Hungarian, but also Romanian, Slovak, Ukrainian, Serbian and later Turkish and Arab folk music, and although he would become recognized internationally as one of Europe's modernist composers, difficult for many to understand in his day, he never lost his interest in folk music and returned to his work as an ethnomusicologist in the 1930s under the auspices of the Hungarian Academy of Science.

In his early years as a professional, before the First World War, Bartók was part of a broad circle of Budapest-based creative intellectuals, which in its time was influential but is virtually forgotten today. Only certain names of individuals involved with it have a resonance—apart from Bartók and Kodály, the circle included the literary critic and later Marxist philosopher György Lukács, the sociologist Karl Mannheim and the film aesthetician Béla Balázs, to name just a few who became renowned internationally in their own fields.

Fortunately, the non-Hungarian reader has today at least two English-language sources which present a picture of that era of Budapest culture: Judit Frigyesi's *Béla Bartók and Turn-of-the-Century Budapest* and Mary Gluck's *George Lukács and His Generation: 1900-1918*. These two excellent works cover some similar ground and overlap to an extent. Both give evidence for their assertions that pre-1914 Budapest was the scene of a dynamic and radical intellectual culture, almost unique in its day.

How and why that cultural flowering came about is a complicated issue. It touches on the speedy urbanization and industrialization of Hungary, and in particular Budapest, in the last quarter of the nineteenth century, the social dislocation which that brought about, the emergence of a newly-educated, sometimes Jewish, sometimes rich, yet hitherto culturally rootless intelligentsia, and the visible social problems which that rapid development had simultaneously generated.

A number of dates pinpoint certain developments of the rapidly changing cultural environment of that era. In 1896 Simon Hollósy left the Academy of Fine Arts to establish a "plein air" artists' colony at Nagybánya, signifying a break with the then established academic tradition. The year 1900 saw the first publication of *Twentieth Century*, a critical sociological journal which counted among its contributors a wide range of scholars. In 1904 György Lukács and others founded the Thália Theatre in Budapest, which was to be devoted to modern trends of the theatrical arts. Two years later, the collection *New Poems* (Új versek) by Endre Ady (see below) took the country by storm. It was in the same year that Bartók and Kodály's *Hungarian Folksongs* appeared and that the Circle of Hungarian Impressionists and Naturalists was formed, to be followed by the more radically artistic group known as The Eight.

If any year might be singled out as special it could perhaps be 1908. This was the year of the first appearance of *Nyugat* (Occident), a journal devoted to exploring and promoting all that was perceived as being progressive, which at the time was associated with "Western" culture. Complementing the works of Frigyesi and Gluck mentioned above, Mario Fenyo's *Literature and Political Change: Budapest, 1908-1919* is an interesting and scholarly account of the early years of *Nyugat*. It is also a sympathetic account, not surprising, perhaps, since the author's father, Miksa Fenyő, was one of the founders of the journal.

Nyugat's yearning for the modern and the progressive inevitably struck a discordant note with the conservative Hungarian establishment, particularly its more nationalistic elements. A comment by a conservative journalist, quoted by Gluck, illustrates the type and depth of feelings the journal generated: "It is treason and slander what they do in *Nyugat* under the pretext of civilizing the barbarian Magyars. They want to ruin our morals, they want to disillusion us of our faith, and they want to crunch into pieces our national pride. A storm of outrage should sweep away all those who commit such deep offences against the nation." Prime Minister István Tisza stepped in and added his criticism. In 1912 he denounced the literature represented by *Nyugat* as "incomprehensible bombast", which was "nothing more than the chaotic exterior of spiritual anarchy and an emptiness of mind and heart."

Interestingly, however, with the outbreak of hostilities in 1914 the journal was by no means unequivocally anti-war, though that would come about as the war progressed. For example, Mihály Babits (1883-1941), one of Hungary's most noted poets and writers of the first half of the twentieth century, was associated with *Nyugat* from its beginnings. Critics have used words like "classical", "decadent" and "ivory tower" to describe the early works of Babits, but all agree that his opposition to the First World War threw him into the political turmoil. "I would rather spill gushing blood for the little finger of my sweetheart, than for a hundred kings, a hundred flags," he wrote in 1915. A strongly anti-war poem of his called "Fortissimo" led to an entire edition of the journal being confiscated in 1917.

The metropolitan cultural elite drawn to *Nyugat* and other critical/progressive journals comprised, by and large, *déclassé* intellectuals and disaffected sons and daughters of the bourgeoisie, though a number of working-class individuals were also involved. Many of these were associated with the urban-based Social Democratic Party, and their mentor in many respects was Ervin Szabó, a social scientist, political writer and activist, and a long-forgotten type of anarcho-Marxist. (The designation appears contradictory, but in the pre-1914 context of Budapest, as elsewhere, it had a certain resonance.) When he died in 1918, work stopped for a while throughout Budapest as a sign of mourning. In his professional life Szabó was a statistician, librarian and library director. The city's main municipal library and its branch network is named after him to this day.

Bartók and other like-minded musicians would occasionally give benefit concerts to support the radical journals and the causes they espoused. That was natural, since, paradoxical though it may seem, Bartók's extensive research into and knowledge of traditional peasant music was the background to his becoming one of the most avant-garde composers of his day. It was natural, too, that Bartók would become somewhat of an outsider, in terms of "official" culture. It was not only that his modernist compositions were at the cutting edge of "difficult" twentieth-century music, his view of folk music was also somewhat anti-traditionalist in that he was critical of over-romanticized, often urban-generated and simplistic views of "puszta culture". "I discovered that what we had known as Hungarian folk songs till then were more or less trivial songs by popular composers and did not contain much that was valuable," he wrote in his autobiography.

Furthermore, he positively acknowledged the multi-ethnic nature and the different, yet interweaving traditions of peasant music and song he found in the region of the Carpathian Basin. One of his biographers, Paul Griffiths, even asserts that Bartók always maintained that musical cultures positively gained from being mongrel. Judit Frigyesi puts it in a rather gentler, though also significant way. Bartók, she believes, "undermined the myth of a unified national musical style," and she describes as "nothing less than high treason" (for its time) Bartók's claim that some of the oldest layers of Hungarian music might have had their origins in the regional music culture existing prior to the ninth-century Magyar "conquest" of the "homeland". No wonder he was never the favourite of the establishment, particularly in the national-minded, conservative era of the inter-war years.

Yet Bartók did not set out to be controversial. "For my own part," he once wrote in 1903, "all my life, in every sphere, always and in every way, I shall have one object: the good of Hungary and the Hungarian nation." Thus it might have come as a surprise to him that, as Paul Griffiths relates, his "Kossuth", composed when he was 22 and due to be performed on 13 January 1904, created a storm. Lajos Kossuth was the political leader of Hungary's abortive 1848-9 independence war against the Habsburgs, and Bartók included in the piece an ironic take-off of the Austrian national anthem. By 1904, however, pride in being part of "the Empire" was something almost patriotic for many. In rehearsal some of the orchestra refused to play and on the night five declined to appear. Five days after the Budapest event the work was performed in Manchester, counting as Bartók's first orchestral performance abroad.

In 1911, together with Kodály, Bartók launched the New Hungarian Music Association, its first recital, with Bartók playing, taking place on 27 November in the hall of the Royal Hotel on Budapest's Great Boulevard. The association had little impact. In that same year Bartók completed his famous *Bluebeard's Castle*, but it would be another seven years before it was performed in Budapest.

Another difficulty concerned his today internationally acknowledged *Miraculous Mandarin*, a mime-play with libretto by Menyhért (Melchior) Lengyel, which was a commentary on modern urban life, involving erotic but hardly pornographic allusions. A planned Budapest staging in 1931 was cancelled after the dress rehearsal. The premiere had taken place five years earlier, not in Hungary but in Germany, in Cologne. It was taken off after one performance on the orders of the then local mayor, Konrad Adenauer, later more famously known as the first chancellor of post-war West Germany.

Throughout the 1930s Hungary drifted steadily in the direction of National Socialism, with 1938 seeing the first of a series of anti-Jewish laws on the German model (for which see Chapter Ten). Although in vain, both Bartók and Kodály, together with other artists and intellectuals, publicly opposed this trend, giving their signatures to protests published in the press. Any notion of racial superiority or exclusivity was anathema to Bartók's way of thinking. In a letter of 1931 he spelt out that his own idea was "the brotherhood of peoples, brotherhood in spite of all wars and conflicts. I try, to the best of my ability, to serve this ideal in my music. Therefore, I don't reject any influence, be it Slovakian, Romanian, Arabic or from any other source. The source must only be clean, fresh and healthy!"

The rising danger of Nazi Germany and the stifling atmosphere at home deeply troubled Bartók. "So much for Hungary, where, unfortunately, nearly all of our 'educated' Christians are adherents of the Nazi regime; I feel quite ashamed of coming from this class," he wrote in a letter of 1938. His thoughts turned to emigration, though he was no longer a young man and he was loath to leave his mother behind. Eventually, after her death, he indeed chose voluntary exile. After giving a final concert in Budapest on 8 October 1940 he left Hungary for the United States, where he spent the last five years of his life.

It was only in death that Bartók returned home, but it was not until July 1988 that his ashes were finally brought to Hungary and interred in Budapest's Farkasrét Cemetery. Today his last home in Budapest, in Csalán utca on the Buda side of the river, is preserved as a special museum in memory of one of the world's greatest musicians of the twentieth century.

Two Writer-Kings

Apart from the Opera House, no major public buildings were erected on Andrássy út (there is not one church, for example), but some places stood out for their elegance and the crowds they attracted. The Theresa Town Casino, one of the many gentlemen's clubs of nineteenth-century Budapest, was one of those. From the ground floor, where there was a popular restaurant, the main staircase led to a two-storey high banqueting hall decorated with Károly Lotz's fresco *The Apotheosis of Budapest*, which featured symbols of civilian professions as well as a centrally positioned allegory of the city. Before the First World War, the building was transformed into the Grand Parisian Department Store, which became one of the city's most fashionable destinations. Its roof boasted a restaurant in the summer and a skating rink in the winter. The "Lotz" hall survived the changes, though at the time of writing cannot be viewed as the building, at no. 39 on the avenue, is closed. There are arguments about its future function, but the hall and its decoration are likely to remain as a reminder of the dream of an elegant city, which the building of Andrássy út stood for.

Surprisingly for a city with much public sculpture, Andrássy út has very few statues. The two which are most prominent, depicting Mór Jókai and Endre Ady (pictured), face each other across the avenue in its innermost section. Yet they were not part of the original plan, being erected here only in 1921 and 1960 respectively.

In his era Mór Jókai (1825-1904) was the Hungarian author most widely published abroad, becoming renowned in England and America, where he was known as Maurus Jókai. He was a prolific author of romantic escapism, creating more than one hundred works of fiction, the stories of which were set all over the world. The son of Calvinist parents, Jókai studied law but turned to literature, writing his first novel, *Weekdays*, when he was twenty-one. Among his works with a political theme his 1854 *A Hungarian Nabob*, set in the pre-1848 Reform Era, is the most famous. *New Landlord*, published in 1862, has as its hero an Austrian general who, after fighting Hungary, settles in the country, adopting it as his own. It was said to be a favourite of Britain's Queen Victoria.

Despite some strong attacks from literary critics, Jókai remained popular, perhaps in the manner of the authors of mass-market pulp fiction today, though the common comparison with Dickens is arguably more appropriate. *Timár's Two Worlds*, which appeared in 1873, is an adventure examining the impact of wealth. This was the work which established his reputation abroad and which is considered one of his best.

Like many Hungarian writers and poets of his time, Jókai was attracted to the ideals of the 1848 revolution in which he participated as a close colleague of Sándor Petőfi, acting for a time as the editor of a newspaper of the young radicals. Consequently, he was driven into hiding after the failure of the War of Independence. Later in life he became a member of parliament, though he maintained his reputation as the "writer-king of his nation" right up to his death.

Endre Ady (1877-1919), who burst onto the literary scene, as it is often put, around the time of Jókai's death, took over the mantle of writer-king, though he was quite different, being much more pugnacious in both his attitudes and his works, outraged as he was by the misery, poverty, economic backwardness and corruption he perceived. "Superstitious, uneducated, sick and in need of change" was how he described Hungarian society in 1902. Ady described his work as the "new verses of a new era". His poems were often unconventional in form, language and content, which with their unusual choice of adjectives could shock the public. The outrage was furthered by their general approach. Ady's long spell as a journalist in Paris had made him see Hungary as narrow and materialistic, and through his poems he unleashed a storm of violent and sometimes abusive attacks upon his country. Inevitably he became the target of counter-attacks, which generated a political tussle, Ady being supported by left-wing radicals and members of the *Nyugat* circle, who hailed him as a prophet, and being condemned by right-wing nationalists.

Ady's more personal verses also irritated the conventional public, as did his lifestyle—he shared many years of his life with a married woman, Adél Diósi, *née* Brüll, who appears in his poems as Léda, the reverse of her first name. As Judit Frigyesi puts it, his themes of love and sensuality, loneliness and estrangement, without the intrusion of any over-sentimental happiness "struck the majority with the force of a manifesto against the conventional image of the Hungarian spirit."

The thrust of Ady's political verse is consistent; Hungary needs renewal or it will continue to wallow in misery.

A peacock takes its perch upon the county hall—
a sign that freedom comes to many folk in thrall.

These simple lines taken from a famous folk song opened one of his poems. The proud, frail peacock, feathers dazzling the sun, proclaims that "tomorrow here all will be undone."

Tomorrow all will change, be changed at last …
New winds will groan laments in the old Magyar trees …

Ady writes of new forges, new fires, new faiths and new holy men.

Either in Magyar words new meanings will unfold,
or the sadness of Magyar life will linger as of old.

Not surprisingly, this poem of Ady's was among the verses declaimed in public during demonstrations on the first day of the 1956 Hungarian uprising.

Ady lived a hectic, unsettled life, often spending long nights at a café. One of his favourites was The Three Ravens on Andrássy út. The café is no longer there, but a plaque by its former entrance at no. 24 near the Opera House recalls the writer's connection. However, we can turn again to Gyula Krudy for the atmosphere:

Ady liked to work in the recess, separated by some boards and hung with tobacco-coloured curtains, whose wine-stained floor had seen the so-called religious disputes of yore and the pub fights of more recent times... While Ady was working, Béla Révész was sitting at a table near the "separated cabinet" welcoming the poet's disciples along with renegades, fools and saints, reformed drunks and pseudo-drunks... arriving under cover of darkness from all over the city on hearing the news that Ady was writing his Sunday poems. But nobody dared enter the poet's sanctuary.

Renegades, fools and saints—Ady's impact was not confined to the literary, educated supporters of the *Nyugat* circles. His many journalistic essays enjoyed a wide readership and he gained a certain popularity, too, even among cabaret audiences. His texts would often be used by Béla Reinitz as the basis of the latter's cabaret chansons.

Ady's journalism could be very hard-hitting. In an article entitled "The Explosive Country", published on Christmas Day in 1910, he lashed out against the status quo. "Till now there was a Hungary which belonged to the few," he wrote, "which struggled with cowering might very often against imaginary enemies. This modern explosive Hungary knows now that the enemy is within, and that this enemy is the one it will have to square accounts with. Stewards and henchmen may organize their armies; pride, rank, illegal wealth, politics, perfidy and superstition may yet find a loophole for a year or two. But the splendid work of creating revolution cannot be held up… The people of new Hungary… will undertake a great clean-up in this huge porch with all its layers of dirt… The gospel of the explosive Hungary fills the towns and villages during this traditional festival of peace."

Not long before he died in late January 1919, Ady had moved into the only apartment he was ever able to call his own, although it was inherited by Berta Boncza ("Csinszka" as he called her), a much younger woman and fanatical admirer, whom he had married in the spring of 1915. Here he lived struck down by illness and worn out by alcohol, acknowledging but not being able to fully participate in the social explosion following the First World War. Today the place, at 4-6 Veres Pálné utca in the centre of Pest, is a memorial museum. The conventionality of the furnishings belies the occupant's character, as was noted by the renowned arts patron Count Lajos Hatvany: "The three rooms [have] nice and cosy family furniture, in a delicate and tasteful arrangement. I was very much surprised and pleased to see the vagabond in such a neat environment."

Avenue of Nightmares
The very mention of 60 Andrássy út is enough to send a chill down the spine of many Hungarians—for two reasons. Firstly, from 1937 the building was one of the bases, later the headquarters of the Arrow Cross, Hungary's fascist party. When the Arrow Cross staged a coup in mid-October 1944 and set itself up in government, the building became a terror headquarters, the site of torture and executions. Secondly, that "tradition" continued after 1945 when the post-war security authorities, originally charged with tracking down war criminals and fascists, moved into the building.

In 1946 the Department of State Security (ÁVO in its Hungarian initials) was officially formed and soon turned its attention to a wider range of people considered to be "class enemies" or "enemies of the people", meaning potential opponents of the ruling party. 60 Andrássy út eventually became a feared address as the centre of a web of state terror. It was from here that the ÁVO ran its network of spies and informers, and it was to here that thousands of its victims were brought for interrogation and often brutal torture.

The ÁVO are frequently referred to as the secret police, which is perhaps a misnomer since its members wore uniforms. "Political police" might be a better term as the organization operated directly under the control of the Party authorities and was known as "the Party's fist". Thousands of "enemies" were held in detention and forced labour camps under the organization's control. Deep hatred of the state security force was one of the motivating factors in the collective psyche of many participants during the 1956 uprising, such that anyone even suspected of being a member was liable to be detained and sometimes mercilessly killed on the spot.

Many harrowing accounts of what happened in the avenue's most feared building have been left by people who found themselves its unwilling occupants. One of the most interesting is by Paul Ignotus, the son of Hugo Veigelsberg, a leading light of the *Nyugat* circle, who wrote under the pseudonym of "Ignotus". The son's memoir, *Political Prisoner*, tackles the thorny question of why many of those taken to 60 Andrássy út confessed to crimes they did not commit—rather in the manner of Nicolas Salmanovitch Rubashov, the protagonist of Arthur Koestler's celebrated novel *Darkness at Noon*, which relates to the show trials of 1930s Moscow.

Koestler, as it happens, was another product of the rich cultural and political atmosphere of early twentieth-century Budapest. He was born in the city in 1905 and according to his biographer, David Cesarani, before his family left for Vienna in 1919 he attended school in a building at the corner of Andrássy út and Szív utca. The family had several homes in the neighbourhood. Koestler is a prime representative of that strange, albeit by no means unusual phenomenon, an internationally celebrated Hungarian, though generally not known as a Hungarian, and better known, too, outside Hungary than within it, in his case no doubt because he quickly ceased writing in Hungarian for Hungarians.

Paul Ignotus acknowledges that some prisoners, in the manner of Koestler's Rubashov, may have confessed because of a twisted loyalty to the Party, which is "always right and on the side of history", even when condemning its own members, and that others may have confessed believing in the (usually but not always false) promises of a lesser sentence. But he is convinced that "in general, torture was surely more decisive."

The confessions were not uniform in their style and it "was comparatively easy to confess lies and conceal the truth." What was common, says Ignotus, was that "none of us could be dignified." Panic-stricken, isolated prisoners, "dirty, miserable and exhausted", broken by humiliation and at the mercy of cruel interrogators, could not stand up to their tormentors in the way the resistance hero of the Italian film *The Open City* spat in the face of a Gestapo officer. "This is just the scene in which such circumstances cannot happen," he asserts. "To be proud and dignified while cigarette ends are stamped out on one's skin is surely more difficult than cinema-goers would think." Reflecting on the anti-heroic responses of most of his fellow prisoners, Ignotus concludes: "We were but human in a sub-human world."

Today 60 Andrássy út is the "House of Terror", containing exhibitions about the history and brutal activities of the Arrow Cross and the post-war political police, mainly the latter. The museum opened amidst a great political hullabaloo in early 2002, having received a tremendous amount of financial backing from the government. Viktor Orbán, the somewhat demagogic prime minister of the then centre-right government, was there at the official opening, as were thousands of his admirers. There was a general election in the offing and presumably it was thought that such an event would remind voters of the country's dark past, encouraging them not to vote for any successors of the *ancien régime*, however "reformed" they might be. In the event Orbán lost the election—just.

Since its inception the House of Terror has generated a great deal of controversy, not only about the massive amount of public money it has and should continue to receive, but also about the appearance of its dominating and rather inappropriate (for the avenue) exterior decoration. Perhaps more importantly, critics have pointed out the imbalanced nature of the exhibitions inside, the victims and era of Hungarian communism being given a disproportionately amount of space relative to the victims and era of fascism in Hungary, when over half a million Jews, gypsies and others perished—the greatest tragedy, simply in terms of numbers killed, of Hungary's twentieth-century history.

One critic, István Rév, has gone on record condemning the display as "a total propaganda space, where death and victims are used as rhetorical devices." He goes so far as to make ideological and stylistic comparisons between the exhibitions created for the House of Terror with the Exhibition of the Fascist Revolution, opened by Mussolini in Rome in 1932.

Gypsies and Princesses on Stage: Puppets and Operetta

Andrássy út and its neighbourhood have by no means been associated entirely either with the spectre of terror or with the seriousness of classical music and deeply stirring poetry. There has always been a lighter side, represented, for example, by the Puppet Theatre and, more generally, by Nagymező utca, a street which crosses the avenue's inner section and which has been known popularly (and in a rather exaggerated fashion) as "Budapest's Broadway", given the number of theatres located there.

The Puppet Theatre is housed in the basement of 69 Andrássy út. In characteristic East European fashion, what you find here, although explicitly produced for children (and the young at heart of any age), is no knock-about, Punch and Judy type of entertainment. Rather it is quality, often "classical" theatre in puppet format. The American poet and writer Michael Blumenthal remembers attending performances with his small son in the mid-1990s as "a cultural experience for children of the very highest artistic and imaginative quality", adding that the "existence of high-quality, low-cost culture (I won't degrade it by referring to it as 'entertainment') for children in Central/Eastern Europe (those poor, deprived Communist backwaters we Americans so loved to hate), of course, far predates the Brave New World of 1989." (Foreign visitors to Budapest, with or without young children, can readily test his thesis, since a visit to the Puppet Theatre by no means stretches the limits of one's purse, nor, due to the format of presentation, is an understanding of the Hungarian language a prime necessity.)

Curious though it may seem, a visit to Budapest's Broadway may also not require knowledge of Hungarian, even though theatre is that most language-oriented of cultural expressions. The reason for this paradoxical notion is that virtually on any one day of the year non-Hungarian visitors to Budapest, at least those fairly familiar with drama and theatre, are likely to find a show in town that they can follow due to familiarity, and which they can contrast with their own previous experiences in the theatre seats of their own countries. At the time of writing, during one week on "Broadway" there were performances or adaptations of Eugene O'Neill's *Mourning Becomes Electra*, Tennessee Williams' *A Streetcar Named Desire*, Christopher Hampton's *The Talking Cure*, Shelagh Delaney's *A Taste of Honey*, Tolstoy's *Anna*

Karenina, and a version of Leonard Bernstein's *West Side Story*—and these were only the "non-Hungarian" productions on one street! Elsewhere in the city during the same week you could find performances of three dramas by Shakespeare, two by Chekov, a couple by Joe Orton, as well as plays by, or based on works by, Gogol, Dostoevsky, William Congreve, Noel Coward, Harold Pinter, Michael Frayn, Martin McDonagh, Martin Sherman, Jean Genet, Neil Simon, Alan Ayckbourn and Milan Kundera, as well as staged versions of works from Agatha Christie to Mikis Theodorakis.

From the theatre point of view, no one can say that Budapest audiences are starved. The total number of more than one hundred and fifty performances available during the week in question was not unusual. The figure is high, since, unlike in some other European cities, a Budapest theatre will have not just one but several plays running simultaneously; in other words, the performances often change from day to day throughout the week.

The variety of performances also applies to operetta, of which Budapest has a rich tradition, stemming from the pre-1914 era. It may seem strange, as Hungarian historian Péter Hanák has pointed out, that a musical theatre genre which has an often primitive and sometimes idiotic libretto, the music of which is a mixture of cheap opera arias, fashionable dance music and easily remembered melodious tunes, could have proved to be so popular not only with ordinary people and the lower middle classes, but also with educated society, creative intellectuals, musicians and writers. Furthermore, he asserts, operetta "effortlessly cuts across regions, countries and nations, and across social strata; it is interregional [and] international." The success he attributes to certain common qualities of operetta: the wit of the music, the uncomplicated nature of the story-line, the escapism tinged with political and/or social satire of varying magnitudes and, of course, the spectacle on a grand scale.

The first major operetta of the late Habsburg era was Johann Strauss' *The Gypsy Baron*, based partly on a work by the leading Hungarian novelist of the day, Mór Jókai, whom Strauss met personally in September 1883. When the operetta premiered two years later, the audiences were presented with a romantic musical play involving Barinkay, a Hungarian nobleman in exile, who will be pardoned by the kind empress and recover his lands. There is hidden treasure, an upstart pig-dealer and kind-hearted gypsies, one of whom, a beautiful girl, turns out to be a princess. The incongruous mixture is typical of the genre. There are also polkas, strains of nineteenth-century Hungarian recruiting music, gypsy songs and Viennese waltzes. The Austrian bureaucracy is mocked and Hungarian patriotism is given some due. According to Hanák, at the seventy-fifth performance in 1886 even the Rákóczi March, banned since the 1848 revolution, was played for the first time on stage in Vienna. By 1900 there had been over three hundred performances in Vienna and more than a hundred in Budapest. Translations were made into many languages, and *The Gypsy Baron* received rapturous applause in cities as far apart as New York and St. Petersburg.

For some, there was a political element about the show which reflected the contemporary reality of compromise in the Monarchy, at least as far as Hungary and Austria were concerned. Hanák quotes an enthusiastic Franz Jauner, director of the Theater an der Wien: "*The Gypsy Baron* is a victory, a demonstration for the Hungarians, for democracy. A wonderful manifestation of fellow-feeling which has been glowing in the air for more than half a century but only exploded now... After the catastrophe [of the battle of Königgrätz] the thought occurred to many responsible: the Hungarian must be conciliated... Consequently they were happy that someone at last stepped out in front of the Hungarian audience, made Barinkay a hero and laughed loudly at the caricature of Metternich censorship." Hanák believes that "it is not an exaggeration to say that *The Gypsy Baron* itself was also part of the compromise process, the reconciliation of hearts, a political agreement narrated in words and music." He further argues that operetta, together with other types of musical production, functioned as an integrating factor in the multi-ethnic, multi-linguistic Empire as a whole, creating in the process "a kind of community of cultural identity".

The big operetta hit in Budapest in the new century was Jenő Huszka's *Prince Bob* (sometimes called *The Vagabond Prince*). With reference to its success, Endre Ady, whom we have met above, once commented that operetta should not be written off as naïve and foolish, since it was "a most serious theatrical genre... the one with which we can freely strike out kings without danger... It can destroy more of this rotten world and better prepare the future than five protests in

Parliament." Ady, it seems, was not only a gifted poet but also an early practitioner of what only decades later would become known as cultural studies.

The king of Hungarian operetta, if anyone deserves the crown, is surely Imre Kálmán, who was born in Siófok by the shore of Lake Balaton in 1882. Kálmán's most famous work, *The Csárdás Princess*, opened in Vienna in 1915 and was premiered in Budapest at the city's Király Theatre on 3 November 1916, right in the middle of the First World War. It says something about the international appeal of operetta that, even while the war was still being fought, there were performances not only in German cites like Berlin, Hamburg, Munich and Cologne, but also in Paris, St. Petersburg and Moscow. As a Viennese critic wrote in 1917: "The whole world resounds with two things—the roar of the cannon and the success of *The Csárdás Princess*."

Kálmán's operetta revolves around the improbable story of a poor girl from a village by the River Tisza, who, passing through the world of the music hall, ends up via marriage as a court princess. Perhaps the escapist element appealed to the war-weary public in all the belligerent countries. Love and song prevailed here, not the powerful and death. In Hungary it was the music which enraptured many. One Budapest daily described the operetta as "bubbling over with blood-boiling Hungarian rhythm, Hungarian songs [and] brilliant orchestration."

The Csárdás Princess maintained its popularity well after the First and even Second World War was over. A film version was one of the biggest box-office draws in Hungary of the 1970s, and the stage version is still regularly performed in Budapest. Yet not all historians, even cultural historians, have given due recognition to this and other operettas in the way that Endre Ady already did a century ago. The extensive index of names at the end of a scholarly English-language collection entitled *A Cultural History of Hungary in the Nineteenth and Twentieth Centuries*, written by Hungarians and published in 2000 by Corvina, a respectable Budapest publishing house, has no entry at all for Imre Kálmán. But his name still rings out—and not only on the operetta programmes. Anyone happening to be at the Eastern Railway Station about nine o'clock in the morning will hear Kálmán's name being repeatedly announced. The Imre Kálmán Express is one of the regular trains on the Munich-Salzburg-Vienna-Budapest route. It arrives in the Hungarian capital every day around nine.

Champagne Louise and Miss Arizona

The Budapest Operetta Theatre has occupied 17 Nagymező utca since the early 1920s. Prior to that the building was the home of the Somossy Orfeum, one of several noted music-hall-type variety theatres which flourished in the city in the pre-1914 era and even beyond. Gyula Krúdy, that seasoned chronicler of the times, has left a description of the Orfeum and its atmosphere, which could well apply to any of the fashionable music halls of the day. To get a real sense of the place, he says, "the latter-day reader would have had to sit at one of the tables laid with damask and silver in that hall where the air was thick with tobacco smoke. The silver bucket with a bottle of bubbly and the equally frosty lily-of-the-valley complexion of the lady of the night would have been *de rigueur* by the tableside."

A true gentleman, says Krúdy, would show up wearing tails, as a mere dinner jacket would not do for the aspiring man-about-town. The flower vendor would place her bouquet on the table without asking and the waiters would serve a variety of dishes without being ordered, since "they knew just about every guest's taste and spending power." Moneylenders were on hand, "seated with the friendliest of smiles at an inconspicuous table somewhere near the cloakroom," to replenish the dwindling supplies of customers' thinning wallets. It was not just the show on stage, then, that was important. It was the atmosphere, the spectacle, the experience of seeing and being seen, particularly if you were observed in the company of the owner.

Some of the owners were almost institutions themselves. One such was "Queen of the Hungarian Broadway" Louise Wabitsch, who opened her Jardin d'Hiver theatrical nightclub in Nagymező utca in 1910. Wabitsch came to Budapest in the mid-1890s from Kliening, a small village in Austria. She started out as a flower girl, working the night clubs and restaurants. Her lucky break came when she was just 18. Through the connections she had shrewdly made she obtained a concession to operate a champagne pavilion in the City Park during the massive millennial celebrations of 1896 (see Chapter Four). From then on, Champagne Louise, as she became known, started to make money. She opened her first nightclub, the Jardin de Paris, on the far side of the City Park. It remained fashionable through to the 1930s. Guests, it is said, were only to arrive by carriage, later by automobile, and the gentlemen were to be served only champagne. The music played until five in the morning, and, according to one enthusiastic journalist in 1936: "The variety theatre owners from Paris come here to copy the Jardin. It is so beautiful..."

When the post-1945 nationalizations began, Champagne Louise liquidated her fixed assets, transforming them into gold, jewels and other movables which she surreptitiously smuggled out of the country to her home village of Kliening hidden in the coffin of her younger brother, Leonard, who had died of excessive drinking. Yet Louise herself was caught up in the wave of deportations to the countryside of former bourgeois and other "undesirables". She returned to Budapest in 1953 and then lived a solitary and quiet life until 1956, when, now in her mid-seventies, she took the opportunity to slip out of the city, head for the border and cross into Austria.

Even more famous was "Miss Arizona", a former dancer who performed under the name Mitzi Sugár and who, with her husband Sándor Rozsnyai, purchased 20 Nagymező utca in 1932 and opened the Arizona revue theatre-cum-nightclub. The furnishings and, in particular, the equipment were spectacular for Budapest, rivalling the Moulin Rouge on the other side of the street. The revue girls flew through the air, or were lowered onto the revolving stage from a chandelier. The prima donna of the show was Miss Arizona herself. Every night she and her Parisian-style girls changed several times, all wearing costumes she had designed herself.

In his *Between the Woods and the Water* the English traveller Patrick Leigh Fermor recalled a visit he made to the Arizona in 1933. The floor seemed to revolve, he remembered, and white horses with feathers careered around it. There were rumours of camels and even elephants. Acrobats flew through the air, then formed massive human pyramids. "The most glamorous nightclub I have ever seen," was his verdict. He was not alone—in the 1930s the Arizona was certainly one of Budapest's most celebrated night spots.

It all came to an end with the war and the German occupation. Sándor Rozsnay was Jewish and found himself under pressure. He eventually perished in a concentration camp, but while she could Miss Arizona stood by him, refusing to divorce him. Like Champagne Louise, she liquidated her assets, investing in diamonds and other gems. But she did not survive. One night she was taken to the banks of the Danube, from which she never returned. A legendary figure, her story is told in the 1988 film *Miss Arizona*, directed by Pál Sándor and starring Hanna Schygulla and Marcello Mastroianni.

chapter three
CITY OF CAFÉS

Coffee House Castles

Before the Second World War Budapest was noted for its coffee house culture. Hundreds of cafés served as meeting places for writers, artists, poets and journalists, as well as other citizens who had the available time to while away gossiping or playing cards, or both. The image of a "coffee house Charlie" type of character, cracking jokes, commenting on the news, decrying the government and generally idling away his time with his friends for hours over one or possibly two cups of coffee has been standard in cabaret, film and on the stage in Hungary for years, and the caricature still appears occasionally in theatre and on television, even though the days when such figures could be found in real life have long gone.

Café society, an essential ingredient of old Budapest life for certain social groups, virtually disappeared after the Second World War, but in a few places the ambience of old times can still be felt, and in recent years there has been a revival of café society, even though a great deal of it is of the international "cappuccino culture" variety.

A century ago there were 500-600 cafés in Budapest, the exact figure depending on which source you consult. It is difficult to overestimate the role they played and the function they performed in former times, particularly for the literary elite. As the writer Dezső Kosztolányi, paraphrasing the famous English saying, once put it: "My coffee house is my castle."

Coffee was introduced to Hungary by the Ottomans, and the first coffee houses in Buda were frequented by Turks rather than by Hungarians. Hungarian cafés took off in the eighteenth century, but their heyday was in the late nineteenth and first half of the twentieth century. Even before that, however, some cafés managed to get themselves into the history books. In the 1840s the poet Sándor Petőfi and other young radicals used to frequent the Pilvax Coffee House in central Pest. "If you write," Petőfi once advised his fellow poet János Arany, "then address the letter to the Pilvax. It is more likely to reach

me, as I am more often here than at home." It was from the Pilvax that Petőfi and the revolutionary youth set out on 15 March 1848, the first day of the anti-Habsburg revolution. Petőfi's rousing "National Song" for freedom was allegedly written by him in the café. The original coffee house was pulled down in 1911, but inside today's Pilvax Restaurant, which more or less occupies the same location in Pilvax köz, there are archive pictures and other items recalling the nineteenth-century atmosphere.

The café scene burgeoned following the 1873 formation of Budapest as the unified capital and the tremendous building activity which followed. It was boosted by the emergence of a cultural elite frequenting restaurants, cafés, galleries and concerts, and using cafés as meeting places, information centres and "editorial offices". One of the most famous such places was the New York Café, which opened on Erzsébet körút in 1894. With its rich interior of marble, bronze and Venetian ground glass and its frescoes and paintings, it had and still has one of the most sumptuous interiors in the city as well as a rich history.

When the New York opened, the writer Ferenc Molnár is said to have demanded the keys from the head waiter and to have thrown them into the Danube, so that the café's doors would never close. (Molnár would have been about sixteen years old at the time, and given that the river is some distance away the story is probably one of the many legends of Budapest.) What is incontestable is that the New York was one of *the* literary and artistic cafés par excellence and a centre of intellectual and creative life for a number of decades. Customers included writers, poets, painters, sculptors, composers, singers, actors and, later, film directors. "Here you could see everybody," commented the writer Gyula Krúdy. The café played an outstanding role in the literary, artistic and cultural life of Budapest up to the Second World War. In its later period, the *Nyugat* (Occident) circle was one group which used to meet here, and the publication's editor-in-chief for many years, Ernő Osvát, would often work at a reserved table. A memorial tablet commemorates this inside the café, and there are also caricatures of various literary figures inside.

As with the other "writers' cafés", waiters provided pen, ink and paper, and would often be the source of news and gossip for journalists, in the manner of today's taxi drivers. Similarly to other cafés, the New York served food as well as drink. Some places stayed open all night and were popular for the "hangover soup" you could obtain in the early hours. A speciality of the New York was the *irótál* (writer's plate), a collation of simple cheap edibles: ham, salami, cheese, etc., only for writers. Poorer guests could order a *kis irodalmi* (a smaller version, literally a "small literary").

In the 1930s it was common for visiting foreign artists and performers to pay at least one visit to the New York, though at this time it was less of a "literary" centre and more a place of entertainment with music and cabaret acts. After 1945 the New York was closed' and subsequently became a warehouse and then a sports shop. In 1954 the café reopened under the name Hungária, though the original name crept back into use in the late 1980s. Many of the journalists who frequented the place in the post-war decades worked in editorial offices in the building above, so that it became popularly known as the "Press Palace". On 23 October 1956, the first day of the uprising, some of the journalists and writers close to Imre Nagy met here in the evening, not to plot but to have a meal—they were unaware for a while of the momentous events unfolding on the streets outside.

Up to and during the 1990s the New York was a popular tourist attraction, highlighted in all the guidebooks as the most opulent of the remaining coffee houses from the pre-1945 era. Yet unfortunately it often felt more like a museum than a vibrant café. Occasionally you could still see a journalist or writer poring over a script before handing it in upstairs, but the atmosphere was cold, as was often the coffee. As this book was going to press, the café, after being closed for some time so that the building which houses it could be renovated and converted into a top-class hotel, reopened in all its splendour.

Twists of Fate

Women had started to frequent cafés from the 1910s in line with moves for female emancipation. At first it was mainly those from the theatrical and bohemian worlds who did so. Upper-class women continued to frequent *cukrászda* (cake shops or patisseries, though with coffee and drinks). Nevertheless, cafés started to introduce special women's rooms or special women's hours, practices which lasted until the 1920s.

The First World War brought many changes. At first cafés became places to discuss the war, with maps, flags and diagrams on the wall. From here emerged the caricature figure of the know-it-all Kávéházi

Konrád, spouting his opinions about the war. (The figure was not entirely mythical. Coffee House Conrad was named after the military commander Konrad von Hötzendorf.) The war produced new social dynamics, partly since men were subject to recruitment. Thus the period saw a rapid rise in the number of waitresses employed. Not surprisingly, the names of some cafés changed because of the war, the London, for example, becoming the Berlin. At the same time, war-time poverty and deprivation affected business and some supplies dried up or became very expensive. Cream was the first to disappear, then milk, then Pest's famous pastries. Coffee itself was expensive, sugar became unavailable, tobacco was hard to find, then even games became rare (apart from cards, cafés had often had games sections or rooms for billiards, dominoes and other similar pastimes). In the end conversation, the very fuel which drove the café society, dried up. Only the cafés with music near railway stations saw business continuing reasonably well. They became known as "death cafés" as they were the scenes of partings as men went to the front.

Many cafés had always had food available at all times of the day, which was one of their attractions for the bohemian elite, but in September 1915 an official directive obliged cafés to serve cheap food for the poorer classes. They immediately lost their "intellectual" character, becoming little more than feeding centres. After coffee had disappeared, so too did electricity and heating. By the end of the war, society had become completely impoverished. Throughout 1919 cafés continued to serve as feeding centres, and many were used as political offices during the Council Republic period.

The 1920s saw a revival of café life, with new types appearing. Café-restaurants with fashionable music opened, singers appeared, cafés had bridge rooms or ping-pong tables, though in parallel there was also a revival into the 1930s of the "writers' and artists' cafés", such as the Japán and the Centrál. The Japán was one of the most famous of them all. It was located at 45 Andrássy út, on the corner of today's Liszt Ferenc tér. Today there is no café there, though the place is occupied by the Writers' Bookshop, which does have a small "café corner" and a number of old photographs of the Japán and its clientele on the wall.

Like the New York, the Japán Coffee House traced its origins to the mid-1890s. The name referred to its "oriental" decorated wall tiles. At the turn of the century this was a meeting place for painters, sculptors, other artists and art collectors. The noted architect Ödön Lechner could often be found here. A colourful description of the café at that time would be written years later by the painter Lipót Hermann in his booklet *Artists' Table*:

> *The artists' table at the Japán was behind the window looking onto Andrássy út to one side of the café... It was perhaps Ödön Lechner who insisted that the table be by a window... Though continuously busy translating his artist's dreams into architectural designs on the marble table-top, he would always keep an eye on the life of the street, the men, women and pretty girls passing by and the forever changing wonderful view in general. With his fine grey beard trimmed in the French style, his pink cheeks, and the obligatory house-cap on his pate, he was one of the leaders of the whole company, a tribal chief of this realm made up of all sorts of colourful individuals.*

In 1909 the café was bought by a certain Richárd Weisz, who maintained strict order but was very kind to the artists. In the autumn of 1919, after the fall of the Council Republic and with the rise to power of the Horthy regime, there was an outburst of anti-Semitism, including many violent attacks. Weisz, it is said, walked the streets of Budapest with a board proclaiming: "I am Jewish." No one touched him. He was a wrestler and weight-lifter, and had been an Olympic champion in London in 1908.

In the inter-war period the Japán became a popular meeting place of writers, poets and artists. A speciality of the Japán was a *javító* (improving) coffee; poorer customers could ask for a little "improving" milk or sugar, for which there was no charge. Apart from writing and gossiping many regulars, such as the poet Attila József, would eat bean soup and play chess. And, if rumours are to be credited, it was "at the coffee-house corner" here that József wrote his famous poem "On My Birthday". The writer Ernő Szép, who also frequented the café, recalled in 1931:

> *We had a café on Andrássy út in those finer days: the Japán Café with its walls covered with majolica tiles painted over with bamboos, chrysanthemums, vases and dream-like birds...We, who*

went to the Japán, are likely to have traversed a greater distance than we would have done if we'd gone to Japan itself; the café was a more distantly exotic place than the world of white lotus, green tea and the golden Buddha, because the Japán was the fairy land of youth. That was where I went in the afternoons, ignoring novels, horse-races, and even love sometimes; such a sacred need of life that was in the time of amicable fraternisation."

The Japán may be no more, but the Centrál lives, or rather has been revived, re-opening as it did in early 2000 after a gap of over fifty years. In contrast with the New York of recent times, the Centrál attracts not only tourists but also locals. At the corner of Károlyi Mihály utca and Irányi utca in the centre of Pest, it is a lively place, open from early morning to late at night, serving food throughout the day.

The original Centrál Café opened in 1887, occupying the entire ground floor of the building, with eight rooms and two games rooms. The surrounding area contained the university, a library, a printer's office and publishing house, so it vied in importance as a "literary café" with the New York. The *Nyugat* circle was based here for a while. Another important publication which was mainly written at the Centrál (its Athenaeum printers being nearby) was *A Hét* (The Week). The so-called "folk writers" or "village explorers" of the 1930s also met here. One of the most famous books of the inter-war period, Frigyes Karinthy's *Travels around My Skull*, has its opening scene in the Centrál.

In the post-1945 era the Centrál continued to be a meeting point for people working on various publications, as well as for art historians, artists and academics, but only for a short while. The café was closed in July 1949, subsequently becoming a company headquarters, a student club and a gaming machine hall before being restored, on the initiative of a private businessman, to its original function. The reopening of the Centrál at the start of the twenty-first century, with its splendid interior, marks a relatively successful attempt to recreate the Budapest atmosphere of a century ago.

The Second World War and its aftermath represented the final blow for Budapest's traditional coffee house. In the post-war period cafés were nationalized and the whole ethos of coffee house culture was scorned as part of a bourgeois reactionary lifestyle. After all, everyone was now supposed to be working in order to eat, not idling away the time sipping coffee and chatting. Yet the decline of café life did not occur overnight in 1945 with the end of the war. As with the economy, what might be called the nationalization of social life in Hungary only really took hold in 1948. Before then there was a certain revival of old-style café life, but it was extremely limited for two obvious reasons: many of the cafés had simply been destroyed during the 1944-5 siege of the city, and demand had largely disappeared given that obtaining potatoes or bread was a higher priority than consuming coffee in public places. The post-war black marketeers could, of course, afford the time and money to hang around cafés, but this only added to the suspicion that such places generated in the mind of the authorities.

The Belvárosi Kávéház (Inner City Coffee House) in what is today called Ferenciek tere was the first to attempt to reopen amidst the ruins of Budapest on 18 February 1945, just a few days after the siege was over. Although no longer housing a café, its building today still has a plaque on the wall testifying to this fact (the café was on the ground floor of the left-side twin, as you face the river, of the so-called Klotild Palaces). From 1910 the café was owned by three generations of the Rónai family, of which Egon Ronai (or Ronay), the noted restaurant and gastronomic expert, is a descendant. In fact, he was there himself in 1945 on re-opening day, writing the sign "We are open!" The passers-by were incredulous, he recalled. The walls of the café were charred with fire, the windows were blown out, the furnishings were in ruins, there was no electricity or water, but it opened. Hot soup was made on a stove, which had a small chimney going out to the street.

Even when the cafés reopened, the clientele and the resulting atmosphere were quite different from the old days. In his *Memoir of Hungary, 1944-48* the writer Sándor Márai records a curious scene he witnessed at the EMKE Café in December 1945. The famous EMKE (the letters represented the Hungarian for "Hungarian Transylvanian Association for the Promotion of Learning"—the association received a small cut from every bill paid) used to occupy the ground floor of the large corner building on the north side of Blaha Lujza tér in central Pest. The 1910s and the 1920s witnessed its heyday, its clients associated with the National Theatre, which used to stand in the square. Márai says that owing to some freakish chance the café had managed to escape serious wartime damage and even its furnishings were intact.

At that moment of historical change, this café resembled the
nostalgic hallucination of a fever-ridden patient suffering chills, his
teeth chattering; in unheated, frigid Budapest… where the insides
of many houses hung out, and among the loitering Russian looters,
the toughs of Pest and the patrols of Russian infantry pretending to
maintain order, a peacetime café, the EMKE, opened a few months
after the siege in all its synthetic and nickel-silver splendour.
Festoons of electric bulbs glittered in the lukewarm restaurant [and]
artificial palms flaunted their imitation oriental luxury…

Márai's vignette describes how into this scene one night strode a
leather-coated Jewish police officer wearing a gold-braided cap with a
colonel's insignia. There was something potentially disturbing,
potentially frightening about his arrival. The man, a distant relative of
Márai, had lost all his family in the Holocaust. Like many other Jews
who had miraculously managed to survive, he had joined the new
authorities and now wore their uniform. What was he doing here now
in this former haunt of bourgeois writers, actors and actresses? Was it a
raid or inspection? The policeman approached a table in leisurely
fashion, sat down and ordered. As the gypsy *primás* approached the
guest to ask what he would like to hear, the onlookers watched and
waited in awe. Surprisingly, he chose a popular irredentist tune of the
pre-war era, "You Are Lovely, Most Beautiful Hungary". The other
guests, says Márai, listened, alarmed and aghast at this "stridently false
and ridiculously business-like expression of phoney patriotism". But the
gypsy played with feeling. Was it a cruel joke? Was he about to inflict
some revenge? Nothing of the sort. After the music he finished his meal,
paid generously without checking the bill, tipped all and sundry and
left, turning only briefly to salute the amazed clientele he was leaving
behind. The café world had certainly turned upside down.

Revival
Apart from the New York and the Central, there are still a handful of
cafés in Budapest which recall the old times. The pre-1914 Astoria
Hotel, for example, has an impressive Art Nouveau coffee lounge on its
ground floor. The Művész, located at 29 Andrássy út since about 1910,
is a small café, traditionally popular with Budapest's gentlefolk. The
furnishings of the Lukács, also on the avenue at no. 70, are like museum

pieces. The occasional afternoon piano music here sends you back in time. The city's oldest café, however, the tiny 1820s Ruszwurm (pictured on p.62), at 7 Szentháromság utca, near the Matthias Church in the Castle District, pre-dates the golden era of literary coffee house culture.

The famous Gerbaud on Vörösmarty tér in central Pest is, like the New York, packed with tourists in the high season, its outside seating being particularly popular. Here since 1870, it still boasts turn-of-the-century furnishings inside. The Gerbaud, noted for its cakes, is strictly speaking a grand *cukrászda*, a term sometimes applied to a large café but which usually refers to a small patisserie, cake shop or confectioner's, where coffee and other drinks are also available.

Some *cukrászda* have tables where you can sit, others simply "stand-up" bars. There are many throughout the city, some with a high reputation. A good sign is if you can see through to a back room where cakes and other delicacies are being made. Then you know that what you see on sale is home made and probably fresh. Locals often pop in to buy cakes to take away and eat at home. The Szalai at 7 Balassi Bálint utca, near the north side of parliament, is a family business of many years' standing and a typical Pest *cukrászda*.

Any decent *cukrászda* will have a variety of strudel (*rétes*) on offer. The idea of building up thin layers of dough is so basic to the Middle East that it is assumed it came to Hungary with the Turks. As the saying has it, the filo pastry must be made so transparently thin that you can read a love letter or a newspaper through it. Late in the spring and in the summer it is filled with sweet or morello cherries, at other times, with apples, cabbage, curd-cheese or ground poppy seed. Other *cukrászda* favourites are creamy gateaux, tortes, tarts and pies. A popular cake is *Dobos torta*, which bears the name of József Dobos, who invented these thin layers of buttery cake, sandwiched between mocha cream, decorated with chopped hazelnuts and covered with a hard caramel glaze.

The *presszó* is another type of Budapest café. Appearing on the scene in the late 1930s, this more modern, often smaller café, offering quicker service, survived the post-war changes and indeed came to dominate café society, such as it was, from the 1950s on. Ferenc Bodor's *Pesti presszók*, published in 1992 by the city council, is an elegy to this fast-disappearing element of Budapest life. "Beneath the grey and scarlet coating of the fifties it was in [these] cafés that office love affairs blossomed and lonely gentlewomen found company," he writes.

After 1956 a young generation of interior designers and decorators was given a free hand in the planning of public catering. "Modern style" was introduced: "Cell-shaped tables, metlachi tiles, Klee-patterned curtains, cone-shaped lamps, counters done up in mosaic. And fantastic streamlined espresso machines," writes Bodor. The hallmark of the genre, however, was neon: "neon signs, neon lemonade with neon bubbles and straws, neon women with neon coffee-cups!" A few of these—now evocative for some—cafés, neon signs and all, survive. The Bambi at 2 Frankel Leó út, at the corner of Bem tér in Buda, is a "classic". "Few interiors dating back to the sixties have remained so untouched," enthuses Bodor. Also in Buda are the Déryné (3 Krisztina körút) and the Rózsadomb (7 Margit körút), the latter rather run-down in its atmosphere, but nonetheless "authentic".

Other places which struggled to survive the economic changes of the early 1990s are now gone, if not forgotten: the Kisposta, always good for a quick drink before catching a bus or tram home from Moszkva tér, or the popular Mignon, just off Deák tér, which in the evening turned into a rare (because cheap and in the city-centre) drinking place, complete with catchy tunes played on an electric keyboard, and even dancing among the drunks.

In his 1992 work Ferenc Bodor wrote that "coffee houses and cafés have had their day, in present-day Budapest at least." It is always risky to close the book on any theme with such certainty, and as it has turned out Bodor was wrong. The past dozen or so years have seen a revival of café life in the city, so much so that in some periods it has seemed that a new café would open its doors almost every week and that the outside tables were encroaching further and further on to the pavements.

Pride of place as the new café quarter must surely go to Liszt Ferenc tér, a long rectangular square running off Andrássy út behind the statue of Endre Ady. Some years ago you would have been hard pressed to find a cup of coffee anywhere here. Today, particularly on a warm summer's evening, the problem is rather passing through the outside tables spread across this pedestrian-only precinct. Almost every building here now houses a café, bar or restaurant, and with music emanating from a number of interiors the atmosphere is certainly vibrant. Close on its heels as a fashionable place is Ráday utca, which runs off Kálvin tér. Up-and-coming entrepreneurs have taken advantage of this now partly pedestrianized long street to establish a multitude of theme bars and restaurants. Elsewhere in the city, though not in such concentration, new bars and cafés continue to open. Something, at least, of the old times has returned.

chapter four

HEROES AND OTHERS

Budapest has a multitude of impressive sights, utterly eye-catching in their grand magnificence. Many of these sights are associated with the riverside majesty of the city and the view to be had from different vantage points. Away from the river, one of the most impressive locations is undoubtedly Heroes' Square (Hősök tere), which opens out at the end of Andrássy út and acts as a gateway to the City Park beyond. Whether you approach the square by foot along Andrássy út or emerge from the underground railway at the end of the avenue, the grand, almost super-human scale of the square cannot fail to impress.

Heroes' Square, with its massive expanse flanked on each side by an imposing neo-Classical building, and with its Millennial Monument comprising a tall central column and two curved colonnades with statues at the rear, is one of the most remarkable and striking large public spaces in Europe, on a par with Trafalgar Square in London and Palace Square in St. Petersburg, even though their histories and significance are quite different, and Budapest's square is, unjustifiably, by no means as well known.

That Heroes' Square is still entirely commanding, more than one hundred years after its initiation, would please its early planners. Whether today's viewer standing in the square and looking around would regard its symbolism and meanings in the same way as those who envisioned it, however, is quite another matter. It is an issue which cannot perhaps be neatly resolved, if only because the symbolism and attributed meanings of this constructed space have changed over time. Indeed, what you have been able to see here has also changed.

Now You See It—Now You Don't
The history of Heroes' Square takes us back to the early 1880s. It was then that the idea was born of creating a prominent national monument to celebrate the 1000th anniversary of the arrival of the Magyars from the east in the area of present-day Hungary, and therefore one thousand years of Hungarian nationhood in the Carpathian Basin.

The tricky and intriguing nature of that project is more than hinted at by the fact that at the time, in the 1880s, Hungary was still part of the Habsburg empire, or more precisely, it was one of the two major parts of the revealingly entitled Austro-Hungarian Dual Monarchy, established in 1867 with the so-called Compromise between the political elites of Budapest and Vienna. Hence, the project aimed to stress not only the glory of a millennium of often independent Magyar nationhood in Europe, but also the pride that many Hungarians then felt about apparently being equal partners in the Monarchy and loyal citizens of the Empire.

There were also problems of detail, such as when the millennium should actually be celebrated. In time-honoured fashion, in 1882 the government appointed a committee composed of members of the Academy of Sciences to determine the exact year of the Magyar Conquest (that is the arrival of the Hungarians) so that a celebratory year could be established. The response was also rather committee-style, though given the nature of the difficulty perhaps it is not surprising. The learned members of the Academy reported that all that could be stated with any certainty was that the area known as modern Hungary had not been settled by the Magyars before the year 888 and that the occupation of the territory was complete by 900.

After much debate, it was not until 1892 that the government decided that the "millennium" would fall in 1895. Great plans were drawn up for many public building projects and a series of celebratory events for the designated year. Perhaps inevitably, it turned out that the planning time allocated was too short, and this was one reason why the government decided to postpone the date of the millennium to 1896. Thus 896 became the "official" year of the Hungarian Conquest, and the number 96, although clearly of human, even bureaucratic creation, assumed a certain mythical significance. As many sources are fond of pointing out, the dome of Budapest's largest church, St. Stephen's Basilica, completed in 1905, reaches a height of 96 metres (315 feet), as does the peak of the dome of Hungary's parliament building, completed one year earlier.

A historically accurate anniversary or not, 1896 was the year when Budapest embraced its millenary celebrations, a main feature of which was several-months-long great exhibition held in the City Park (see below). Yet the Millennial Monument itself, with all its planned statuary, did not even begin to appear in that celebratory year. In fact, the monument in its entirety was actually completed only in 1929, by which time Hungary had experienced a certain number of changes, not least of which included the collapse of the empire, the end of the Dual Monarchy, a revolution and a counter-revolution. What fate then for the meaning of a public monument?

As planned, the central feature of the Millennial Monument is a 120-foot column, on top of which stands a double life-size statue of the Archangel Gabriel. The statue was ready in mid-1897, but a major dispute about whether the column was strong enough to hold it led to its erection being delayed by several years. In the meantime, it was shipped to Paris where it deservedly earned a prize for its sculptor, György Zala, at the 1900 World Exhibition.

Around the base of the central column are a number of equestrian statues. To the fore is Árpád, the chieftain who led the Magyar tribes into the Carpathian Basin in 896, or thereabouts. He is flanked by six of his fellow leaders. It is not so important that the statues are somewhat inaccurate (for example, the Magyars rode much smaller Asian horses than those depicted here). After all, the essential representation of the Hungarian Conquest is clearly symbolized. "Conquest" is the historically clear term traditionally employed in English to designate the arrival of Árpád, his fellow chieftains and their tribes. However, a more literal translation of the traditionally employed Hungarian term, *Honfoglalás*, would be "occupation of the homeland", which seems like a rather convoluted linguistic attempt to justify retrospectively what was, indeed, a conquest of a land inhabited, albeit not densely, by Slavs and other non-Magyar peoples. Nevertheless, it was the arrival of the Magyars one thousand years previously which provided the justification for the planning of the Millennial Monument.

It is interesting to note, however, that the symbolism of Gabriel at the top of the central and dominating column refers to another event separated from the Conquest by over one hundred years. Legend has it that the Archangel once appeared in a dream to István, or Stephen, Hungary's first monarch, exhorting him to persevere with the conversion of the Magyars to Christianity. Stephen was crowned around the year 1000 at Esztergom on the Danube bend, with a crown sent by the Pope. In the statue the archangel holds aloft a double cross in his left hand, and in his right hand the Hungarian crown. The symbolism of the unity of Hungarian statehood and (Western) Christianity is clear.

Árpád or Stephen? Which to emphasize—the Eastern origins of the Hungarians or their Western orientation? The Millennial Monument cleverly does both, though there has often been some confusion over the definition of dates. In 1996, for example, there were again celebrations in Hungary, this time to mark the 1,100[th] anniversary of the Conquest, though the term used then was often, rather inaccurately, the "anniversary of the foundation of the Hungarian state". The confusion was laid bare four years later, when in the year 2000 the millennium of Stephen's coronation was also marked, more accurately, as the anniversary of the foundation of the Hungarian state. It became even more complicated when pundits pointed out that Stephen's millennium, strictly speaking in terms of the calculation of years, should have been marked in 2001!

On the top of the double colonnade, behind the central column, are two large, imposing statues of the chariots of war and of peace. There are also two pairs of figures, one pair representing work and welfare, the other pair knowledge and glory. These are undoubtedly finely sculptured and certainly eye-catching, but curiously they do not relate specifically to any particular Hungarian theme. They, or something similar, could equally be found in any major European city. The statues below them, however, standing between the columns of the colonnades are all figures of Hungarian history. There are fourteen statues in all and, beginning with King Stephen on the left, they were all bar one intended to represent monarchs who had ruled Hungary over the centuries. By 1914 and the start of the First World War, barely half of the monument had been completed, but that half included five Habsburg rulers—Ferdinand I, Charles III, Maria Theresa, Leopold II and the still ruling Francis Joseph, who was depicted wearing full military dress. Thus, paradoxically, a monument to celebrate one thousand years of Hungarian nationhood gave the Habsburgs a major place. Reflecting the official mood of the time, there was no figure which might allude to the Hungarians' anti-Habsburg revolt of 1848.

In 1919, during the "Bolshevik" Council Republic period following the post-war democratic upheaval when Hungary became independent, the Habsburgs were removed from the Millennial Monument. The mood was now much more dominated by the sentiments of national independence and 1848. Perhaps unsurprisingly, the figure of Francis Joseph in his military uniform was smashed to pieces. He had been the ruler of Hungary since 1848 and had overseen the repression which followed the suppression of the revolt after 1849. Yet this was not the end of the story of the Habsburg statues. After the victory of the counter-revolution of 1919-20, and the consolidation of the new regime under Miklós Horthy, the Habsburgs were put back, though this time Francis Joseph was portrayed in coronation robes. Yet the paradox continued, since now Hungary was supposed to be a republic.

This period also saw growing demand among sections of the public for the creation of some kind of war memorial in honour of those who had fought and died in the First World War. The country had not only lost the lives of many of its soldiers, but had also, under the post-war 1920 Trianon Treaty, been obliged to relinquish a great deal of territory. The ambition to regain that territory was a prime motivation of the Horthy regime, thus the memorial to lost soldiers was mixed with the idea of a memorial for the heroes who had fought, as it was now seen,

77

to preserve the boundaries of the old Hungary.

Eventually, the large, simple block of the National Heroes' Memorial was officially dedicated on 26 May 1929. The inscription in front, "1914-1918", marked the years of the war, while the one to the rear was "Dedicated to the 1000-year-old national borders". The memorial was placed on the ground immediately in front of Árpád and the other chieftains. The meaning of the Millennial Monument was thus slightly modified. To the complacent patriotism of the pre-1914 era was now added a touch of the irredentism which marked Hungarian public policy throughout the 1920s and 1930s. Three years after the Heroes' Memorial was dedicated, the square itself was officially named Heroes' Square. Yet even this did not mark the end of the whole matter of the meaning and appearance of the square.

Soon after the Second World War the statues of the Habsburgs were once again removed, four of them being replaced by noted Hungarian figures in the history of Transylvania—István Bocskai, Gábor Bethlen, Imre Thököly and Ferenc Rákóczi II—all of whom had in one way or another struggled against Habsburg domination. The statue of Francis Joseph was replaced by one of Lajos Kossuth, the leader of the 1848-9 anti-Habsburg Hungarian War of Independence. Now the dominant theme of the Millennial Monument was clearly national independence, in a way in which its original planners had not intended.

At the same time, even though some of the unchanged statues of Hungarian monarchs referred to earlier chapters of Hungary's greatness and territorial extent, the National Heroes' Memorial was removed (though the name of the square remained). The memorial was too clearly associated with the irredentist policies of the inter-war era. Such policies and their accompanying chauvinistic sentiments were now condemned outright in the new era of alleged brotherly friendship between the nations of Eastern Europe. Furthermore, while nations on the winning side of the Second World War could conveniently "update" their First World War memorials to encompass remembrance of their dead in the second war, in Hungary that was impossible, given the new domestic and regional political configuration. Hungary had, after all, fought against the Soviet Union, and there was a tendency on the part of the new ruling elite to condemn the Hungarian nation as a whole for being guilty of siding with the fascist enemy.

It is a wonder that when the Hungarian communists gained full ascendancy after 1948-9 they did not remove more statues from the Heroes' Square colonnades (or even change the name of the square). Perhaps part of the explanation for their restraint was their desire to appropriate for their own purposes Hungary's national traditions. (See the story of the Kossuth statue in Chapter Seven for a revealing example of how a statue group was changed, but where the national theme remained.)

All this, once again, might have been the end of the matter—but not so. The block of the National Heroes' Monument eventually returned to its original place in the summer of 1956, some time before the uprising of that year. Now, however, there was no specific reference to either of the two world wars. The inscription on the front, which remained for some time, referred to all those "who have given their lives for the freedom of the Hungarian people." (Today it simply says: "To the memory of our heroes.")

Temples of Art
Each side of Heroes' Square is dominated by a large neo-Classical building. On the north side stands the Museum of Fine Arts (Szépművészeti Múzeum), the country's main collection of non-Hungarian art (Hungarian paintings are housed in the National Gallery on Castle Hill). Designed by Albert Schickedanz and Fülöp Herzog and formally inaugurated on 1 December 1906 in the presence of Emperor Francis Joseph, the main façade of the huge Fine Arts Museum features a portico with columns; at the top of the tympanum is a copy of a sculptural group of Centaurs and Lapiths on the Olympian Temple of Zeus. Elsewhere, in and around the building are all the historicist elements deemed appropriate at the time for a temple of the arts— Classical, Romanesque, Renaissance and Baroque revival can all be found. At the time, art historian Ervin Ybl believed there was an overall "effect of reserved monumentality, which is expressive of the exalted, sacral aura associated with a museum's functions."

The idea was not unique to Hungary. Indeed, the last two decades of the nineteenth century had seen the completion of the Kunsthistorisches Museum in Vienna, the Bode Museum in Berlin, the Statens Museum for Kunst in Copenhagen, the Rijksmuseum in Amsterdam and the Narodniho Museum in Prague. In addition to any element of imitation, the "international" appearance of the Fine Arts Museum was no doubt influenced by the fact that, as well as leading figures from the world of Hungarian arts, the jury appointed to evaluate the tenders submitted for its design included A.W. Weissmann, the designer of Amsterdam's Stedelijkmuseum, the Swedish architect Skjöld Nekelmann and Prussia's Privy Councillor for architecture.

Furthermore, the style adopted suited academicism, then in favour among official circles in Hungary. There was not even a nod in the direction of echoing any kind of revived national style, or perceived national style, which had happened with Ödön Lechner's Museum of Applied Arts, completed in 1896. Little wonder there was ample criticism when the Fine Arts Museum was completed, though as a writer in a 1906 issue of *Vasárnapi Ujság* (Sunday News) put it:

> *Everybody who habitually expressed his views on artistic matters had formed his opinion in advance. The conservatives, who insist on the architectonic forms of old, praised its impressive proportions and its balanced style, while the moderns, who embrace the slogans of a renewed architectural style, berated it without having had a single look at the building... The opinions voiced on the matter do not concern the fact of the matter in any case, but reflect their proponents' various preconceptions, over which no dispute can pass judgement. Such a decision can only be made by the natural evolution of the arts.*

This view is perhaps applicable to any of today's architectural controversies.

The original contents of the Museum of Fine Arts had been brought together from the former collections of the aristocracy, the high clergy and wealthy individuals. Government purchases and various donations made additions in later years. The most important collection is the Old Masters Gallery, the core of which came from the private gallery of Count Miklós Esterházy, who sold his works to the state in 1871. The thirteenth-to-eighteenth-century European paintings here include Italian works such as Correggio's *Virgin and Child with Angel* (1520s), Titian's *Portrait of the Doge Trevisani* (1553), Bronzino's *Venus, Cupid and Jealousy* (c 1550), Raphael's *Esterházy Madonna* (1508) and

Portrait of Pietro Bembo (c 1504), and Tiepelo's *St. James Conquers the Moors* (1759).

A Spanish section of around seventy works is one of the largest such collections outside Spain itself. There are several El Greco's, including his *Mary Magdalene in Penitence* (c 1580), *Study of a Man* (1590s) and *Agony in the Garden* (c 1614), and five works of Goya, including *The Water Seller* and *The Knife Grinder* (both c 1810). Works by Velásquez, Murillo, Zurbarán and Ribera can also be found here. In the Flemish and Dutch sections there are paintings by Rubens, Van Dyck, Jordaens, Pieter Bruegel the Elder, Frans Hals, Jan Steen and Rembrandt. The German collection includes works by Dürer and Altdorfer.

The nineteenth-century collection is not extensive, although there are a number of interesting French Impressionist and other works by Cézanne (*Sideboard,* c 1875), Monet (*Fishing Boats,* 1886), Gauguin (*Black Pigs,* 1891) and Camille Pissarro (*Pont-Neuf,* 1902), as well as Delacroix, Courbet and Manet. The even smaller collection of twentieth-century art can at least boast some significant painters including Kokoschka, Chagall, and Vasarely.

Facing the Museum of Fine Arts and closing the south side of Heroes' Square stands the Hall of Arts (Műcsarnok), a large palace with a three-part basilica-like interior devoted to major temporary exhibitions of mainly contemporary works of art. Like the Fine Arts Museum, the neo-Classical red-brick Hall of Arts was designed by Schickedanz and Herzog, though it was actually completed in 1896, in time for the millenary celebrations. The building is somewhat smaller than the Fine Arts Museum, but its external appearance is more attractive, partly due to the incorporation of coloured glazed tiles invented and manufactured at the famous Zsolnay factory in Pécs in southern Hungary.

Behind the portico's six Corinthian columns is a colourful three-part fresco by Lajos Deák Ébner depicting *The Beginning of Sculpture,* with figures of Vulcan and Athene; the *Source of Arts,* with Apollo and the Muses; and *The Origins of Painting,* with images from the mythology of antiquity. The two smaller ones in between show allegorical figures of Painting and Sculpture. Originally the tympanum was plain. The present design, by Jenő Haranghy and depicting St. Stephen as patron of the arts, was added between 1938 and 1941.

Funerals for Heroes

The steps of the Hall of Arts in Heroes' Square have been the scene of a number of major events going all the way back to 1 May 1900 and the massive ceremonial funeral of the painter Mihály Munkácsy, which took place on that day. Interestingly, historian John Lukacs begins his celebrated work *Budapest 1900* with a description of the Munkácsy funeral. Placed in front of the Hall of Arts, the painter's sarcophagus rested on a catafalque, which was forty-five feet high. The organization of the funeral, as Lukacs describes it, was equally impressive. Present were government ministers, the mayor and other dignitaries of the municipality, as well as bishops, hussars and heralds in costume. As the funeral procession got under way in the middle of the afternoon, the hearse was drawn by six horses and was followed by eight carriages packed with wreaths. Black flags flew in Pest, and some public transport came to a halt. The minister in charge of education had ordered schools to close for the day so that pupils could line the funeral route. Gypsy bands and choirs provided music as the hearse passed by. Who was this man, for whom it seemed the entire city was mourning?

The question is significant, if only because Munkácsy, who was born in 1844, spent the most productive years of his life, from 1871, in Paris, where his reputation as the most famous Hungarian painter of the nineteenth century was already made in his lifetime. Part of that fame rested on the fact that he was both appreciated and bought; he became commercially successful and his paintings commanded the attention of some of the wealthiest collectors from all over Europe and America. He was also commissioned to decorate some important public buildings. A ceiling fresco of his, *The Apotheosis of the Renaissance*, can be found, for example, above one of the main stairwells in Vienna's Kunsthistorisches Museum (a large study he made for it is displayed in the Hungarian National Gallery).

In his home country Mukácsy's fame was boosted by the fact that he proudly declared himself a Hungarian all along. Like members of other relatively small nations, Hungarians are more than happy to bask in the achievement of successful sons and daughters of the country, even when such people have chosen, for whatever reason, to leave their homeland. Indeed, as a brochure issued by the Hungarian National Gallery in 2005 claimed: "To this day Munkácsy has continued to be the best known and most successful representative of Hungarian painting." The brochure was published in connection with a major exhibition, which brought together for a few months works of Munkácsy held in private and public collections throughout the world. Sure enough, people flocked to the exhibition.

The paintings of Mihály Munkácsy include landscapes, but his tendency was to portray people and their settings. Many of them depict peasants, outlaws, poor people, prisoners or drunks, sometimes from a rather romanticized perspective. Yet he also painted many conventional family scenes, often showing children and animals. Everyday bourgeois life was reflected in scenes of family members playing instruments, organizing birthday celebrations, or simply dozing on settees. The realism of his skilful painting was easily understood, and there was nothing particularly challenging about it. It was popular and, to use today's term, marketable. His works thus ended up all over the world, and hence the National Gallery in Budapest only has a selected Munkácsy collection in its permanent exhibition.

Outside Budapest, the Déry Museum in Debrecen, in eastern Hungary, has a special Munkácsy collection centred around three large canvases he created and known as his "Christ Trilogy", the components of which have an interesting history. *Christ before Pilate* was the first of the three works to be completed, in 1881. While it toured Europe in a special train, Munkácsy began work on the second, *Golgotha*, which was ready in 1884. Both went to America to be displayed and the artist himself was given a great reception there, even being invited to the White House. Self-made entrepreneur John Wanamaker bought both pictures, and from 1911 they were kept in a special room in his large Philadelphia store, being shown to the public every year around Easter, a tradition which continued even up to 1988.

In 1894 Munkácsy finished *Ecce Homo*, which in the Passion chronology actually comes between the events portrayed by the other two paintings. The original idea had been a representation of the Resurrection, but Munkácsy chose to return to the theme of Christ and Pilate. This third work was displayed in Budapest in 1896 during the millenary celebrations of that year and later went on tour. James Joyce, who viewed the painting at the Royal Academy in Dublin, commented: "It is a mistake to limit drama to the stage; a drama can be painted as well as sung or acted, and *Ecce Homo* is a drama." In 1914-15 the painting was once more exhibited in Hungary, following which it was bought by art collector Frigyes Déri and taken to Debrecen.

In 1988 the two pictures in America were sold at Sotheby's in New York. *Golgotha* was bought by a New York gallery owner of Hungarian descent who loaned it to Hungary in 1991. Three years later, after restoration work, it went on display in Debrecen. *Christ before Pilate*, the first of the trilogy, was bought at Sotheby's and taken to Canada to be displayed in Toronto. In 1995 it, too, returned to Hungary. It was only in the mid-1990s, then, that Munkácsy's three works actually appeared together, something no one had seen before, not even the artist himself.

In 1904, four years after Munkácsy's burial ceremony, the bier of Károly Lotz also started its last journey from the steps of the Hall of Arts. Lotz was Hungary's most noted fresco painter of the nineteenth century. His works can still be seen all over the city and include major items such as the ceiling fresco of Olympus in the auditorium of the Opera House, a ceiling fresco depicting an enthroned Justitia surrounded by allegories of Justice, Peace, Sin and Revenge above the main hall of the Museum of Ethnography in Kossuth tér (the building originally housed the Supreme Court), large ceiling frescos above the ceremonial staircase of parliament, and a painting on the north wall of the Matthias Church showing Pope Calixtus III ordering church bells to be tolled at noon every day in memory of the Hungarians' victory over the Turks at Nándorfehérvár (today Belgrade) in 1456. At the same time, there are also hidden gems of Lotz's work which can be found or even just stumbled across. The attractive decoration of the stairway of 3 Andrássy út is his work (the building today houses the Postal Museum, so there is public access). Similarly, a fresco of his can be seen above the steps leading down to the Blaha Lujza tér metro station, by 2 József körút.

In 1914 the burial ceremony of the influential architect Ödön Lechner similarly began on the steps of the Hall of Arts. Over six decades later, on the morning of 16 June 1989, an important and symbolic event took place on the same steps, though it had a political rather than artistic significance. The façade of the building was decorated in black and white, and over 100,000 people packed Heroes' Square to witness a ceremony marking the public reburial of Imre Nagy, the prime minister during the 1956 uprising who was secretly executed on 16 June 1958. Nagy's coffin was flanked by five others. Four belonged to colleagues who had also been executed or who had died in prison after 1956, while one was empty, representing the unknown victims of the period. In the afternoon the coffins were taken to plot 301 in a far corner of Budapest's Új köztemető cemetery, on Kozma utca in eastern Pest, where Nagy and over 200 others had lain in unmarked graves for three decades. The reburial ceremony, with the concurrent political "rehabilitation" of Nagy and positive reassessment of the 1956 uprising, was the most publicly symbolic event of Hungary's political changes of 1989-90.

A piece of public sculpture, the destruction of which played a major role in 1956, was the gigantic statue of Joseph Stalin, erected in 1951 in Dózsa György út, a broad sweep running from the side of the Hall of Arts for more than half a mile to the south (at the time the expanse was labelled Stalin Square). In the evening of 23 October 1956, the first day of the Hungarian uprising, crowds pulled the statue down with the help of industrial cutting and other equipment. It was one of the most symbolically potent events of the entire rebelliom, though not without a touch of humour. Given the strength of the bronze statue, the crowds only managed to topple its top three-quarters, leaving Stalin's massive footwear, the height of a man, in place. The area was known as "Boots Square" for some time after, and those who eventually found themselves imprisoned for their alleged role in the toppling of the statue were known to their fellow inmates as "the sculptors". The statue was smashed to bits, but a surviving piece of it, the hand, can today be seen in the Hungarian National Museum. Stalin's enormous fist gives some idea of the monumentality of the original creation.

A People's Park

Behind Heroes' Square stretches one of the largest and most popular public parks in Budapest, the City Park (*Városliget*). Like Margaret Island on the Danube, this is one of the "playgrounds" of the metropolis. Around its perimeter can be found the Zoological Gardens, which has become much more animal-friendly and indeed visitor-friendly in recent years, the Municipal Circus, housed not in a "big top" but in a permanent building, the Fun Fair, also in permanent operation, the massive complex of the Széchenyi Baths, with its many pools of varying temperatures, and the Transport Museum. In the interior of the park stands Petőfi Hall, which with its indoor and open-air stages is a popular venue for pop, rock and folk music concerts. The striking form of Vajdahunjad Castle (for more of which see below) is just into the park beyond Heroes' Square. In the winter months the lake in front of the castle complex is transformed into a large artificial ice skating rink. Viewed from the bridge linking Heroes' Square and the City Park, the stooping skaters appear like matchstick figures from a painting by Lowry. When floodlit in the evening the ice rink, with the towers of the Vajdahunjad Castle in the background, is an impressive sight.

The park was laid out in stages throughout the nineteenth century. The transformation was celebrated by a poem of János Arany, "Song of the City Park", written in 1877.

You have reeds here and hillocks and soggy-wet earth
And maybe the reason I like it so well
Is that I followed for twenty odd
Years as it washed off its dust and its dirt...

The park's facilities have often provided the backcloth for Hungarian filmmakers, and dramatists have used the park as a setting for plays. One of the humorous scenes in Péter Bacsó's renowned film *The Witness*, set in the dark days of the early 1950s, involves changing the character of the Fun Fair, which used to be called the "Angol" (English) Park. Ferenc Molnár's play *Lilliom* (made famous later in the West as *Carousel*) is set in the City Park.

The popularity of the City Park among ordinary citizens is reflected in the fact that it has been a traditional focal point for the labour movement. In the pre-1914 era a number of restaurants with large gardens on its far side became known as workers' meeting places and even strike headquarters during disputes. On 1 September 1930, with demands for work and bread, the largest workers' demonstration of the inter-war period headed along Andrássy út and assembled in the park. The park has also seen many May Day labour celebrations, which date back well beyond 1945. Budapest's first great May Day demonstration was in 1890, when up to 40,000 marched in the park. The tradition continues today with festivities every 1 May, though without the orchestrated demonstrations of the post-1945 decades. The park is taken over by crowds who come to enjoy the traditional sausages

and beer, the paprika chicken and the *gulyás* soup, all prepared in and served from makeshift tents set up for the occasion. Other customary food on sale from stalls include *perec*, large salted pretzels, *kürtös kalács*, a sweet, sticky hollow roll, and Hungary's own traditional "fast food", *lángos*, a fried dough—a cross between a pizza base and an English "Yorkshire pudding", eaten with or without various toppings.

There are also political stalls, where pamphlets and books are on sale, and there are some organized political discussions, too, but the bulk of the crowd each year seems to come for the atmosphere and the entertainment. On different stages are singers, dancers, bands and cabaret turns. The live music covers folk, jazz and pop. There are children's games and attractions, ranging from the traditional to bouncy castles and fairground rides. A visitor to Budapest wishing to see ordinary Hungarians "at play" could do worse than to visit the City Park on May Day.

The Throbbing Hearts of 1896

The biggest spectacle ever to be staged in the park was undoubtedly the National Exhibition of 1896, a major part of that year's millenary celebrations. For six months, from May to October, crowds from all over the country flooded into Budapest and the City Park. Over 200 pavilions were erected to display the agricultural, industrial and commercial life of the country. Hungary's first museum village was built, and "real" peasants were on hand to demonstrate authenticity. A great attraction was the balloon that rose over 1,500 feet in the air, providing its passengers with a panoramic view of the city—at least until the day when it was unfortunately ripped to pieces during a storm.

Sponsored by the Ministry of Commerce and Hungarian State Railways, a commemorative pictorial volume was published about the National Exhibition and about some of the major attractions of provincial Hungary. The language and tone of its introduction are revealing.

> *One thousand years have passed since the noble and gallant Hungarians left their ancient home in the far East and, led by Árpád the Founder, crossed the forest-clad border hills of this sunny land, and now millions of hearts are throbbing in the expectation of this eventful anniversary.*

How many millions of hearts, throbbing or not, agreed with the introduction's reference to "the mild and glorious rule of our beloved King Francis Joseph I"? There were probably many more than might be guessed at, given that it was less than half a century since the Hungarians' doomed War of Independence, which aimed to throw off Habsburg rule and which led for several years to severe repression, in no way "mild and glorious", under the rule of Francis Joseph. Yet all that seemed to be forgotten as the nation's leaders proudly cheered the Emperor-King who attended the official opening of the exhibition on 2 May.

Elsewhere in the volume the text informed readers: "The dimensions of [the Exhibition's] whole arrangement give correct conceptions of its extraordinary magnitude, proving how well founded those cherished hopes are, which every true Son of the Fatherland justly entertains as to its entire success, as in reality it will reflect, so to say from a huge Mirror, the Greatness and the Fame of a Thousand years of History..."

That thousand years of Hungarian history included two hundred years of Habsburg domination, preceded by around 150 years of Ottoman rule. Generously, it might seem, Ottoman rule over Buda and much of Hungarian territory was acknowledged with a special section of the exhibition called "Ancient Buda", which aimed to reproduce what the city must have looked like in Turkish times. There was a Turkish fountain with columns, a bazaar and even a functioning mosque with its own minaret. Across the river, on a large area to the south of Gellért Hill, a "Constantinople in Budapest" was constructed, seeking to produce in miniature the Turkish capital and Turkish life. Despite the positive images, however, the pictorial volume could not resist making at least one mention of the "bleak times of abject servitude" which characterized the country under Ottoman rule.

In 1896 Hungarians, as an ethnic group, constituted just under half the total population of the country and thus the dress, lifestyle and types of dwellings of the non-Magyar groups living in the Hungarian part of the Dual Monarchy were, understandably, given a prominent place in the National Exhibition. Yet the contemporary attitude of the ruling Magyar elite towards other national and ethnic groups is well reflected in the words of the commemorative publication. Romanians, for example, were described as "steadily advancing in culture under the brotherly protection of the Hungarians," and though they are "still shepherds and agriculturalists", they are "quick-witted, their customs are modest and their wants easily satisfied." A gypsy camp established at the exhibition called forth a description of "brown grizzly men, uncombed" and "dirty children in tattered dress". An elderly bearded man was pictured hammering a piece of iron, a child appears at the side with a large pail, a woman is stirring a pot with a stick, a pipe hanging from her mouth; she is observed by a boy in dirty clothes, his eyes staring blankly from underneath a cap. "This is one of the bleak, but at the same time romantic moments of nomadic life," declared the accompanying caption. "But in spite of the misery that pervades this scene, the spirit of Liberty floats over these figures."

The exhibition included three specially commissioned cycloramas, or circular paintings. One depicted a panoramic view of Pest and Buda in 1686, the year the Ottomans were driven out of Buda. Another took Dante's *Inferno* as its theme. There were souls of the departed crossing the Styx, the rock of the spendthrifts and of the misers, a river of blood and rain of fire, a land of snakes and a world of ice. A contemporary English-language advertisement described it as an "unrivalled and greatest work of sensational painting", but gave no explanation as to its link with Hungarian history. By far the most renowned and subsequently celebrated cyclorama, however, was Árpád Feszty's massive circular painting *The Arrival of the Magyars*, which measured an incredible 400 by 50 feet. The subject of the cyclorama, one of the largest in the world, is a romanticized impression of the arrival of Chief Árpád and the conquering Magyars through the Verecke Pass in the Carpathians. Feszty, with a group of fellow artists, actually went to the historic site of entry to make sketches of the region. These were then blown up with optical enlargements. The work was ready in 1894 and went on display in a specially constructed building, originally on the site of today's Museum of Fine Arts. It was one of the major attractions of the Millennium Exhibition. A reproduction of part of the cyclorama featured near the start of the commemorative publication mentioned above. It was preceded only by a picture of an almost-smiling Francis Joseph.

At the time of its creation, scholars could not agree about the authenticity of the cyclorama's detail, though the intention was to create a factual visual history—perhaps undermined by the fact that Feszty immodestly chose himself as the model for Chief Árpád. Despite the official attitudes alluded to above, the 1890s in Hungary was a time of intense dispute over the relations between the ethnic Hungarians and the country's Slovaks, Serbs, Romanians and others. What is one to make of this major artistic statement at the time of an important celebration, which takes as its subject matter the conquest of the Slav inhabitants of the area, depicted as living in caves, making human sacrifices, the women being dragged off into slavery or, alternatively, shown bowing down accepting the rule of the newly arrived conquerors? On the other hand, in one sense this was what the 1896 millennium was all about. The painting's original sub-title was "Under the leadership of Árpád the nation conquers the fatherland", itself a rather convoluted notion and one which hides the reality as experienced by some at the time, namely the arrival of marauding bands and their warlords.

In 1898 the cyclorama went to London and only returned to Hungary eleven years later. It remained on display in Budapest more or less permanently until 1944 when a bomb caused serious damage. After 1945 the strongly nationalistic theme of the painting and the enormous cost of restoration both meant that it was "forgotten" and left to rot. As 1996 and the 1100th anniversary of the Conquest approached, the idea was revived of restoring the huge canvas. Specialist Polish restorers undertook the work from 1991 to 1995, following which it was put on display in another specially constructed building at the National Historical Memorial Park at Ópusztaszer, some ninety miles south-east of Budapest. It is believed that Ópusztaszer is the site where Árpád and the other Magyar chieftains met soon after their arrival in the Carpathian Basin to settle the affairs of their newly conquered territory and to distribute land.

Following the closure of the Millennium Exhibition in early November 1896, the pavilions and buildings were removed and the park reverted to its more or less natural state. An exception was the fairy-tale-like Vajdahunyad Castle, which had been designed by Ignác Alpár with the aim of presenting in one building the different architectural styles which could be found in Hungary. Due to its popularity, Alpár was later commissioned to rebuild the structure in a permanent form. That was completed in 1907.

The section facing the lake, which becomes the ice rink in winter, is a copy of part of a fifteenth-century Transylvanian castle in Vajdahunyad (today Hunedoara, Romania), from which the whole complex of buildings takes its name. The noted Hunyadi family were associated with the area. János Hunyadi (1407-56) held high political and military office during his lifetime. He is attributed with the famous victory against the Turks at Nándorfehérvár in 1456, in the final year of his life. His son Mátyás (1440-90) became the renowned King Matthias (see Chapter Eleven).

On either side of the main gate of the edifice are copies of towers of former castles in Upper Hungary (Slovakia) and a copy of the tower of Segesvár (today in Romania). Inside the courtyard is a Romanesque wing and the "Chapel of Ják", an imitation of the still-standing thirteenth-century Benedictine church at Ják in western Hungary, one of the country's oldest monuments. Actually, only the doorway decorated with the twelve apostles is a copy. The rest is both smaller and different from the original church. Beside the chapel is a cloister featuring elements echoing Hungarian architecture of around the twelfth century. Opposite the chapel, around a small courtyard, is the façade of the so-called Palace section, containing a mixture of Romanesque and Gothic styles, and the "Vajdahunyad" section. Further along, Renaissance style appears in a small building with a balcony copied from Sárospatak Castle in eastern Hungary. Beyond that, the large sprawling "Baroque" building is based on details of various eighteenth-century mansions. This section today houses the Museum of Agriculture.

Alpár's Vajdahunyad Castle can be compared with the Museum of Applied Arts, designed around the same time by Ödön Lechner. Alpar's work represented the then official viewpoint whereby what counted was Hungary's cultural heritage as derived from Western European artistic developments. Hence although purporting to reflect Hungarian styles as a whole, there is nothing traditionally Magyar or "folkish" about the constructed castle complex. Lechner, however, looked rather to the Eastern sources of Hungarian tradition, which partly explains his estrangement from the establishment of his time (See Chapter Seven).

chapter five
HEARTS AND MINDS

Over the past one hundred years the atmosphere and indeed the very appearance of Budapest have changed a number of times more or less in line with, and reflecting, changes of political ideology in different periods and at different turning points. This chapter focuses on certain aspects of four diverse periods in the city's twentieth-century history, which have been selected to highlight this phenomenon and which illustrate, in different ways, Budapest's role as a battlefield in the struggle to win over hearts and minds. The aspects and the periods chosen are: cultural policy and activities during the Council Republic of 1919; elements of everyday life during the inter-war years; literary politics in the Stalinist era of the 1950s; and the removal of statues and changing of street names in the early 1990s.

1919: Revolutionary Interlude
One of the strangest looks ever assumed by Heroes' Square appeared during the period of Hungary's Bolshevik-type Council Republic in 1919. For May Day that year the entire two-part colonnade at the rear of the square was wrapped in red drapery covered with slogans such as "Proletarians of all countries unite!", while the square's central column was transformed into a gigantic red canvas-covered obelisk, in front of which stood a specially-made statue of Karl Marx flanked by two suitably proletarian-looking figures.

The government of People's Commissars, which had only been in power a little over one month, commissioned artists literally to paint the town red for the celebrations on 1 May, billed as the country's first free May Day. Heroes' Square was a major rallying point as demonstrators wound their way along Andrássy út and into the City Park; in the eyes of the revolutionary authorities it would not have been appropriate for the masses to pass by statues and memorials devoted to the monarchs of what was now seen as a bygone age.

Public art and art for the public were taken seriously by the commissars and the various artistic "directories" they set up to manage and promote culture for the masses. These bodies also sought to ensure the livelihood of the artists themselves, who now had become state employees with substantial guaranteed income, freeing them, it was believed, from the vicissitudes of capitalist art market relations.

The political history of the 1919 Hungarian Council Republic is, by and large, ignored by many Western historians. The reasons are arguably twofold. So much was happening elsewhere in that fateful year of 1919 that Hungary has been overlooked. This omission has been exacerbated, of course, by the language difficulty. How many historians have been familiar enough with Hungarian to make research a practical possibility? Partly to redress that imbalance, what follows is an overview of the (even lesser-known) cultural aspects of the period.

It was the modernist artists who were at the forefront of the battle of ideas, recruited to visually publicize and dramatize the new order and its proclamations. Revolutionary placards were everywhere, and a genuinely outstanding poster art developed. Specialists working in this field included Róbert Berény, Mihály Biró and Bertalan Pór. Their images of red fists smashing through the old bourgeois order and nailing down the coffin of parliamentary humbug, or of Cézanne- or even early Picasso-inspired figures marching under slogans such as "Forward Red Soldiers!" were plastered around the city. Biró's already by then classic image of a massive, naked, red proletarian figure wielding a hammer—originally a Social Democratic Party icon—was reproduced countless times to advertise the 1919 May Day.

The poster artists were also encouraged to produce images with what were seen as socially useful messages. Anti-alcoholism was one theme. The new regime banned the sale and consumption of alcohol in its early days, though it was forced to relent after a short while. Another motif involved hygiene. "Before and after eating, and after work, wash your hands under running tap water!" exhorted one poster.

Finding examples of this innovative poster art in today's Budapest is not easy. Postcard reproductions of some of the striking images of 1919 used to be readily available in bookshops up to the late 1980s, but no longer. Until then there was also a Museum of the Hungarian Labour Movement in one of the wings of the former Royal Palace on Castle Hill, which concentrated to an extent on the 1919 period. The whole display tended, however, to conflate and confuse "labour movement" and Communist Party, so perhaps it is not surprising that it has disappeared. (Revealingly, the exhibition's final item was a Hungarian-made television set, as if this represented the culmination of the Hungarian labour movement's aspirations!) The Hungarian National Museum in Pest also used to have a substantial section about 1919, including its poster art. In the early 1990s a new permanent exhibition was installed in the museum, the part about revolutionary 1919 being reduced dramatically.

In 1919 the process of involving the artists was not without its problems and tensions. Bertalan Pór, a member of the artists' directory, later recalled how he was working on a huge 26-foot-high canvas for May Day, decorating the façade of the Hall of Arts in Heroes' Square. The slogan at the top (in the male-oriented fashion of the time) read: "Forward for your wives and children!"—as if no women were involved in the political and labour movement, which was not the case, even if no woman had emerged as a People's Commissar. In the event, according to Pór, nature intervened and his work was destroyed by a huge storm which raged before the May Day celebrations.

Pór also records a rather amusing and, at the same time, telling anecdote concerning Tibor Szamuely, one of the more hard-line of the People's Commissars, officially designated to look after matters of defence. Szamuely once telephoned Pór to say a poster was needed to portray the following themes: "1. The land belongs to those who till it; 2. The factory belongs to those who work in it; 3. The power belongs to those who struggle for it. Work and Struggle!" Pór told Szamuely that as a member of the artists' directory he was fully occupied and did not have the time, to which the latter replied that it was a very important matter and that he had to have the placard by the following morning. "I went home and did it," says Pór, adding that for someone like Szamuely it was absolutely normal to dictate a theme to an artist.

The commissars certainly exercised enough dictatorial power to enable them to appropriate (they called it socialize) notable works of art from private collections and organize a public exhibition of them in the Hall of Arts. The display was opened by György Lukács, who had been appointed Deputy People's Commissar for Education. More than half a century later, in a filmed interview of 1971, he was still enthusiastic, recalling of "socialized art treasures" his views of 1919: "we take over into state—i.e. proletarian—ownership every valuable work of art; and the time will come when the proletariat will be in a position to declare what it considers, and what it does not consider, as its own." It is strange, with the passing of time, to consider how a celebrated Marxist philosopher could have had such a naïve view of the relationship between the state, even a nominally socialist one, and the working class.

The world of theatre in 1919 was no less affected than the world of art. All theatres were nationalized, turning actors into state employees. A "Decree on Theatres", issued on 24 March, just three days after the Council Republic was formed, declared: "From now on, the theatre belongs to the people! Art will not any more be the privilege of the leisurely rich. Culture is the rightful due of the working people." Lukács' Education Commissariat ordered that two days before each performance two-thirds of all tickets should be submitted to the central ticket office of the Trade Union Council for distribution to workers at substantially reduced prices. Lukács himself issued a decree to the effect that anyone trying to sell on such cheap tickets for profit would be punished.

The theatres were crowded, whatever the performance, and even though the idea was to encourage theatrical innovation, old plays with an emphasis on what was perceived as progressive were the order of the day. At the same time, there was a rather cruel joke going the rounds, as recorded by Artúr Bárdos, a theatre producer and director, according to which audiences were not supposed to applause during classical productions, "in case the proletariat woke up."

The music scene of 1919 is of particular interest in terms of modern-day perceptions of the personalities involved. Both Zoltán Kodály and Béla Bartók were involved in the activities of the revolutionary music directory. Kodály, in particular, suffered from this participation afterwards, not being permitted to teach at the Academy for two years (he had been appointed its deputy director during the revolution). Bartók wrote strongly-worded letters to the press in his defence in 1920. According to Tibor Hajdu, who has chronicled the cultural policies of the Council Republic, the many worker concerts were well attended and it was during this period that Bartók gave a public recital for the first time in nine years. The British journalist H. N. Brailsford, in Budapest at the time, was particularly enamoured of the public music festivals he encountered. "One had the irresistible feeling," he wrote, "in those bright days of spring, as the music of these festivals floated on the lilac-scented air over the Danube, that youth and art and talent and creative impulse were with this spirited movement." Film culture, despite being in its youth internationally, was perceived as being of supreme importance, perhaps as a reflection of the Soviet experience; Lenin is often quoted as a firm supporter of film and cinema as the most modern and effective means of mass propaganda. As with theatres, film production and distribution were nationalized, but that did not mean an end to financial backing. On the contrary, film was subsidized to a great extent. The first issue of the magazine *Red Film*, published on 12 April 1919, spoke of getting rid of old-style films full of false capitalist ideology, and producing instead films appropriate to the current revolutionary times. Yet interestingly, its long list of envisaged new films was dominated by proposed cinematic versions of Hungarian literary works, many from established authors such as Mór Jókai, Kálmán Mikszáth, Mihály Vörösmarty and Ferenc Molnár. Among foreign authors whose works were deemed worthy of film treatment were Zola, Tolstoy, Ibsen, Gogol, Hugo, Stendhal, Verne, Maupassant, Dickens, Mark Twain and even Charlotte Brontë. It was an ambitious project and to help realize it a special "Proletarian Academy" was established to give crash courses in all aspect of film technique, both behind and in front of the camera.

During the 133 days of the Council Republic about twenty films were completed, including a version of Upton Sinclair's *Samuel the Seeker*, one called *Money*, based on writings by Maxim Gorky, and another called *Hail Caesar*, directed by Sándor Korda. When the regime fell in August 1919 a further fifteen or so films were being made. These included Dickens' *Oliver Twist* and Victor Hugo's *Marion Delorme*. All this was no small achievement, given the circumstances (as a comparison, by the 1980s, after Hungarian cinema had been established for decades, on average twenty feature films a year were being produced in Hungary).

Of a more immediately propagandistic nature were the documentary cinema newsreels of 1919, which went under the name of *Red Report*. These concentrated on issues like the disparity of wealth before the revolution and how the Council Republic was changing such imbalances. Proletarian children, for example, were shown happily consuming food in the Park Club, a formerly exclusive gathering place for the gentry. There were also reports from the front, about the red army and its successes. The 26 April issue of *Red Film* enthusiastically described how *Red Report* was preparing to record for posterity Budapest's first May Day celebration under the proletarian dictatorship. All available camera operators would be stationed to capture the atmosphere in front of the Millennium Monument, on Andrássy út, on Margaret Island and elsewhere. Others would be following events from moving vehicles. It was expected that over six thousand feet of film would be used to record the events, after which the compiled documentary would be shown throughout the week in the six largest cinemas of Budapest. "After the extraordinary long film has played in Budapest," *Red Film* concluded, "it will be sent to Russia."

Due to their involvement with filmmaking during Hungary's "Red 1919" period, many of the artists involved thought it better to leave the country soon after, particularly in view of the growth of extreme right-wing nationalism in the early period of the Horthy regime. As happened with many intellectuals and scientists who emigrated in the inter-war period, Hungary's loss was the rest of the world's gain. Sándor Korda would eventually become better known as the "British" filmmaker Sir Alexander Korda. Mihály Kertész, a member of the artists' committee of the Central Council of the Socialized Cinema Industry in 1919, became famous as Michael Curtis, the director of *Casablanca*. Even Hollywood's favourite Dracula, Béla Lugosi, had gone into exile after having participated in the 1919 events.

In the field of literature, writers were divided concerning the degree and consistency of support they afforded the Council Republic, though many rallied to its defence. The official line, on the surface at least, was one of tolerance, although couched within a certain ambiguity. "The Communist cultural programme," wrote Deputy Commissar Lukács in the *Red Gazette* on 19 April:

> *only makes a distinction between good and bad literature, and is not prepared to throw out Shakespeare or Goethe on account of their not being socialist authors. Nor is it prepared to let loose dilettantism in art, under the pretext of socialism... The People's Commissariat of Education does not want any official art; it does not want a dictatorship of party art either. The political point of view will remain a criterion of selection for a long time, but cannot dictate the direction of literary production. It should be a filter but not a source.*

How this might have worked out in the long run we cannot say; the Council Republic did not last long enough for any "filtering" to fully take effect. One interesting step was represented by an announcement in *Red Gazette* on 2 July concerning the setting up of a translators' bureau. "Valuable works of the old, along with standard works of modern and modernist literature, will be translated," it said. Perhaps surprisingly, it continued: "It goes without saying that the first thing will be to translate all Dostoyevsky's works."

Behind such developments we can probably detect the hand of Lukács—and not just because the article indicated that "the introductions to the [translated] books will probably be written by Comrade György Lukács." At that point, Commissar Lukács played a role somewhat similar to that of Anatole Lunacharsky, the People's Commissar for Education in revolutionary Russia. Both were committed Marxists and leading functionaries of their respective parties, bound by their rulings. But both were also cultured intellectuals, appreciative of broad European traditions and trends. They did their best to defend and uphold the best literary and cultural standards, irrespective of party lines (though Lukács could be quite ruthless in non-literary matters, defending, for example, the summary execution of deserters from the Red Army). In practical political terms, Lunacharsky had the harder time of it, if only because his revolution lasted much longer and therefore had to face deeper and longer-lasting problems. Yet in later times Lukács also experienced difficulties with his comrades on the cultural front, notably in post-1945 Hungary (see below). Lukács, incidentally, also had another taste of governmental power, since he was appointed minister of culture and education in one of the swiftly-changing cabinets of Premier Imre Nagy during the 1956 uprising. Yet his position then and, indeed, the government itself, lasted for an even shorter period than the Council Republic of 1919.

The failure of the Commune, as the Council Republic is often called in an echo of the Paris Commune of 1871, was not primarily due to its cultural policies, though their implementation did cause some dissatisfaction and disagreement. The nationalization of all cultural production perhaps inevitably led to bureaucratization and, within that, charges of favouritism and even corruption. It was not particularly well-liked, for example, at least according to Artúr Bárdos, that the wife of party leader Béla Kun was given an influential position, making her *de facto* in charge of the theatres of Budapest.

In his 1971 interview, Lukács himself remembered the accusations of privilege. "Once, when I delivered a lecture in Budapest, someone took the platform after the lecture and said: 'Well, it's just like old times. Comrade Lukács came by car and will leave by car, just like the leaders of the old regime.'" Lukács claims he retorted by explaining what he had to do the following morning, offering to give up his car and leave on foot if someone else would undertake his tasks. His rather patronizing response seems to have worked: "The workers laughed and said that I was right..."

The speed with which measures were applied also tended to create disorientation, particularly as many of the comrades entertained rather utopian ideas of what could be achieved in a short time. As Ervin Sinkó, a twenty-year-old activist in 1919, wrote in his novel about the Commune, *Optimisták* (Optimists), what was needed, as he described the reasoning of "Comrade Vértes" (modelled on Lukács), was "the strength of faith". This apparently non-Marxist, non-materialist trait was not necessarily a shared attribute of every participant of the time. Faith in what, after all? Sinkó completed his novel in 1934 while in exile in Paris. He then experienced great difficulty in getting it published, even in the Soviet Union where he lived from 1935 to 1937. His diary notes of that period were eventually published as *A regény regénye* (The Story of a Novel). The work not only describes the monotonously repetitive and often farcical obstacles he encountered with the Soviet literary bureaucracy, which reflected a certain Soviet ambiguity towards Hungary's Commune, but also offers a revealing and informed account of life in Moscow on the eve of Stalin's great purges.

One cultural issue which did cause much resentment was the clamp-down on press freedom. Using the genuine paper shortage as an excuse, many publications were closed down. The closures were seen as blatant political censorship and aroused strong opposition from the journalists' union.

What was not the subject of any major criticism, according to Frank Eckelt, whose essay on the domestic policies of the Commune was published in America in 1971, was its overall cultural policy in relation to children. A genuine attempt was made to improve the lives of the many deprived children of proletarian families. Eckelt recounts that aside from trying to reform the education system (an impossible task given the shortage of time) the revolutionary regime established feeding centres for children, both in a material and cultural sense. The legal stigma of illegitimacy was abolished. Compulsory, free, medical examinations were ordered for all children between six and fourteen year of age. Dentists were paid to give two hours a day free care to school children recommended to them. Public spas and baths were nationalized and formerly fashionable resorts by Lake Balaton were commandeered to give urban children the chance to have at least one holiday. "The Children of the Proletariat are Bathing" declared *Népszava*, the Social Democrats' daily in its issue of 5 April. *Red Gazette* carried similar articles.

The government, says Eckelt, planned to establish a "Child's Protective Office" to deal with delinquent and morally depraved minors. Homes, sanatoria and dispensaries were planned, but shortage of time prevented their realization. Specialists were recruited to help psychotic and maladjusted children. Kindergartens were renamed "play schools", and poems glorifying war were to be eliminated in favour of texts asserting peace, brotherly love and equality. A special theatre was established for children and, according to Tibor Hajdu, in May five cinemas in Budapest were allocated especially for the screening of films for children.

Even so, the "memory" of 1919 in Hungary has ranged from the extremely negative to the ambiguous. The right-wing Horthy regime which followed the Commune understandably wanted to erase all positive memories of what had happened. From its perspective, this process was helped by the fact that a large number of the people's commissars were Jewish, or of Jewish descent. Indeed, that fact enabled the post-1919 regime to conflate Bolshevism and Jewishness, conveniently mixing anti-Semitism and anti-communism, even though the majority of Hungarian Jews cannot be said to have been out-and-out Commune supporters, and nor did the commissars act in the name of Jews as such. This mattered little to the right-wing nationalists. The Commune experience, from their point of view, justified not only the physical atrocities which accompanied its downfall but partly also, as described elsewhere, Hungary's *Numerus Clausus*, one of the first anti-Jewish laws of twentieth-century Europe.

The post-1919 Hungarian Left also had problems with the Commune. It was not just, as is often explained, that Kun and his comrades had not followed Lenin's example of distributing the land to the peasants (in this sense they were more "radical" than Lenin, preferring, at least in theory, collectivization). More important, certainly from a psychological point of view, was the fact that the majority of the Hungarian people's commissars who in various stages had emigrated to Moscow fell victim to the Stalinist purges of the late 1930s. In the early post-1945 era, how could a communist proclaim the glories of 1919 if many of its leaders had lost their lives under Comrade Stalin, who continued to rule in Moscow until his death in 1953?

Foreign writers were not hidebound by such prejudices. The British journalist H. N. Brailsford was an early enthusiast, as were the American reporters Alice Riggs Hunt and Cyril Eastman. All three wrote positively about their experiences in the Budapest of 1919. Such enthusiasm could perhaps be explained by the "politically friendly outsider" factor, famously exemplified by the Americans John Reed and Louise Bryant, and reflected in the former's dramatic eyewitness account of the Russian Revolution, *Ten Days that Shook the World*, and in the 1981 evocative film *Reds*.

A positive reflection of the Hungarian events by a then youthful insider has been left by Arthur Koestler, who in 1919 was a thirteen-year-old Budapest schoolboy. In his autobiographical volume *Arrow in the Blue*, Koestler emphasizes his upbeat impressions of the time. He was impressed by the music in public places, whether it was Chopin's *Funeral March* being played during communist burial ceremonies, or the then ever-present *La Marseillaise* and *Internationale*. He was struck by the new teachers who appeared in his school, dealing with subjects that were new to him, ranging from the life of farm workers to economics and constitutional government. On May Day 1919 a schoolmate of his gave a speech praising Danton and Saint-Just, leading figures of the French Revolution. He was also impressed after attending a workers' class his cousin Margit had given at a factory in Újpest, on the north side of Budapest. It seemed to him, on reflection years later, that something exciting was happening and that the world was gloriously being turned upside down.

How far can we trust this cheerful recollection of a teenager's experience? In his monumental and scholarly biography of Arthur Koestler, David Ceserani shows that Koestler wrote and re-wrote his autobiographical essays and works with a view to the context in which they would be published and with an eye to particular readerships. *Arrow in the Blue* was written not in the early 1930s, when Koestler was an ardent communist, but twenty years later, when he was well into his anti-communist and Cold Warrior phase, and so it is of some interest to quote his summary of the Hungarian Commune. While remarking that the Commune "would in due course have degenerated in a totalitarian police state, forcibly following the example of its Russian model" and believing that "no Communist Party in Europe has been able to hold out against the corruption imposed on it from Moscow," Koestler admits that this later "knowledge" does "not invalidate the hopeful and exuberant mood of the early days of the Revolution in Hungary…"

The Inter-War Years: Irredentism and Everyday Life

To compare a whole country with the suffering Christ might seem hyperbolic, but this is what was often done in Hungary in the inter-war period. The territorial division imposed by the 1920 Treaty of Trianon had, in the mind of many, crucified the country, but there was always hope of a resurrection, and this attitude became a key component of the period's official culture. It was a culture which managed to penetrate many otherwise ordinary elements of everyday life, and thus was not restricted to propaganda statements issued on national holidays and at political meetings. "Revisionism" or "irredentism", the campaign for the restitution of territory lost through the Trianon Treaty, became part of the mainstream.

The widely used slogan "No, No, Never!" appeared first between 1918 and 1920. Later it was joined by others proclaiming "Everything back!", "Hungarian justice", "Hungarian resurrection" and "Broken Hungary is no Country; Whole Hungary is Heaven." These slogans not only gained an official identity, but were reproduced countless times on posters, postcards and badges. At the beginning and the end of a school day pupils had to recite the *Hungarian Credo*, which won the first prize of a patriotic poetry competition organized by a Hungarian revisionist group in 1920.

I believe in one God,
I believe in one Homeland,
I believe in one divine eternal justice,
I believe in the resurrection of Hungary.
Amen.

Hundreds of examples of "Trianon literature" appeared, representing very varied standards. The authors of these literary pieces ranged from self-appointed amateurs to representatives of high culture. The writer Ferenc Herczeg was the president of the Hungarian Frontier Readjustment League, though at one point he felt compelled to complain about the cheap mass-marketing methods employed by many promoters of "Trianon culture".

Numerous songs were composed and written in a revisionist spirit. They were usually march-like or sentimental pieces, but revision as a topic appeared even in popular dance music. Alongside fashionable foreign hits, love, frivolous or pub songs, the sounds of "patriotic foxtrot" also filtered through from bars. One curiosity was a Transylvanian march entitled *Despite It All,* which the composers, Lajos Krajcsi and Imre Koltay, instrumented for a jazz orchestra.

According to cultural historian Miklós Zeidler, revisionism was expressed not only through cultural productions but also in the culture of objects.

> *The head of a family with irredentist feelings, if he felt like it, could pour soda water in his wine from a soda bottle with the inscription "No, No, Never!", use an irredentist ashtray and keep his valuables in a decorative box with the outline of historic Hungary. There was an irredentist candleholder on his table. He presented his children with a puzzle depicting historic Hungary and when the school year started he bought them "No, No, Never!" pencils and irredentist exercise books.*

He might have a neck chain with a locket containing some soil from the lost territories, and, using "national drawing pins", he could put an irredentist poster on his door proclaiming the "No, No, Never!" of the Hungarian National Alliance. He could send postcards depicting the lost territories, while his table clock would be inscribed with the

Hungarian Credo. Irredentist wall hangings could decorate his home, as might a statuette entitled *Hungary's Bouquet*, which looked like an everyday flower composition but, if lit from a certain angle, cast a shadow in the form of historic Hungary on the surface below.

On the streets of Budapest, the true irredentist might even speak to people in a special way. Zoltán Várady, a zealous Catholic priest, developed a new form of greeting to deepen patriotic feelings, which he expounded in a special booklet in 1938. The detailed description, accompanying poems and the included photograph assert that in order to greet someone in an irredentist way the person must make a small step forward with his right foot, lift his right hand with the open palm turned inwards and with a friendly look say "Resurrection!" or "Justice!", to which the other person should answer with similar motions, declaring "May God grant it!"

Such gestures, slogans, verses and other paraphernalia, says Zeidler, were the result of "simplifying voices, which, on the one hand, provided an understandable, comforting and self-absolving explanation for the break-up of historical Hungary and, on the other, offered a tempting programme for a triumphant and deserved territorial revision." The formula of an honest victim and a cruel enemy, he believes, was suitable for demonizing opponents, while at the same time it reduced the problem of the partition of the country to a moral level, generating a virtual world divorced from political realities.

Into this world there came, of all people, a member of the British House of Lords, Viscount Lord Rothermere, who befriended Hungary and used his *Daily Mail* to campaign for revision of the 1920 Trianon Treaty. Rothermere's article of 21 June 1927 under the heading "Hungary's Place in the Sun" won him tremendous praise in Hungary and led to an enthusiastic "Rothermere campaign". On the spot in Szabadság tér where today the Soviet Army Memorial stands there used to be, from 1928 to 1945, another quite different symbol: a flag permanently at half-mast mounted on a pedestal inscribed with pro-Hungarian quotations from Rothermere and from the Italian dictator Benito Mussolini. Rothermere contributed towards another memorial for Szabadság tér entitled *Monument of Hungarian Grief.* The work of French sculptor Émile Guillaume, it featured a nude bronze figure of a mother radiating despair and vulnerability, mourning for her children.

Such was the popularity of the British lord that a street was named after him in Budapest. But that was by no means all. A song was composed with the title "Lord Rothermere Sent the Message" (a reference to the famous "Kossuth Song" hailing the great Hungarian revolutionary leader of 1848-9). The music score had a striking colourful cover depicting Rothermere, in reality rather plump and nearing sixty, as a heroic knight in full armour protecting a Hungarian warrior with a broken sword. A former prime minister, Károly Huszár, compared Rothermere to Simon of Cyrene carrying Christ's cross, by which he equated the British lord and Hungary with the passion story. There was even a cartoonist who depicted Rothermere as the eye of God.

Incredibly, Rothermere received a letter of gratitude signed by over one million Hungarians and, even more amazingly, at one point was even offered the Hungarian crown. Today one can still see a piece of stained-glass work with a Rothermere connection in Budapest's Church of St. Margaret, which stands in Lehel tér, just to the north of the West End City Centre. The ornamented window was placed in the northern aisle of the church, which was consecrated in 1933. Rothermere himself was one of the church's benefactors. The window bears the inscription

"Viscount Rothermere 1933" and shows his coat of arms and motto, "Bene qui sedulo" (He lives well who lives industriously).

It was one thing for official Hungary to have Mussolini on its side, as it did in its campaign to regain territories lost in 1920, but it was quite another potentially more prestigious matter to have the support of a prominent British press baron and member of the House of Lords. What many Hungarians failed to appreciate, however, was that Rothermere was arguing not for a return of all of Hungary's lost territory, but for a revision of the borders on ethnic grounds, so that as far as possible tightly-knit Magyar communities close to the post-1920 border of Hungary but living in another country could be re-united with their homeland.

After 1945 Rothermere's donated statue and the flag-pole with his inscription were removed from Szabadság tér. The irredentist ideas of the inter-war period were now taboo and all thoughts about revision of the borders, even in part, had to be forgotten. Also removed from the square were four statues entitled *North*, *South*, *East* and *West*, which had stood there since January 1921. They had symbolized, sentimentally, the lost territories. *West*, for example, showed a figure holding the coats of arms of the lost counties tumbling on the Hungarian crown. On the triple-figure composition of *North* a Slovak boy seeking protection was leaning on a crucified Hungaria, and a well-built Kuruc soldier was protecting both with his sword.

The 1950s: The Stalinist Era

On 8 March 1952 a packed audience in the Hungarian State Opera House on Andrássy út (then known as Sztálin út, after the Soviet leader) cheered and clapped wildly at great length. The object of the adulation was the lead performer of a very special type of orchestration—Mátyás Rákosi, the leader of the ruling Hungarian Workers' Party, who had orchestrated the party's rise to power in the years following the Second World War. It was Rákosi's sixtieth birthday and the gala performance at the Opera House was one of a number of events organized to generate adulation for Hungary's own great leader in the manner of the celebrations which had taken place three years previously to mark the seventieth birthday of Joseph Stalin. An exhibition about Rákosi's life was organized, for example, in the Institute of Working Class History (today the Museum of Ethnography in Kossuth tér). The display included hundreds of gifts which had been sent to Rákosi from all parts of the country.

In March 1952 the cult of personality was at its height in Hungary, and literary figures were at the forefront of its promoters. A birthday volume was published with the title *Hungarian Writers on Mátyás Rákosi*. Thirty-three well-known poets and writers made their contribution in essays with titles such as "The People's Hope", "The Example of Rákosi", "When Rákosi Speaks" and "We Give Our Hearts". The cult of personality might have been at its height, but the quality of post-war Hungarian literature was probably at its lowest.

Writers and intellectuals in general had welcomed the winds of change which began to sweep across Hungary following the end of the Second World War. There was a genuine hope that the country could be rebuilt, not only physically but also culturally, and many writers regarded the communists as being in the vanguard of that change. In the background was the prestige of the victorious Soviet Union and the knowledge that the Soviet system, at least in theory, put culture and its producers on a pedestal.

For its part, the new Hungarian political leadership did indeed treat writers in a special way. Poets, novelists and essayists were now paid a stipend (the condition was membership of the newly-formed Writers' Association, firmly under the control of the party), and if a work was issued by one of the state publishers the print-run could reach hundreds of thousands of copies. Successful writers, including non-party members, could live very well in the late 1940s and early 1950s in Hungary. Villas in the Buda hills were allocated to them, and resort homes by Lake Balaton and in the Mátra Hills were at their disposal. Invitations to attend official events were a regular occurrence. In 1948 a new state honour, the Kossuth Prize, was introduced and awarded to those deemed to be innovators in the fields of culture and science. Recipients of the prize were engulfed by extra praise and adulation. It was all part of tying the cultural elite more closely to the state. (The prestigious Kossuth Prize is still awarded every year.)

At first writers were more or less free to write what they wanted, only extreme reactionary and clearly fascist themes or works exhibiting nostalgia for the Horthy era being outlawed. Conservative writers who had opposed the pro-Nazi trends of official Hungary in the 1930s were particularly welcomed. This pluralistic approach to culture was reflected in other fields such as architecture and was itself a reflection of the political realities in the early post-war years

It is a common misconception that the iron fist of Stalinism, one-party rule and the police state, as elsewhere in Eastern Europe, must have begun immediately in Hungary with the end of the war in 1945 and the Soviet presence. In reality, the immediate aftermath of the war saw a period of coalition, both politically in that there was a multi-party system and a coalition government, and culturally, in that different trends co-existed. It is only from 1948-9 that we can speak of a one-party, Soviet-style system in Hungary, and even then a relatively open attitude to culture persisted for some time.

The death-knell of cultural pluralism was sounded in the summer of 1949 with an article published in one of the party journals in which the author, László Rudas, a long-standing communist and one of the party's "official philosophers", made a zealous and unexpected attack on György Lukács. Lukács, now aged 64, had spent the years 1933-45 in the Soviet Union, returning to Hungary after the war with the other "Muscovite" Hungarian communists who had managed to survive Stalin's purges. Himself a respected philosopher and literary critic with a prominent political past as a commissar in 1919, Lukács was a kind of father figure of the post-war cultural scene and a supporter of its relative tolerance.

Lukács published an article refuting the attack, and the dispute could have ended there had it not been followed by a second assault in the autumn, published in the party's widely-distributed daily *Szabad Nép* (Free People) and written by the paper's editor-in-chief, József Révai, one of the leading communist officials and, in effect, the overall dictator of Hungarian cultural policy. According to the new line, Lukács' ideological failing—although he was recognized as a staunch party member—revolved around his view of literary realism, which included the idea that some politically reactionary writers of classical European literature had nevertheless produced works which, in view of their style, insight and content, could be considered progressive. A further point of contention was that Lukács had had little positive to say about Soviet literary output.

In the background was the new, hard-line policy being pursued in the Soviet Union under the leadership of cultural boss Andrei Zhdanov. Western influences, modern music, naturalism and in general "cosmopolitanism" were condemned, while "socialist realism" was being promoted exclusively as the accepted aesthetic. What was now required in Hungary, as in the Soviet Union, was a greater emphasis in literature on class struggle, the positive development of proletarian characters and, in particular, the leading role of the communists and their party.

An example of what this meant involved the noted left-wing writer Tibor Déry, who had come from a relatively wealthy background but had been attracted to communism during the 1919 events. In the inter-war period he had experienced problems in getting published, but when his *Unfinished Sentence*, a trilogy about different individuals living through the political crises of the 1930s, eventually came out in 1947, he was the recipient of loud acclaim, Lukács calling his work "one of the greatest creations of our century".

In 1948 Déry was one of the first to be awarded the prestigious Kossuth Prize, though he was no stranger to trouble. A collection of short stories he had written about the siege of Budapest had been pulped under Soviet pressure after publication. The problem was that Déry had written realistically about the behaviour of Soviet troops towards Hungarians in 1944-5, behaviour which was part heroic and generous and part brutal and oppressive. Exposing the latter aspects could not be tolerated. Furthermore, before the war Déry had translated André Gide's *Return from the USSR*, a critique of the Soviet Union as Gide had experienced it during his travels there in 1936. This would later be held against Déry as "suspicion of Trotskyism", although, ironically, after its publication Déry had been sentenced to three months imprisonment, since Gide's work, albeit critical, was regarded by the authorities of the Horthy era as still being written from "within the Soviet camp".

Déry was one of the writers who contributed to the 1952 birthday eulogy of Rákósi; his had been the essay entitled "The Example of Rákosi". Yet soon afterwards he found himself in serious trouble, which came to a head in the summer following the publication of the second volume of his planned four-part *The Answer*. It was an epic work, intended to highlight the development of progress in Hungary by following the story, from the 1930s to1948, of its working-class hero, Bálint Köpe, who rises to become the director of the nationalized factory in which he had once worked. Déry had spent much time visiting factories and talking to people in order to make his background as authentic as possible. What better socialist-realist theme with which to portray the new Hungary?

But then in stepped József Révai again. He attacked the work in a *Szabad Nép* article entitled innocuously "Comments on the Margin of a Novel". Far from being marginal, there then followed an invitation to writers, both party members and others, to Budapest's Akadémia utca headquarters of the Hungarian Workers' Party to discuss "the state of our literature". Déry's work was a prime item on the agenda.

The problem for Révai lay with Déry's portrayal of the underground Communist Party in the inter-war period. The picture painted was realistic. Before the war the party was small, sectarian and splintered, and by no means a mass left-wing organization with influence. If anything, that role, though limited by circumstances, had belonged to the Social Democrats. In his novel Déry has Köpe joining the Communist Party only in 1945. This was too much, or rather too little and too late for Révai and the new line on literature. The party should have been portrayed as much stronger than it was, and much more heroically. The "historical truth" of the party's eventually victorious role was, according to the line, much more important than the actual truth of its former impotence. As Tamás Acél and Tibor Méray pointedly put it in their fascinating account of literary politics in Hungary in the early 1950s, *The Revolt of the Mind*, paraphrasing Révay's position: "Déry falsified by telling the truth; but he would be telling the truth if he falsified." In addition, Déry was accused of "petty-bourgeois moralizing" in so far as he had portrayed characters facing personal dilemmas of responsibility and conscience, issues which were not resolved by following the party line.

Yet this was not the end of the matter. Acél and Méray's account of the lengthy meeting at party headquarters has Révay going so far as to suggest changes to Déry's work. The class struggle and the role of the party should be given more prominence. There should be more Communist Party characters in the novel, with greater influence on Köpe. The love story between a female party member and a bourgeois professor should be modified to have both of them joining the party before the war. Révay's attack ended with a curious compliment, according to Acél and Méray: "What makes this novel particularly dangerous is its high literary level."

Suggesting changes to cultural works was one thing; actually changing them was another—but it did happen. According to Acél and Méray, when Italian director Vittorio De Sica's classic 1948 film *The Bicycle Thief* was shown in Hungary, the Ministry of Culture intervened with the effect that the last scene, which showed the depressed proletarian hero walking into the distance, was inter-cut with documentary film shots of an Italian Communist Party meeting and its leader Palmiro Togliatti, implying that the downcast hero, both victim and perpetrator of theft, need not despair—the movement was at hand to help. Imagination, of sorts, was certainly the order of the day.

After Stalin

On 5 March 1953 something happened that had an enormous influence on the political climate in Budapest, and indeed elsewhere in Eastern Europe and the Soviet Union. Joseph Stalin died in his dacha at Kuntsevo, on the eastern outskirts of Moscow.

There used to be a popular saying: "When it rains in Moscow, the umbrellas go up in Budapest." Now, with the slowly emerging "thaw", as it was called, following Stalin's death, a little bit of sunlight appeared over the towers of the Kremlin and the umbrellas in Budapest came down for a while. In June, at a specially convened meeting in Moscow, the new Soviet leaders, recognizing that many errors had been made by Stalin and, in Hungary, by Mátyás Rákosi, "Stalin's best Hungarian pupil", ordered that the premiership of Hungary be passed to Imre Nagy. The New Course, the name given to the changes which the new premier intended to implement, was announced by Nagy in parliament on 4 July. Nagy's speech resounded like a bombshell, both in parliament and in society at large.

Lending a human touch to the proceedings with his colourful country accent, Nagy outlined his programme for change. Pressure on the farms would be eased, peasants would be free to leave the collectives if they so wished, the balance of economic planning would shift in favour of consumption at the expense of the recent over-emphasis on investment in heavy industry, there would be a partial amnesty for prisoners, internment and labour camps would be closed and "class enemies" deported to the countryside would be allowed to return to the urban centres, even religious believers would experience a greater tolerance. Intra-party democracy was to be encouraged and a certain level of press freedom would be allowed.

Although Nagy's speech had little to say specifically about cultural matters, the announcement of his Hungarian thaw generated a new, relatively hopeful atmosphere in the country and contributed to various movements for reform, particularly among party dissidents, critical journalists, writers and intellectuals generally, which were to provide the backdrop to the uprising in October 1956.

On 7 November 1953, the anniversary of the Russian Revolution, an article appeared in *Irodalmi Ujság* (Literary Gazette), the publication of the Writers' Association, called "Nyírség Diary". The author, Péter Kucska, had spent the summer travelling through the Nyírség region in north-east Hungary, investigating conditions there in the manner of Hungary's critical "village writers" of the 1930s. Previously Kucska had been one of the writers who could find no fault with the system, but now his exposé of the real conditions in the countryside not only came as a shock, but encouraged further critical journalism, essay writing and poetry. The free cultural cat had been let out of the bag.

Nagy remained premier until April 1955. Internal struggles (Rákosi had remained as general secretary of the party) and a shifting balance of forces in Moscow finally led to his downfall and an attempt to put the brakes on reform. But the writers and journalists were not easily cowed. According to Acél and Méray, the only party organization that failed to enthusiastically adopt the new hard line of the Central Committee was the Writers' Association. There were attempts to browbeat the writers and attacks on journalists, leading to demotions and dismissals, but there were no arrests.

Irodalmi Ujság became the country's favourite newspaper, selling out immediately on the first morning of its publication. It was something new in Eastern Europe at the time for writers not to slavishly follow the party line in all matters, even though such writers were, in the main, party members or communist sympathizers. In September 1955 an entire edition of *Irodalmi Ujság* was confiscated, an action that led to further protests from the writers, including the production in early November of the so-called Writers' Memorandum, a document criticizing the party's literary and cultural policies and its "anti-democratic interferences", such as the ban on Imre Madách's nineteenth-century Hungarian classic *The Tragedy of Man*, which includes elements critical of a socialist utopian vision.

Fifty-nine well-known writers and artists, all party members, signed the memorandum. In this instance, however, the pressure to conform and not to "peddle the idea of the freedom of literature" was such that eventually all but a handful withdrew their signature. This pressure has been vividly described by Gyula Háy, one of the writers who tried to remain steadfast and who was summoned along with others to face a hostile audience of party officials on 6 December. The venue was the Metal Workers' Union Headquarters on Koltói Anna utca in Pest (today Magdolna utca). It was the same venue where the infamous show trial of foreign minister László Rajk had taken place just over six years previously. As he sat down, Háy was handed a piece of paper, ominously by one of Rákosi's bodyguards. He saw his name on it and the words: "peddling the idea of the freedom of literature." Even more ominously, the outcome of the proceedings, the words of a resolution of condemnation that the meeting was to pass, was already in print on the paper he had been handed. In the presence of Mátyás Rákosi, Háy tried to respond to the accusations. "My very first sentence was interrupted," he recalls. "Rákosi himself echoed my vocative 'Comrades' in a tone of mockery." This was the signal for barracking and catcalls. "Yells and cries of derision came at me from all sides." Háy was gripped by fear. A number of thugs were sitting in the front row, ready to pounce. "All at once I knew what it felt like to be delivered up to lynch justice." He was rescued by Hilda Gobbi, a renowned actress at the National Theatre and an old communist from the underground years. Even though her powerful voice was drowned in the uproar, her appearance calmed the atmosphere. The union official rang his bell and called time-up for Háy. He was pleased to get away from the rostrum and the hall.

Though many individuals gave in to this type of pressure, writers' resistance remained quite strong. They were to receive a great boost in February 1956 from an unexpected source—the XXth Congress of the Communist Party of the Soviet Union, during which the Soviet leader Nikita Khrushchev denounced Stalin. When news of this event swept through Eastern Europe it had a dramatic effect, boosting currents in favour of reform. In Budapest many young intellectuals and professionals began to flock to the meetings of the Petőfi Circle, which had been established in 1955 as a discussion group by the official youth organization of the ruling party. By the summer of 1956, however, its meetings had become a forum for a variety of oppositionist elements, "a second parliament" some might say.

One of the most dramatic of the Circle's meetings took place on 27 June at the Officers' Club (today a bank building, 38 Váci utca). The theme of the meeting was information and the press, and the hall was packed and full of anticipation well before the appointed time for it to begin. In the end so many tried to attend (a figure of 5,000 is often quoted) that loudspeakers had to be rigged up in the foyer, on the staircase and outside in the courtyard. One of the speakers at the meeting, which lasted until the early hours of the following morning, was Tibor Déry, who not only criticized those in power but raised the issue of structural defects in the political system itself, an outspoken and daring move in the context of the time.

When it came to the uprising in October, however, the writers were somewhat overshadowed. True, on the first day of the events, their association's president, the peasant writer Péter Veres, led a march from its Bajza utca headquarters to join the protest at the Petőfi statue by the Pest embankment, from there moving across the river to the larger gathering at the statue of the Polish general Josef Bem. Veres himself spoke, or tried to speak, at both gatherings despite the fact that the Writers' Union had issued a statement, published in that morning's *Szabad Nép*, saying that it was not organizing any demonstrations, nor did it agree with such. From then on the impetus moved to the streets, due to the fighting, and eventually to parliament, where Imre Nagy, now reinstalled as premier, tried to find a political solution to the crisis.

When the Soviets intervened for the second time, on 4 November, and crushed the uprising militarily, the writers continued the struggle in their own way. A number of outspoken declarations in defence of the revolution and condemning the Soviet intervention were adopted, notably the Manifesto of the Revolutionary Council of Hungarian Intellectuals of 24 November and the statement *Gond és hitvallás* (Sorrow and Confession), adopted almost unanimously by a special meeting of writers on 28 December.

Even more worrying for the post-uprising, Soviet-imposed Kádár regime was the fact that links were established between intellectuals and workers, whose factory-based workers' councils also represented centres of resistance. In response, the authorities legally dissolved the Writers' Union on 17 January 1957. Many intellectuals were arrested and served time in prison, both for their earlier activities and for their resistance and refusal to bow down before the new regime. Tibor Déry, for example, was arrested in April 1957 and would spend three years behind bars.

The 1990s: Changing the Face of the City—Statues and Street Names

In the post-1945 period statues of figures regarded positively during the Horthy era were removed and over time new ones more amenable to the new regime appeared. Sometimes they, too, disappeared. The pulling down of the monumental statue of Joseph Stalin in Budapest's City Park on 23 October 1956, the first day of the uprising, was one of the most emblematic episodes of that eventful day. Following the political changes of 1989-90 it was no surprise to find another about-turn in terms of public sculpture, and the issue soon began to excite the minds of Budapest's newly elected municipal representatives.

In the midst of much argument a compromise solution was found concerning what to do with all the highly political statues that had been erected in the post-1945 decades and still stood. Almost all of them were removed, but they were not destroyed. They were instead taken to a specially constructed Statue Park, which now serves as an open-air museum. The museum is a long way from the centre, on the south-west outskirts of the city and thus well "out of sight" and potentially "out of mind". On the other hand, those who argued against the removal or at least against the destruction of these by-now historical creations, whether on aesthetic or political grounds, also had some satisfaction. Today the Statue Park is a popular destination for locals and visitors alike.

Burnt into the metal plates of the park's main gate are the words of a poem by Gyula Illyés called "One Sentence about Tyranny". The poem was first published during the uprising on 2 November 1956 in *Irodalmi Ujság* (Literary Gazette), the paper of the Writers' Union, though it had been written a number of years before during the darkest days of Hungarian Stalinism. One sentence indeed it is, but a long one, consisting of fifty four-line stanzas. The basis of tyranny is the theme. Illyés asks us not only to look for guns and prisons, but also to seek the roots of tyranny in our everyday lives and in our own attitudes.

On either side of the neo-Classical entrance gate, which recalls both a temple and a mausoleum, stand huge statues of Marx and Engels, and Lenin. Inside, there are dramatic statues such as the memorial to the 1919 Council Republic, based on a famous poster of the time designed by the artist Róbert Berény, as well as small wall plaques. Some are familiar to most of the older generation in Budapest, such as the statue of 1945 Soviet plenipotentiary Ostapenko, which used to stand at the beginning of the Balaton motorway (thus an urban reference point for hitch-hikers and others), and there are others of little-known communists whose images are now familiar only to a few. Then there are those whose removal caused much controversy: the memorial to the Hungarian members of the International Brigades who fought against Franco in the Spanish Civil War, or another to the Budapest volunteers who battled with the retreating Germans in 1944-5. Even the removal of the Marx and Engels statue, which used to stand near the Pest end of Margaret Bridge, generated some hullabaloo. A historical peculiarity is that the overwhelming majority of these mainly socialist realist statues were erected not in Hungary's Stalinist period of the early 1950s, but in the late 1960s, the 1970s and even the 1980s, the more liberal years of the Kádár era.

Another striking peculiarity concerns the monuments that were not removed. The Soviet Army Memorial in Szabadság tér, for instance, remained in its place, as did the Liberation Monument, a 45-foot-high female figure holding aloft the palm leaf of victory, situated prominently overlooking the city at the top of Gellért Hill. The work of the noted sculptor Zsigmond Kisfaludi Strobl, the monument was erected in 1947 to mark the liberation of the capital from the Germans in 1945 by Soviet troops. To the sides are large figures symbolizing progress and destruction.

Following the multi-party municipal elections of 1990 there was much argument as to whether this well-known monument should be removed and, as with the Red Army memorial, about whether the events of 1944-5 were a "liberation" or "occupation" by the Soviets. In the end, the new city fathers decided to leave the monument standing, but removed the figure of a Soviet soldier which had stood in front of the plinth below the main statue (the soldier had been pulled down during the 1956 uprising, but was later put back). Also removed were two side reliefs portraying Soviet army activities and, from the back of the monument, the names of Soviet soldiers who had lost their lives during the siege of Budapest. Gone, too, is the original inscription on the front of the pedestal referring to the glorious, liberating Soviet forces. In its place appeared a new text in honour of all those who have given their lives for Hungary's freedom, independence and progress. At the same time, the authorities decided to officially re-name the monument the Freedom Monument, perhaps echoing New York's Statue of Liberty. Hence here, instead of being removed on political grounds, a statue remained with an attempt to change its political meaning. Effective or not in terms of mass psychology, it was certainly a much cheaper way of going about things.

This is only part of the intriguing story of the Liberation/Liberty monument. One of the most persistent and telling anecdotes of Budapest relates how the female figure of the statue was, ironically, originally intended as a monument to Regent Miklós Horthy's son, István, who was killed in a plane crash in 1942 on the Russian front. After the siege of Budapest the Soviets, so the story goes, discovered the statue in the sculptor's workshop and requisitioned it for its "pro-Soviet" function. Yet the original Horthy memorial, although bearing similarities, was different from the Liberation Monument (the Horthy memorial, for example, would have shown a male figure with no palm leaf). What is true, however, is that the sculptor Kisfaludi Strobl managed to win favour and commissions from both the pre-1945 and the post-1945 authorities, despite their conflicting political approaches to public sculpture.

The Gellért Hill statue is large and inescapable. There are other, smaller, relatively unnoticed monuments that tell similar stories. The history of one, or its labelling, shows that the "changing game" has been played in Budapest for quite some time.

To the left of the broad steps leading up to the main entrance of the Hungarian National Museum in Pest is a single, not particularly eye-catching column standing on a plinth, which is actually a column from the Forum in Rome. This genuine Roman remain has been standing here since 1929 and was presented to Hungary by the Italian dictator Mussolini, who was a "friend" of Hungary and one highly regarded since, as we have seen, he supported Hungary's claims to revision of the notorious 1920 Trianon Treaty. Pre-1945 guidebooks described the column in the museum garden, quite correctly, as "a gift from Mussolini". In the post-1945 period, however, it was clearly thought inappropriate to highlight a gift from a fascist ruler, so guidebooks then preferred the phrase "from the city of Rome". The current plaque on the plinth, which appeared in the 1990s, indicates the most recent change. It now describes the column as "a gift from the Italian nation".

Another of the (more immediately noticeable) changes after 1989-90 was something that happened on the ground, literally at street level: the names of a whole wave of streets and squares also changed. The vast majority of roads, streets and squares in Budapest are named after a noteworthy person regarded as important for some reason or another. Who decides who is important, and why? Politics usually supplies the answer. Not surprisingly then, just about all the names of political personalities that had appeared on the street signs in the post-1945 decades were quickly changed, most reverting to their former names. A passion, almost a mania, for re-naming streets grew among the new municipal and district representatives, as if changing the names actually changed society—which it perhaps did in a subtle way, as an attempt to reassess the past and redefine who was and was not significant.

Predictably, streets and squares named after Marx, Engels and Lenin soon received new plaques. Marx tér by the Western Railway Station became Nyugati (Western) tér, while a stretch of the Great Boulevard that had carried Lenin's name since 1950 reverted to its earlier title of Erzsébet körút. Engels tér in central Pest also took on the name Erzsébet, referring to Elizabeth, wife of Emperor Francis Joseph.

The four streets named after the Red Army had no chance of survival. Similarly, Felszabadulás tér (Liberation Square) in the city centre, an allusion to the victory of the Soviet army in Hungary in 1944-5, once again became Ferenciek tere (Franciscans' Square) after the church standing there. Tolbuhin körút, named after a Soviet commander, became Vámház (Customs House) körút, though the street named after Soviet Marshal Voroshilov had already changed in 1961. The name of the well-known junction Oktogon reappeared after forty years of being called November 7th Square, a reference to the anniversary date of the Russian Revolution.

It was not only names with a Russian or Soviet connection that were perceived as being in need of change. In fact, although there were some prominent ones there were not that many, and there were many more named after Hungarian communist activists. In 1989 there were still seven streets or squares (there had been more) named after Imre Sallai, a communist executed in 1932 and six named after his co-defendant, Sándor Fürst, also executed. Six plaques bore the name of Zoltán Schönherz, an activist of the international communist movement, executed in 1942 aged 37, while twelve carried the name of Endre Ságvári, a communist youth activist shot dead by police in 1944. Almost all of these were changed. In Kispest, a district in the south-east of the city, a square was re-named Square of the 56ers, with reference to the 1956 uprising. It had been known since 1962 as Chlepkó tér, which sounds as if it had been named after a Soviet. Ede Chlepkó, however, had been a Hungarian Social Democrat turned Communist Party member and an activist in the 1919 Council Republic. In 1936, while in exile in the Soviet Union, he was caught up in the Stalinist purges and executed two years later. Prior to 1962 the square had borne the name of Joseph Stalin.

Since 1989 over 400 street names have changed in Budapest. That represents about five per cent of the city's total, so it is not a large proportion. Nevertheless, the changes caused a stir, partly because some familiar city-centre names were seen as losing their "identity", partly for political reasons, and partly since, for some, the mania for name-changing was judged both superficial and driven by ideology involving much public expense.

Yet, as with the statues, it had all happened before. In the 1920s many streets and squares in Budapest and its suburbs were named after places and regions of pre-Trianon Hungary, and although there was then a regulation stipulating that a public place in Budapest could be named after someone only ten years following his or her death, the vanguardists of territorial revision were often treated as exceptions.

Public places were named after Regent Horthy, Prime Minister István Bethlen, peace delegate Albert Apponyi and others while they were still living.

Post-1945 Budapest street names changed once again, in line with the new political times. Before the war, for example, not only was the currently named Petőfi Bridge called Miklós Horthy Bridge, but there were altogether twenty-one streets also named after Horthy. Those names all disappeared, and although the issue has been raised, none of them has reappeared on any street plaque in recent times. Twenty-one was a high number. Even today, the most common names to be found in a Budapest atlas—those of Kossuth and Petőfi, leading figures of the 1848-9 anti-Habsburg rebellion—appear just sixteen times each. After 1945, the earlier names naturally had to go to give way to all the new street plaques bearing names of communist heroes. Street names referring to Hungarian saints or to royalty were a common target, though, interestingly, the "Habsburg" names of Elizabeth Bridge and two sections of the Great Boulevard named after Francis I and Joseph II respectively remained untouched throughout the decades of state socialism. Even within the period 1945-89 there were changes. For a number of years today's Árpád Bridge, along with six streets and squares, used carry the name of Soviet dictator Stalin. All those disappeared following the 1956 uprising.

The game of amending street names continues, albeit without the fervour of the early 1990s. Yet in some areas away from the centre you can still find the old "communist" street names, as if they have escaped public attention. At the time of writing, for example, there are still two streets in Budapest named after Imre Sallai and three with the name Endre Ságvári. In District IV there is still a square named after György Kilián, a communist activist of the 1930s. Perhaps his surname now resonates more closely with the Kilián Barracks, a major location of fighting during the 1956 events, though the barracks was nowhere near the square.

Sometimes there does not seem to be any clear reason why the name of a location has not changed. The most prominent example is Moszkva tér. This major junction in Buda has had the name "Moscow" since 1951. Before then it was called Széll Kálmán tér, in honour of Széll (1843-1915), a politician who had a long career as a member of parliament. For three years in the 1880s he was the minister of finance, and for three years at the turn of the century he was even prime minister. Even so, his is not a name that reverberates strongly in the public consciousness today. There have been a number of suggestions for renaming the junction. There was a move some years ago, for example, to have the square named after József Antall, Hungary's first prime minister after the 1989-90 political changes who died before his four-year term of office expired. Members of his family were not keen, but there was also a regulatory difficulty. Before a street or square in Budapest can be named after someone, twenty-five years now have to pass after the person's death. Today it is not so easy to name a place after a recently deceased "favourite" of the current ruling party.

chapter six
CITY OF BATHS

It is cold. In fact, it is freezing, but people are wearing next to nothing. They are running, dashing past the snow and ice, in a hurry to gently ease themselves into the water and its all-embracing warmth of over 30° Centigrade, the steam slowly rising around them. It is a typical winter-time scene at one of Budapest's major attractions, the Széchenyi Baths in the City Park.

The Széchenyi has both indoor and outdoor pools, and even the latter stay open throughout the year. The extensive neo-Baroque baths complex, dating from 1913, has been undergoing a facelift in recent years and now looks superb with its striking yellow façades. This is the place made famous by the many photographs taken of swimming-cap bedecked, stocky men playing chess in the water of the open-air pool. Yet the Széchenyi is not alone in Budapest. There are many baths and pools in the city, based on the Hungarian capital's most valuable natural resource—its numerous thermal springs and underground waters.

Local bathing culture has a history of two millennia, reaching back well beyond the time of the arrival of the Magyars. The territory of today's Hungary, west of the Danube, used to be part of the Roman Empire. The Romans, who were here from around the time of Christ until the end of the fourth century, established a number of encampments along the Danube, particularly at Aquincum on the right bank, where both military and civilian towns were developed. They brought with them their love of bathing, the traces of which can be found today.

Aquincum is now the name of the museum of Roman remains on the Buda side, a few miles north of the city centre. The museum was established in the 1890s following excavations that had unearthed a large part of the former civilian town. It had been an important place in Roman times, visited by every Emperor who ruled during the town's existence. The population, consisting of migrants from places as far apart as Syria and north-west Europe, at its height numbered over 40,000, a considerable figure for those times.

Today at Aquincum you can see the excavated remains of a private bath, which belonged to the villa of a wealthy resident, and the town's central public bath house with different sections for cold, tepid and hot water, together with the infrastructure for underground heating. Part of the former aqueduct, which brought the water from springs a few miles to the north, can also be seen. Inside the museum building the pride of the collection is a reconstructed example of an early third-century small Roman organ, which worked with a hydraulic system. The museum guards sometimes flip a switch to enable "reconstructed" Roman-era music to be heard. All in all, the remains at Aquincum are not spectacular like those of Herculaneum or Pompey in Italy, but they can certainly be recommended for anyone interested in traces of antique culture.

Some scattered remains of the Roman military town can be found to the south of Aquincum. The most spectacular of these is the second-century military town amphitheatre (at the junction of Nagyszombat utca and Pacsirtamező utca). The walls of the amphitheatre, which could seat up to 15,000 spectators, no longer stand, only their bases, but the huge size of the arena is clear—it was actually larger than the arena of the Colosseum in Rome.

Following the end of the Roman period, centuries passed in which bathing was not one of the main social activities, though a special section of Buda's legal code during the time of King Sigismund (ruled

1387-1437) was devoted to the issue of baths, declaring that public bathing houses were important elements of the town's infrastructure. Some scholars believe that the present-day Rác Baths at the foot of Gellért Hill (currently being developed as part of a new hotel complex), date from Sigismund's time. Later, during the time of King Matthias (ruled 1458-90) the complex was known as the "Royal Bath" as it was connected to the monarch's palace by a covered corridor.

The next great, perhaps golden age of bathing culture came with the Ottoman occupation. The Turks built baths by their mosques and caravanserais, above springs abounding in hot water. The Turkish baths in Buda were rather different from their traditional style. In contrast to the original layout of a typical Turkish bath, here the central space was not a steam or sweating chamber, but a hall with several pools. This design can be seen most clearly in the central, domed section of the four-hundred-year-old Rudas Baths, by the Buda end of Elizabeth Bridge. The Rudas is a rare remaining architectural relic of the Ottoman period, which lasted in Buda from 1541 to 1686. The small, dark vaulted interior, with its several warms pools of varying temperature (from warm to extremely hot) generates an authentic Turkish atmosphere. For many years that atmosphere could only be experienced by male visitors, since the "Turkish" section of the Rudas was not open to women. That changed following the latest renovation of the baths, completed in late 2005, following which mixed bathing sessions were introduced for parts of the weekend as well as some women-only sessions in mid-week.

Robert Townson, a British traveller who visited Buda in the early 1790s, over a century after the Ottoman period had ended, noted that "some of the baths, and the greatest, are Turkish remains." It seems, however, that the single-sex rule did not apply in his day, as he recorded, somewhat humorously:

There are large common baths for the lower order of the people, and commodious private baths for those who can afford to pay for them. In a common bath I saw young men and maidens, old men and children, some in a state of nature, others with a fig-leaf covering, flouncing about like fish in spawning-time. But the observer must be just. I saw none of the ladies without a petticoat, though most were without their shifts. Some of the gentlemen were with drawers, some without; according, no doubt, to the degree of their delicacy, and as they thought themselves favoured by nature or not. But no very voluptuous ideas arise in these suffocating humid steams; and as a further sedative, the surgeon is seen hard at work cuping and scarifying...

The next upswing in the history of bathing culture occurred in the wake of scientific progress. The nineteenth century saw significant developments in balneology, medicine and, importantly, in the technologies of deep drilling. In 1867 the mining engineer Vilmos Zsigmondy bored his first artesian spring on Margaret Island, creating a well about 400 feet deep, yielding thermal water at a temperature of over 43 degrees. This was followed by the establishment of a well at what is now Heroes' Square. Drilling began in late 1868, also under the supervision of Zsigmondy, but the well was only completed ten years later. It was an incredible 3,200 feet deep with an original yield of 528 litres per minute at a temperature of around 74 degrees. It was this well which made possible the development of the first thermal water medicinal complex in Pest.

The year 1860 had seen the Császár Baths, on the Buda side opposite Margaret Island, reconstructed in neo-Classical style to plans by József Hild. The same decade also witnessed the construction of the island's Saint Margaret Medicinal Baths designed by Miklós Ybl (in its place today stands the Hotel Thermal). 1893 was the year when the Lukács Baths was rebuilt, while in 1913 the Széchenyi Baths and in 1918 Gellért Baths, behind the famous hotel of the same name, were opened. It was also at this time that the first swimming pools and hygienic baths were built. The cult of open-air bathing emerged at the turn of the century and, following a trend set by Vienna, it was at this time, too, that swimming pools opened by the Danube.

Spa City

The development of Budapest as an international tourist "spa city", however, proceeded—and is proceeding—in fits and starts, even though the city, due to its natural endowments, is well suited for maintaining that title and its associated reputation. In 1891 the "Balneological Association of the Countries under the Holy Crown" (i.e. the "Hungarian" part of the Dual Monarchy) was formed. The association, representing general practitioners, physicians employed by spas, balneology experts, owners and lessees of baths and plants bottling mineral water, endeavoured "to cultivate and popularize balneology and its ancillary sciences and to improve the treatment of the country's baths and mineral waters." It managed to focus public interest, as well as professional and official attention, on baths and watering places.

1922 saw the founding of the Budapest Spa City Association, working to bring the issue of tourism into the public arena and it was in the inter-war period that the concept of Budapest as a spa city really took off, as reflected in the many colourful posters of the time advertising the Hungarian capital's thermal waters, medicinal treatments and public lidos. In October 1937 the founding meeting of the International Congress of Balneology was organized in Budapest with the participation of 342 delegates from thirty countries. During the event the International Spa Federation (the forerunner of Fédération Internationale du Thermalisme et du Climatisme) was founded with Budapest designated as its permanent centre. Professor Heinrich Vogt, director of the Reichsanstalt für das Deutsche Baderwesen, explained the reason.

There is no metropolis with a better claim for this than Budapest, a city gifted by nature, in its singular magnanimity, with splendidly efficacious medicinal waters and a wealth of beautiful natural scenery. In addition, the high standards of the medical profession as practised here, together with the quality of the city's medical facilities and the remarkable achievements of its scientific research qualify Budapest as the centre from where the international concerns of the world's great baths be administered.

One of the world's great baths is undoubtedly Budapest's Széchenyi Baths, one of the largest bathing complexes in Europe. Until recent times and its revival through careful renovation, it has been outclassed in terms on popularity among foreign visitors by the Gellért Baths, the most internationally famous of Budapest spas. But times are changing. Up-to-date filtering systems, deck-level pools, efficient wave machines, whirl pools and modern slides are all helping to revive and regenerate bathing culture at many different spas, drawing new guests, both local and from abroad. The Lukács Baths is a case in point. Situated to the north of Margaret Bridge on the Buda side, the complex has a tradition of attracting prominent writers, poets, actors, artists and politicians to outdoor swimming and indoor thermal pools. Renovation during recent years has widened their clientele.

It is said that the secret of longevity and good health is a daily swim and/or treatment at the Lukács. Numerous plaques mounted in gratitude on the walls of the inner courtyard of the baths testify to the therapeutic effects. One was placed here in 1996 by Károly Molnár, who, describing himself as "the last Hungarian soldier of the last Hungarian king" (Habsburg Charles IV, crowned in 1916), pays tribute to the beneficial effects of his daily swim here from 1920. He was 102 when the plaque appeared. The drinking well by the entrance of the Lukács on Frankel Leó utca was ceremonially inaugurated in 1937 on the occasion of the International Congress of Balneology. Nicely renovated today, visitors can sample the strange-tasting but apparently health-giving waters of the Lukács.

Széchenyi, Rudas, Gellért, Lukács—the choice does not end there. The huge Palatinus Baths lido complex on Margaret Island, dating from 1937, opens its doors for the summer months. The island's Hajós Swimming Baths, in contrast, are open all year. The Dagály Baths, the Csillaghegy Baths and the Római Baths, are just three more open-air complexes. Internationally recognized or not, Budapest is certainly a spa city with a wide range of bathing possibilities.

chapter seven
WRITTEN IN STONE

Parliament

No picture book or postcard series can be published about Budapest without at least one image, if not several, of the Hungarian parliament, which stands proudly overlooking the Danube on the Pest-side embankment between the Chain Bridge and Margaret Bridge. Viewed from Buda, across the river, it bears a striking resemblance to the Palace of Westminster in London. Both occupy city-centre riverside locations and both were built in the style of Gothic revival. Both are also huge, each being constructed to accommodate two debating chambers, for an upper and a lower house. The length of the parliament in Budapest reaches 880 feet, roughly the same as its London equivalent. Both parliaments have become landmark buildings of their respective capitals.

Work on the Hungarian parliament began in 1884, sixteen years after the completion of Westminster. Although its architect, Imre Steindl, must have been familiar with the British parliament by the Thames—indeed, he was even a member of the Royal Institute of British Architects—there seems to be no direct evidence that he based his plans on the London model. A major difference between the two buildings is his incorporation, above the centre of the totally symmetrical ground plan, of a massive central dome, which echoes Classical and Baroque styles rather than Gothic examples. Nevertheless, the dome is in perfect harmony with the rest of the building's slim towers, pointed arches and decorated arcades.

For centuries the Hungarian parliament had no permanent home. Then in 1843 a resolution was passed at the Pozsony (Bratislava) Diet to erect a permanent building in Pest, though plans were delayed by the events of the 1848-9 Revolution and War of Independence and the resulting political tension between Vienna and Budapest. From 1861 the Lower House met in what is today the Italian Cultural Centre in Bródy Sándor utca in Pest, and the Upper House in the National Museum nearby. In 1880 a law was passed approving the site by the

Danube and three years later work began according to Steindl's plan, which had been accepted following an international design competition. A plan submitted by Alajos Hauszmann for the new parliament was also accepted—as the basis for another massive building, the Supreme Court, erected facing parliament across Kossuth tér. The imposing nature of the court building, with its huge façade columns and high tympanum, appropriately reflects the pomp and self-importance of a legal institution. A visitor passing through its entrance is made to feel small, guilty perhaps, even though today the grandiose building houses, rather incongruously, the Museum of Ethnography, the permanent exhibition of which has displays about Hungarian folk history and folk culture.

The Supreme Court was completed in 1896, but it was not until eight years later that the parliament building was finally ready, though in 1896 a festive joint session of parliament had been held in the completed Dome Hall as part of the millenary celebrations of that year and from 1902 parliamentary debates were able to take place inside. All the interior rooms and passageways were ornamented in a rich and colourful style by the top Hungarian artists of the day. The main entrance from Kossuth Lajos tér leads to a dazzling, broad, ceremonial staircase with large ceiling frescoes by Károly Lotz, including *The Apotheosis of Legislation*, about the rule of law in Hungary, and *Glorification of Hungary*, which incorporates images of historical figures such as István Széchenyi and Sándor Petőfi.

The staircase leads to a sixteen-sided hall below the dome, used today for official receptions and ceremonies. Around the interior walls of the Dome Hall are sixteen statues of rulers. Rather stylized—in 1902 one MP referred to them as "misshapen figures with parrot colours"— they nevertheless say something about Hungarian history. Here is chieftain Árpád, who led the conquering Magyar tribes westwards in the late ninth century. Here, too, is Hungary's first king, Stephen, accompanied by eight monarchs from the era when Hungary was a great medieval kingdom. There are also three Transylvanian princes who spearheaded movements for Hungarian independence from Austria: István Báthory, István Bocskai and Gábor Bethlen. The circle is completed, rather ironically, by three Habsburg rulers, Charles III, Maria Theresa and Leopold II, reflecting the rather ambiguous ruling ideology of the era when parliament was built, which mixed the pride of a thousand-year-old nation with respect for, as well as a certain smugness at being a partner of, the imperial power.

The MPs' debating chamber (formerly the Lower House—the bicameral parliament became single-chamber in 1945) is in the south wing of the building. Here, two large paintings by Zsigmond Vajda behind the Speaker's raised platform also attest to the ambiguous imperial connection. One shows the crowning of Francis Joseph as king of Hungary in 1867 (the most symbolic event of the year in which the Habsburg ruler recognized Hungary's separate constitutionality), while the other depicts the opening of the Hungarian assembly in Pozsony in July 1848, in the wake of the revolution that had erupted in Pest four months earlier.

The pomp and grandeur of Hungary's parliament, one of the largest parliamentary buildings in the world, appealed enormously to official national sentiment at the time of its planning and construction. Although the decision was the subject of much dispute, it was this sentiment that lay behind the acceptance of Gothic revival for the style of the building, the idea being that the Hungarian state had been at its strongest in the medieval era, the heyday of the Gothic style. Government spokesman Sándor Országh put it like this: "It is what we owe to our past, as this style was the style of its most glorious period, and its slender, dynamically vertical forms also express the present goals of the Hungarian nation." Arguing in the Upper House for the choice of style, Bishop Arnold Ipolyi, himself an art historian, claimed that the ruins of Greece and Rome spoke more loudly of their glory than did even classical literature and that otherwise relatively insignificant medieval towns like Florence had become great since they had put their energies into constructing cathedrals of artistic merit. "Really, our new Parliament building should be splendid and monumental, not only to promote art and architecture, but also because the grandeur of the nation and the state demands it."

What did not seem to be an issue at the time was what might actually be going on in the building once it was completed, whatever the style. At the time of its construction less than ten per cent of the population actually had the right to vote, and Hungary's non-Magyar nationalities (Serbs, Slovaks, Croats, Romanians and others), who constituted over fifty per cent of the total, were drastically under-represented in terms of seats. The state might be grand and have a grand new building for its parliament, but it could hardly be called democratic.

Hence, the struggle for the right to vote, including female suffrage, was a hallmark of Hungarian politics in the pre-1914 era. Kossuth tér in front of parliament was the scene of many political demonstrations, as the Social Democrats and their allies persistently agitated for universal suffrage and the secret ballot. "Red Friday" in September 1905 saw 100,000 gather here. Violent clashes often ensued, such as during the mass demonstration of 23 May 1912, known thereafter as "Bloody Thursday".

Photographs of demonstrators and agitators in front of parliament bear witness to a striking resemblance to events elsewhere, for example in Britain, where the movement for democratic reform and universal suffrage involved trade union and labour activists as well as "votes-for-women" campaigners. There were even direct links. In 1913 Budapest's Vigadó Concert Hall hosted the International Women's Suffrage Conference and the following year the famous English female suffrage campaigner and socialist activist Sylvia Pankhurst lectured there. She also visited public welfare projects for orphans, which she found positive, and investigated the conditions of women prisoners, which struck her as "a sad experience".

Sylvia Pankhurst had her own Hungarian counterpart in the character of Róza Schwimmer, whose picture addressing crowds in front of parliament is sometimes found in history books. With her white dress and broad-rimmed white hat contrasting with the dark suits of her male audience, she would not be out of place in a photograph of any British suffragette. Róza, or Rózsika, Schwimmer was born into an upper middle-class Jewish family in 1877 in Temesvár in Transylvania. Perhaps she was influenced by her uncle, Leopold Katscher, who founded the Hungarian Peace Society. In 1897, having been active as a journalist, she began working for the National Association of Female Civil Servants, becoming its president, and in 1903 she helped found the first Hungarian Association of Working Women. After 1904 and a Berlin women's conference, she was a founder of Hungary's Feminist Association (*Feministák Egyesülete*) and for many years she edited its paper, *Woman*. It was through these activities that she became involved in the international women's and peace movements, helping to organize the above-mentioned Budapest international women's conference in 1913.

During the First World War Schwimmer worked in London as the Press Secretary of the International Women's Suffrage Alliance. Like Sylvia Pankhurst, she was a militant anti-war campaigner and by contemporary standards had always been radical in her personal behaviour, smoking cigarettes and drinking wine. Immediately after the war, under the new democratic administration of Mihály Károly, she became Hungarian ambassador to Switzerland, the first female ambassador in the history of Hungary. (Or perhaps of the world; the status is often attributed to Alexandra Kollontai, representative in Sweden of the fledgling Soviet government, but perhaps the designation rightly belongs to Rozsika Schwimmer.)

Schwimmer was not liked by the post-Károly left-wing Kun regime of 1919 and she later fled Hungary under the right-wing White Terror as "a wanted woman". She arrived in the United States in 1921, but was not particularly welcome there either, being shunned by the authorities and denied US citizenship, allegedly for her refusal to sign a document indicating that she would be willing to take up arms for the country. In 1948 she was nominated for a Nobel Peace Prize by parliamentarians in the UK, Hungary, Sweden, France and Italy, but she died before the award could be made, aged 71. Her ashes were scattered in Lake Michigan. Today the name of Róza Schwimmer is by and large "hidden" from Hungarian history (you will not find her name on any street plaque in Budapest). In this respect, she perhaps shares the fate of Sylvia Pankhurst, another unconventional figure whose name is overshadowed by those of her equally active, though less radical mother and sister, Emmeline and Christabel.

Crowning Glory

A main showpiece for visitors to parliament is Hungary's *Szent korona* or Holy Crown, one of the oldest royal crowns in existence. It sits in a glass case, watched over by guards in ceremonial uniform, and comprises an upper crown made up of gold bands set with gems and pearls, and with cloisonné enamel images of eight apostles, and a lower, Byzantine portion. At the top is a gold cross bent to one side (no one truly knows the explanation). For many years it was believed that the crown, or at least its upper part, was the same that, according to tradition, had been sent by Pope Sylvester II to King Stephen I for his coronation in 1000 AD, the event which marked the foundation of the

Hungarian state. Yet, recent research, as detailed in *A Thousand Years of Christianity in Hungary*, published by the Hungarian Catholic Episcopal Conference to accompany a major exhibition of the same name in 2002, indicates that the crown could not have existed in Stephen's time, which obviously leads to rather iconoclastic and controversial conclusions, not readily accepted in the public mind, or at least in the mind of many.

The lower crown was sent to King Géza I of Hungary in 1074 as a gift from the Byzantine emperor. It is a gold diadem set with precious stones and gold enamel images of archangels and saints. Along the upper edge are images of Christ enthroned, the Byzantine emperor Michael Duca, Constantine the Great and Géza I. The upper crown is even later, dating probably from the mid-twelfth century. The two crowns were most likely joined together during the same century.

Whether dating from St. Stephen's time or not, the crown was used for centuries at the coronation of Hungarian kings. Possession and being crowned with it was always a matter of great political, almost mystical, significance. Several times it has been removed from the country, the most recent absence lasting for 34 years. At the end of the Second World War it was taken by Hungarian fascists to Germany, from where it was removed to the US and kept in Fort Knox. It was not returned to Hungary until January 1978, after post-1956 US-Hungarian relations had been normalized for some time. The crown was then kept in the National Museum, along with other items of the historic royal regalia, but in December 1999 it was moved to parliament amidst much controversy.

It can be difficult to appreciate the significance and symbolism which many Hungarians attribute to the crown, for whom it is a symbol not only of royal authority but also, it is argued, of constitutional sovereignty. Hence the dispute in 1999. The then populist centre-right government argued that the crown, as the symbol of sovereignty, should rightfully have its place in parliament, the now legitimate seat of power. Others believed that the mixing of ancient beliefs, royal symbolism and modern democracy was at best mumbo-jumbo, at worst an attempt by the government to use historic symbols to generate legitimacy for itself, and that the crown should remain in the most appropriate place—a museum. The government coalition, with its majority in parliament won the debate, but the issue was so heated that during the subsequent election campaign of 2002 the contending Socialist Party was accused of planning to return the crown to the museum. The Socialists strongly denied the accusation and the crown remained in parliament after they won the election.

The issue had earlier appeared in another guise when, in 1990, the newly-elected parliament debated which coat-of-arms should be adopted for the new Hungary. No one was arguing for a return to a monarchical system, but the decision was made to reintroduce Hungary's traditional coat-of-arms prominently featuring the Holy Crown, or St. Stephen's Crown, as it is inaccurately known, and its leaning cross. Those who argued for a return to the "Kossuth" coat-of-arms, which had no crown and which appeared during the 1848-9 events and, officially, in the period 1946-9 and then again in 1956, lost the debate and so now Hungary is in the curious situation of being a republic with "monarchical" arms.

Every Statue Tells a Story

Two huge statues dominate the main area of Kossuth tér in front of the parliament building. The figures they represent have at least two things in common. In the southern part stands a fine equestrian statue of Ferenc Rákóczi II (1676-1735), the Transylvanian prince who led an anti-Habsburg revolt which turned into a War of Independence lasting from 1703 to 1711. In the northern part stands the figure of Lajos Kossuth (1802-94) the political leader of the 1848-9 Hungarian War of Independence against Habsburg rule. Both were key figures in the struggle for Hungarian nationhood and independence; their other commonality is that they were both defeated.

Rákóczi originally grew up as a young aristocrat loyal to the Habsburgs, but contact with disaffected Hungarian nobles resulted in a changed attitude, and for conspiring against the Habsburgs he was imprisoned in 1701. After escaping, he sought refuge in Poland from where he eventually launched the freedom struggle of 1703-11. Due to both lack of outside help and internal division, Rákóczi and his "kuruc" fighters, although brave, were defeated in every major set battle. In the end a peace treaty was signed behind Rákóczi's back while he was away soliciting support from Russia's Peter the Great. Forced into exile, Rákóczi eventually settled in Turkey, where he died in Rodosto (today Tekirdag) in 1735. His house there is a place of pilgrimage for

Hungarians, helped by the fact that Tekirdag is conveniently situated for tourist coaches running from Budapest to Istanbul. His remains, however, were brought back to Hungary in 1909, passing through Budapest in a massive reburial ceremony. It is from this time that Rákóczi út, one of the main arteries of central Pest, has borne his name. Rákóczi was finally laid to rest in the medieval Cathedral of St. Elizabeth in Kassa, then within the borders of Hungary but which today, as Košce, is in eastern Slovakia.

The Rákóczi War of Independence, as it is called, has gone down in Hungarian history as one of the heroic periods in the country's past, and its leader is extolled as a great national figure. Both Ferenc Liszt and Hector Berlioz composed variations of the popular "Rákóczi March", the playing of which was politically contentious throughout the Habsburg era. The equestrian statue of Ferenc Rákóczi by parliament was unveiled in 1937. It was one of the few public monuments of the 1930s whose erection was financed from the state budget and not out of private fund-raising. Sculptor János Pásztor depicted the prince bareheaded, wearing light armoury and a pair of soft-topped spurred

boots, with a sword on his side and two contemporary pistols by his knees in the saddle of his horse, which rears up on its hind legs. Rákóczi's noble birth is suggested by the prestigious order of the Golden Fleece, whose sash lies across his armoury. In his right hand the prince holds an ornamented mace, indicative not only of his rank as commander-in-chief, but also of his having been elected reigning prince of Transylvania in July 1704.

Pásztor modelled the statue's facial features on a well-known oil portrait made in 1712 by Ádám Mányoki (which today hangs in the Hungarian National Gallery). According to equestrian statue specialist László Prohászka, for the creation of the beautiful thoroughbred Pásztor made on-site sketches of the fine Lipica horses at the Spanish Riding School in Vienna. Noteworthy is how he solved the problem of supporting the huge monument by resting it on the large flowing tail of the horse as well as its hind legs.

The composition bears a resemblance to Étienne Maurice Falconet's famous statue of Peter the Great, "The Bronze Horseman", unveiled in St. Petersburg in 1782, though while Peter is putting his horse at a jump, Rákóczi makes his stallion almost dance with restrained elegance. The overall aesthetic effect is heightened by the fact that the horse looks to the right, while the rider's head is turned to the left, giving their movements opposite directions. Latin inscriptions on the red marble plinth read, on one side, "The wounds of the glorious Hungarian nation are being torn open" (the first lines of Rákóczi's anti-Habsburg declaration), and on the other, "With God for Fatherland and Liberty". The words "With God" (Cum Deo) were removed in the early 1950s, only to reappear in 1989.

The Rákóczi statue, which fits organically into its environment, helping to define the space in front of parliament, is regarded by many as one of the finest specimens of Budapest's public statuary. The statue of Lajos Kossuth at the north end of the square is even more imposing, if only because this is a statue group, Kossuth being the central figure, raised on high.

Lajos Kossuth is the most celebrated leader of Hungary's national independence struggle of the 1830s and 1840s. Born in Monok in north-eastern Hungary, he originally trained to be a lawyer but in 1832 moved to Pozsony (today Bratislava, the capital of Slovakia), then the seat of the Hungarian Diet, a kind of parliament of the landed elite.

Kossuth made a name for himself with his radical journalism and got into trouble with the authorities simply for reporting the Diet's debates in Hungarian. He was arrested and held in custody for three years in the Joseph Barracks in the Castle District of Buda, where he apparently taught himself English using texts of Shakespeare. (A plaque on the wall of 9 Táncsics Mihály utca recalls his imprisonment here.)

Although Kossuth was not present in Pest on 15 March 1848 and so did not participate in the street events that sparked off the rebellion, he soon came to the fore politically. Officially he was minister of finance in the first independent Hungarian government of 1848, though *de facto* he was its leader, a reality recognized shortly afterwards when he was elected Governing President of Hungary following his declaration of the dethronement of the House of Habsburg on 14 April 1849. During the war with Austria, he travelled the country rousing the people to arms, an activity depicted in the statue group in Kossuth tér.

Forced to flee the country after defeat, he spent many months in both England and the US, defending the cause of Hungary. Landing at Southampton on the south coast of England in October 1851, he surprised his audience with an extempore speech in English (perhaps using Shakespearean rhymes?). Although popular in England, he refused an invitation from the Chartists to speak at a working men's dinner, an attitude which prompted Karl Marx to write that Kossuth was "all things to all men. In Marseilles he shouts: Vive la République! In Southampton: God Save the Queen!"

Eventually, Kossuth settled in Turin, in the north of Italy. He would never return to his native land, not even after the Compromise of 1867 when Hungary gained a large degree of autonomy within the Monarchy. For Kossuth this was only a half-measure—which it was in terms of real independence. While most of his contemporaries among Hungary's political elite were happy with the half that gave them extra power and privileges, Kossuth preferred to concentrate on the missing half.

Following his death in Turin in 1894, the city council decided to organize a ceremonial burial in Budapest and to erect a statue in his honour. Despite his "rejectionist" approach to the 1867 Compromise— or because of it for some—in the popular mind Kossuth remained the father figure of 1848 and all it stood for, even if many now believed that "within the Monarchy" was a satisfactory place to be. The funeral was accordingly a tremendous affair. His coffin lay in state on the steps of the National Museum before being taken to the Kerepesi Cemetery. About half a million people took part in the ceremony. Two thousand citizens of Cegléd, the town where Kossuth had first called the nation to arms in 1848, walked the 45 miles to Budapest to participate.

The statue took longer to materialize. Fund-raising problems, bureaucratic delays and the First World War meant that it was not until 1927 that a statue by János Horvay finally appeared in the square by parliament. Yet that is not what you see today. The original was removed in 1952 and replaced by the present statue, which is primarily the work of Zsigmond Kisfaludy Stróbl. The year 1952 was the high point of Hungary's Stalinist period and undoubtedly the reason for the change was entirely political.

The earlier work depicted a despondent-looking Kossuth flanked by his aristocratic fellow ministers of 1848—counts, landlords and leading politicians such as Batthyány, Széchenyi, Eszterházy and Deák. All were looking rather downcast, reflecting the gloom of the 1849 defeat. That image clearly did not fit demands for heroic representations of a socialist realist nature which came to the fore in the early 1950s. Thus the statue group was removed and replaced with one of Kossuth standing proudly aloft, arm outstretched pointing to the future, just like the many heroic statues of Lenin erected throughout the Soviet Union. Interestingly, the nationalistic theme remained, reflecting the tendency to recuperate and utilize national themes in the Stalinist era. But now, instead of the elite, Kossuth is flanked by "the people", enthusiastically responding to his call to arms. They are all here: peasants with children, a foot soldier, an armed blacksmith representing the working class, a youth with a sword, his face the image of the radical poet and March 1848 leader Sándor Petőfi, and even a traditional Hungarian horseman with weapon.

In contrast with the earlier monument, depicting "unheroically" and thus not particularly attractively the reality of the mood of defeat, looking at the 1952 monument you could be forgiven for assuming that Kossuth and the Hungarians were victorious in 1848-9. That was presumably part of the message, though not in a way that might normally be understood. The Hungarian Stalinists aimed to present *themselves* as the true victorious inheritors of the Kossuth tradition. Four years previously, in 1948, there had been huge celebrations in

Budapest to mark the centenary of the anti-Habsburg national revolt. The city was plastered with huge posters of Lajos Kossuth together with Mátyás Rákosi, the post-1945 Communist Party leader.

It is significant that despite being a product of Hungary's Stalinist era, clearly reflecting Soviet-style socialist realism in its form and intention, the Kossuth statue was not removed in the early 1990s, like so many other of the city's political statues (see Chapter Five). The reason was presumably the statue's national theme. Thus, every year on 15 March, the anniversary of the outbreak of the 1848 revolt, wreaths continue to be laid here by the country's leading politicians, just as they were throughout the period of state socialism.

Imre Nagy and the 1956 Explosion

A number of monuments in Kossuth Lajos tér are related to the 1956 uprising. Naturally, all of these appeared after 1989-90, since before then the 1956 events had been officially and unequivocally condemned as a counter-revolution. Even so, it took six years after the multi-party elections of 1990 before Budapest's first central 1956 monument was constructed. It takes the form of a marble block irregularly shaped at the top, where an eternal flame burns. Entitled "The Flame of Revolution", it presumably represents the burning hope generated by the uprising, but the meaning of the monument is not at all clear to the eye, and while its positioning close to parliament is appropriate politically, its form and nature make it aesthetically out of place in its surroundings.

In the central area of Kossuth tér some way in front of the Rákóczi statue is a symbolic grave in memory of the victims of a massacre that took place in the square on 25 October, the third day of the uprising. Hungarian demonstrators had actually been fraternizing with Soviet tank troops when shots rang out and panic erupted. It was believed that members of the Hungarian State Security Authority had fired into the crowd from the roof of the Ministry of Agriculture facing parliament. Some historians now argue that the shots came from other Soviet tanks sent to the square.

A statue of Imre Nagy, dating from 1996, stands by the south-east corner of the square. Nagy was the communist politician who as prime minister during the uprising attempted to steer developments in the direction of democratic reform and national independence. He is portrayed standing on a bridge, looking somewhat wistfully towards parliament and depicted realistically with his characteristic moustache, pince-nez, hat and umbrella. An oddity, however, is that the statue shows Nagy as a rather slim figure, whereas in reality he was quite plump.

All the major events of the 1956 uprising took place in Budapest. On the first day, 23 October, student demonstrations were organized to demand reforms of the political system and in solidarity with developments unfolding in Poland. The demonstrators headed for the statue of Josef Bem, on the Buda side of the Danube, not far from Margaret Bridge. Bem was a Polish general who had joined the Hungarians in their 1848-9 uprising. On the way the students were joined by office and factory workers. The atmosphere heated up and the Soviet-style coat-of-arms was cut out of the Hungarian flag. (The Hungarian national red-white-and-green tricolour with a hole in the middle has since become a well-used symbol of 1956.)

After the demonstration, part of the crowd headed for Kossuth tér to demand the appearance of Imre Nagy, who as prime minister in 1953 had introduced reforms before being removed from office. His return to government was one of the central demands of the demonstrators. Nagy appeared and addressed the crowd, rather ineffectually, from one of the windows of parliament at around 9 pm. An hour earlier, the hard-line party general secretary Ernő Gerő had spoken on the radio denouncing the demonstrators in vitriolic language. The broadcast only served to inflame passions. Shortly after Nagy's speech demonstrators used industrial cutting equipment to pull down the massive statue of Stalin by the City Park. Around the same time, others were besieging the headquarters of Hungarian Radio in the narrow Bródy Sándor utca. It was here that shots were first fired and people killed in Budapest. Overnight, barracks and factory warehouses were raided for arms and several public buildings were attacked. In the early hours Soviet tank units stationed in provincial Hungary appeared on the streets of the capital. For the next few days there would be armed clashes between the Soviets and groups of spontaneously formed armed civilians, notably at Corvin Passage, by the junction of Üllői út and the Great Boulevard in Pest.

Nagy spent the early days at party headquarters at 17 Akadémia utca, about 250 yards south of parliament. Having been named prime minister with Soviet backing, he faced the task of finding a political solution to the crisis that was rapidly developing in a revolutionary direction as workers and citizens took control of their own factories and communities. By now the main political demand, which had appeared already on the first day, was the removal of Soviet forces from Hungary. At first Nagy appeared hesitant, but eventually on 28 October, in the name of his new coalition government formed from representatives of the communists and non-communist parties of the 1945-8 coalition period, he announced that the uprising was now officially regarded not as a counter-revolutionary, even fascist, development, but as a national democratic uprising. Nagy moved to parliament, which then became the focus of political events (though power still lay elsewhere, in the streets and factories).Within days the abolition of the political police, plans for a multi-party system and even the country's withdrawal from the Warsaw Pact and its neutrality were announced. A cease-fire was put into operation and, following negotiations, Soviet troops withdrew from Budapest. At this point many believed that a revolution had occurred and that it was victorious. That view was shattered in the early hours of Sunday 4 November, when Soviet tanks returned to Budapest and within days had dealt with the remaining pockets of armed resistance. Non-violent resistance continued for some time, led by the many workers' councils that had been established during the uprising. By means of threats and legal measures, they too eventually succumbed.

On 4 November, in the wake of the second Soviet intervention, Nagy and others in his political entourage took refuge in the Yugoslav Embassy, at the corner of today's Andrássy út and Heroes' Square. There they stayed until 22 November, when they were tricked into leaving and taken to Romania, where they were held under house arrest. Having been brought back to Budapest, Nagy and others were tried in secret in mid-1958 at the Fő utca prison in Buda. Following a death sentence for treason, Nagy was executed on 16 June, a date which reverberated during the political changes of 1989, when his rehabilitation and reburial (on the anniversary of his execution) and a general reappraisal of the uprising were a central feature of that historic year.

Márta Mészáros' 2004 feature film about Imre Nagy, *A temetetlen halott* (The Unburied Man) covers the last period of his life in almost documentary fashion. It has been issued on DVD with English subtitles.

In Place of a Prison

It is often said that Budapest is a "turn-of-the-century" city, meaning the turn of the nineteenth and twentieth centuries. Certainly much of the city's present form was built up as part of an extensive process of urban development which took place over four decades, between 1870 and 1914. Extensive areas of central Budapest, at least on the Pest side, were created then and still retain more or less the same look today. In the wake of serious war damage, the authorities of the post-1945 era insisted that replacement buildings should reflect the style of those around them, should not have flat roofs and should not exceed to any extent the height of neighbouring buildings. Even today, you will not find a dominating skyscraper anywhere in the central area of Pest. A number of early plans were drawn up by enthusiastic modernist architects to reshape the city centre and the Danube embankments in a grand scheme echoing works by Le Corbusier, such as his own post-war "Unité d'Habitation" in Marseille. Perhaps it was simply luck that there were not enough financial resources to realize such designs. Perhaps it was also lucky that Budapest, unlike Warsaw, was not the recipient of a post-war "gift" from Joseph Stalin in the shape of the huge Palace of Science and Culture that came to dominate the skyline of the Polish capital. Stalin's "wedding-cake skyscraper" architecture is arguably not out of place on Moscow's immensely wide outer ring road, but an example of it would have looked very incongruous, to say the least, anywhere near the centre of Budapest.

A good mixture of Budapest's architecture can be found in Szabadság tér, a large square close to Kossuth tér and parliament in the heart of the Lipótváros (Leopold Town) district. In recent times Szabadság tér has been freed of traffic, and it is now easy and relaxing to stroll here, or just to sit and soak up the atmosphere. Just over a century ago, however, no one would have wanted to stroll in the area of today's Szabadság tér, since here stood a massive prison complex covering an area of over twenty acres, which the Habsburgs had built in 1785. Rather strangely, they had christened it the New Building.

After the 1848-9 War of Independence many of the imprisoned Hungarians were held here and some, like Lajos Battyány, the prime minister of the first independent Hungarian government of 1848, were executed inside its walls. Today an eternal flame burns on the site of his execution as part of a monument erected to his memory in 1926. The monument stands in a small square at the end of Aulich utca, leading off the north-east corner of Szabadság tér. That this point was then inside the prison walls gives an idea of the enormous size of the New Building.

Representing Habsburg absolutism, the prison was understandably an object of hatred to Hungarians. After 1867 and the Compromise, it was also rather out of place in Pest, and it is not surprising that the prison was demolished in the mid-1890s. The name Szabadság tér, meaning "Freedom Square", dates from that time. The buildings that replaced the prison were all planned more or less simultaneously and so Szabadság tér is a good example of unitary urban development in the Hungarian capital in the period immediately preceding the First World War. Earlier in the nineteenth century this part of the city, at least to the south of the New Building, had been characterized by straight streets containing impressive neo-Classical town mansions, many of them designed by a leading architect of the day, József Hild (1789-1867). The regular pattern of these Leopold Town streets survives to this day, as do some of Hild's works, for example, 7 Október 6. utca, which dates from 1832, the former Tigris Hotel (1839) at 5 Nádor utca, and no. 12 in the same street, built in 1844.

When it came to the construction of Szabadság tér some neo-Classical elements were adopted, but tastes were now much more eclectic. The buildings were certainly all grand. Indeed, "Grandiose Eclecticism" is a good description to apply to Szabadság tér, as to many other buildings that appeared in Budapest at the turn of the nineteenth and twentieth centuries. The largest and most grandiose building in the square, stretching for the entire length of its west side, exhibits elements of both Greek and Assyrian temples, and is one of the most imposing structures in the whole of Budapest. Designed by Ignác Alpár, it was built in 1905 to house the Budapest stock and commodity exchanges. That a building of this size and nature was constructed for this function indicates the importance of Budapest as a financial centre in the pre-1914 era.

Other major buildings of the period erected for financial, often insurance institutions, include the 1907 Gresham Palace facing the Pest end of the Chain Bridge (today the Four Seasons Hotel), the Anker Palace, dominating Deák tér and built in the same year, the 1913 Adria

Insurance Building in Erzsébet tér (today the Le Méridien Hotel) and the Hungarian General Credit Bank in József nádor tér, also built in 1913 (today the Ministry of Finance).

The Szabadság tér exchanges continued to operate until 1948, when they were both closed down. Since the mid-1950s the building has been the headquarters of Hungarian TV, though there are proposals for it to move. Much of the interior was drastically reconstructed to produce a maze of corridors, cutting rooms and studios, but a glimpse of the original grandeur can be had from the small public waiting area just inside and to the left of the main entrance. From here you can see the massive entrance hall with its dramatic stairway.

The large Eclectic building dominating the east side of Szabadság tér though not taking up its entire length was also the work of Ignác Alpár. It was completed in 1905 to house yet another financial institution, the Austro-Hungarian Bank. Eight prominent architects from Hungary and Austria were invited to take part in the tender competition, which the Hungarian press treated like a football match, acclaiming the commissioning of Alpár as a national victory. A series of vivid limestone reliefs stretches around three sides of the building on the first-floor level. These show a variety of scenes illustrating the history of money, commerce and industry, as well as the arts and sciences. One relief modestly depicts the architect himself dressed as a medieval master builder (sixth from the right on the façade overlooking the square). After the First World War and the collapse of the Monarchy, the Hungarian National Bank was established here, where it still functions to this day.

The National Bank has some impressive stained glass windows, the work of glass master Miksa Róth. Róth (1865-1944) was a prolific craftsman of colourful stained glass and mosaics. His works can be found all over Budapest, but often, as with the National Bank, they are in parts of buildings to which the public does not have access. The National Bank, however, like a number of other sumptuous buildings of its period, is usually open to the public during the annual European Architectural Heritage Days, which fall on the third or fourth weekend in September. At other times a sample of Róth's work and designs can be seen in the memorial museum established in his former apartment at 26 Nefelejcs utca, not far from the Eastern Railway Station.

The Embassy of the United States stands to the north of the National Bank at 12 Szabadság tér. The building was constructed in 1899-1901, along with the neighbouring nos. 11 and 10, on which the Vienna-style Secessionist (Art Nouveau) decoration is more prominent. The embassy is famous, though not for its architectural qualities. During the Second World War, when US interests in Budapest were looked after by the Swiss, this was the original base for the operations of Carl Lutz, a Swiss diplomat who helped save the lives of hundreds if not thousands of Jews. Lutz later established his rescue base at the so-called Glass House at 29 Vadász utca, in the neighbourhood to the rear of the embassy. At the time of writing there is no reference to Lutz on the façade of the embassy building, but apparently there are plans for a Lutz memorial to stand nearby in the square. There is a plaque, however, in memory of another internationally-known figure who had long-term, albeit involuntary, connections with the embassy—Cardinal József Mindszenty.

It was within the walls of the embassy that Hungary's Catholic Primate, Cardinal Mindszenty (1892-1975), spent fifteen years in "internal exile" following the 1956 uprising. Mindszenty had been badly mistreated in prison during and after a show-trial in 1949. Released in 1956, he was only free for a few days before receiving refuge at the embassy on 4 November. His subsequent presence here, publicized around the world, and his uncompromising attitude were a problem in Church-state relations until, as he writes in his own memoirs, the Vatican persuaded him to leave for Austria in 1971. Following his death six years later, Mindszenty was buried in the ancient pilgrimage centre of Mariazell in Austria. In 1991 his remains were brought back to Hungary and reburied in the crypt of the cathedral at Esztergom, by the Danube, thirty miles from Budapest.

Why was Mindszenty not buried in Budapest? Following the coronation of Hungary's first monarch, Stephen, around the year 1000, which in effect marked the establishment of the Hungarian state, Esztergom was both the ecclesiastical and the royal centre of the country. After the Mongol invasion of 1241-2, however, King Béla IV decided to move the royal seat to Buda, where he established his castle and court. The central ecclesiastical authorities remained, and are still resident, in Esztergom, and so that town is the centre of Hungarian Catholicism and not Budapest.

Art Nouveau and Romantic

Immediately behind and adjacent to the US Embassy is one of the most unusual buildings in Hungary, the former Post Office Savings Bank, designed by Ödön Lechner and built in 1900. The building, with its colourful, extravagant shapes and floral ornamentation, almost defies categorization. Perhaps pure "Lechnerese" would be best, exemplifying as it does Lechner's individualistic attempt to fuse Art Nouveau and Hungarian features.

Note the bees crawling up the columns to beehives at the roof level, symbolizing savers accumulating pennies. Lechner once asked why the birds should not also enjoy his buildings, and in fact the roof, with its serpents and winged dragons, is perhaps the most astounding part of the whole. You need to fly high like a bird to fully appreciate it.

The former Post Office Savings Bank and its designer, Ödön Lechner, occasionally manage to creep into histories and encyclopædias of European architecture, which otherwise tend to ignore Hungarian innovations. Lechner arguably has his place on the European scene, but he certainly occupies a prominent position in the history of Hungarian architecture.

Towards the end of the nineteenth century and in the following decade growing dissatisfaction with officially sponsored Eclecticism produced a feeling that something more Hungarian should be developed. A significant figure in this trend—one could almost say the father of it—was Lechner (1845-1914), who turned to Eastern influences in his search for Hungarian roots, reflecting a contemporary belief that the sources of Magyar culture were to be found primarily in Asia. The Budapest Museum of Applied Arts on Üllői út, completed in 1896, is Lechner's most striking Asian-influenced legacy to the capital, the entrance and much of the

interior clearly reflecting "Mogul" forms. At the same time, Lechner also made use of Hungarian folk art motifs as dramatic decoration on his otherwise Art Nouveau buildings. His colourful Geological Institute (1899) on Stefánia út and the striking Post Office Savings Bank are the best examples of this cultural synthesis. But Lechner's views failed to find favour with the authorities and eventually official commissions dried up. Even so, he had started something that others were able to take up.

One trend emerging from Lechner's work is represented by Béla Lajta (1875-1920) who began with an Art Nouveau style but soon turned to a type of functionalism which enables him to be described as the first Hungarian modernist architect. His 1911 "Rózsavölgyi" building in Budapest's Szervita tér has become the classic example of early Hungarian modernism. The folkish decoration on this building and on some of his other creations also betrays the earlier influences of Lechner.

Modernism itself, at least of the Bauhaus, pre-1945 type, played a relatively minor role in Hungarian architecture. In the inter-war conservative period it was seen as rather too "internationalist", though some typical "white cube" dwellings were erected in the Buda Hills and elements of modernism can be detected in the 1931-2 experimental Napraforgó utca project in Budapest's Pasarét district.

Another post-Lechner trend, though critical of the master, was in a way more faithful to his concepts. A truly Hungarian architecture, the argument went, could not be developed simply by using folk decoration as ornamentation, as Lechner tended to do. What was required was an adaptation of traditional (which here meant mainly peasant) styles of design. Thus was born Hungarian National Romanticism, which had similarities with other national fashions in architecture appearing throughout Europe at the time. The attempt to rediscover a genuinely Hungarian architecture drew on Transylvanian building techniques, with high-pitched roofs and much wood, suggesting that here was the area where Hungarian culture had suffered least disruptions over the centuries.

While there are some examples of National Romantic architecture in the capital, notably the attractive Áldás utca School in Buda, designed by Dezső Zrumeczky and built in 1912, much of the building in this style took place outside Budapest. One of the main adherents of the National Romantic tendency and a major figure in twentieth-century Hungarian architecture was Károly Kós (1883-1977). In keeping with his attachment to the roots of Hungarian traditions he mostly lived and worked in Transylvania (today part of Romania), but some of his early works can be seen in modern-day Hungary. His ensemble of buildings in the central square of the Wekerle Estate survives as an example of garden-city type development constructed between 1908 and 1925 in Kispest, a district to the south-east of the centre.

Neither Hungarian Art Nouveau nor National Romanticism, however, found favour in the inter-war period. This was a time when Classical and Baroque revivalist tendencies emerged almost as if to counter the loss of heritage caused by the 1920 Trianon Treaty. A good example of the spirit of Baroque revival in Budapest is the St. Imre Church, built for the Cistercians in 1938 on Villányi út in Buda. Post-1945 there was a brief period when modernist trends were tolerated; noteworthy in this connection is 84/b Dózsa György út in Pest, at the corner of Városligeti fasor, built for a trade union headquarters in 1947-50. With its airy interiors, light, open spaces and circular glass lifts, the building has retained its appeal.

Eventually, however, socialist realism and "Stalinist neo-Classicism" emerged triumphant. Prime examples are represented by the building of the then new town of Sztálinváros (today Dunaújváros) south of Budapest and in the capital itself by the massive People's Stadium, completed in 1953 (and today named after Hungary's most famous footballer, Ferenc Puskás). Yet there was no excessive imitation of grandiose Moscow styles and later, as elsewhere throughout Europe, a uniform "tower block" culture came to dominate. This has been complemented by the equally ubiquitous post-modernism, represented prominently in Budapest by the latest office buildings. The enormous glass block of the International Bank Centre, by the south-east corner of Szabadság tér across from the National Bank, is a good example. Completed in 1995, it was designed by József Finta, who with his associates has been responsible for some of the largest and most attractive post-modern buildings of recent times, including the luxury Kempinsky Hotel (1992) in Erzsébet tér and the enormous, yet not overwhelming Westend City Center by the Western Railway Station. With its nearly 400 retail outlets, this is one of the largest shopping malls in Central Europe. It opened in 1999 after an incredibly short construction time of just over one year.

Almost all of Budapest's large shopping centres have appeared in the last ten years or so, and together with the appearance of large foreign-owned supermarket chains located on the outskirts have transformed the shopping habits of the capital. Yet not all the city's contemporary urban creations are on a huge scale. The Bellevue Plaza (1999), at the corner of Kossuth Lajos utca and Szép utca in central Pest, has a rich mixture of steel-and-glass surfaces and shapes which give it prominence, while at the same time its height and overall appearance blend well with its neighbours in this old city-centre neighbourhood.

Interestingly, as noted by the architectural historian András Ferkai: "1989 fails to represent a real change in architectural terms; the most significant changes had already made their appearance around 1980." In this sense, the imagination of the designers and planners perhaps preceded that of the politicians, but it may also suggest that some aspects of culture were already fairly autonomous before the end of state socialism in 1989-90.

A quite different trend to have emerged in recent decades harks back to Kós-style National Romanticism and usually goes under the name of "organic" architecture. The prominent use of natural elements like wood, of curving features and echoes of animal forms are characteristic of the style. The leading representative of this school is Imre Makovecz, who has been the subject of international attention. His 1977 mortuary chapel in the Farkasrét Cemetery in Buda, for example, is the only work in Budapest included in architecture critic Jonathan Glancey's pictorial survey of nearly 400 "structures that shaped the twentieth century". Makovecz's representation of the human rib cage is described as an "extraordinary and moving interior".

As Glancey points out, Makovecz and his followers were out of favour in the 1980s, but his assertion that "since 1989 [they] have been national heroes" is not entirely accurate, even though the nationalistic tone of some of Hungary's organic theorizing might have appeared to dovetail neatly with the policies of the centre-right coalition that formed the new government in 1990. Certainly, Makovecz was chosen to design the Hungarian pavilion for Expo '92 in Seville, the almost completely wooden structure described by Glancey as "memorable". But arguably this was a significant but nevertheless *ad hoc* commission, motivated by a mixture of politics and prestige-seeking. The new buildings appearing in 1990s Budapest were mostly constructed as commercial and office developments and have copied the international post-modern orthodoxy that emerged in the 1980s. Even the election in 1998 of a much more populist centre-right government under Premier Viktor Orbán did not basically change the situation. Neither of the two major prestigious public building projects initiated during the Orbán period, the National Theatre (2002) and the Palace of Arts (2005), standing close to each other by the Danube, were built to "organic" designs.

Perhaps the Makovecz style by its very nature is more suited to smaller-scale, primarily non-commercial construction. A number of family houses have been built in Budapest to the designs of organic architects, while larger projects have been mostly confined to the provinces. Makovecz's Church of the Holy Spirit (1991) in Paks to the south of Budapest and his Árpád Secondary School (1993) in Sárospatak in the north-east of Hungary are two striking examples. There is also one large, even commercial, example in Budapest itself— the Swan House on Hattyú utca near Moszkva tér, designed by Ervin Nagy and completed in 1998.

Soviet and American

Of all the monuments in Szabadság tér the most prominent is the Soviet Army Memorial, a 45-foot limestone obelisk placed in the central area of the northern part of the square. Raised in 1945, it stood, ironically, in front of the American Embassy right throughout the Cold War period and beyond. Reliefs at the base depict on one side Red Army soldiers in the vicinity of (the old) Elizabeth Bridge during the siege of Budapest in 1944-5, and on the other Soviet soldiers near the parliament building. The plinth contains the names of those who lost their lives. The hammer-and-sickle symbol can be seen above, and there are inscriptions in Hungarian and Russian glorifying the "liberating Soviet Heroes". Such symbolism and language, though common throughout the city in the post-1945 decades, are rarely found today.

Following the political changes of 1989-90 and the election of a new municipal council, there was much argument about the fate of the monument, the largest of several such Soviet Army memorials in the city. A central dispute was partly linguistic: whether 1945 should be regarded as "liberation" by the Soviets from German occupation and fascist Arrow Cross rule, or "occupation". (Few seemed to take the view that perhaps it could be both.) In the end the city council decided to remove all the Red Army monuments except this one.

Near the Soviet obelisk stands a statue of a US Army general, Harry Hill Bandholtz. A member of the Allied Military Mission, Bandholtz was present in Budapest in 1919 after the fall of the Hungarian Council Republic. He intervened to prevent the looting of the Hungarian National Museum by Romanian troops and came to be regarded as hero by the Hungarians, who erected his statue in Szabadság tér in 1936. Bandholtz's own memoirs, *An Undiplomatic Diary*, give a rather prosaic account of the matter. He says the Romanians claimed many items in the museum as theirs since they had been taken from Transylvania, which now belonged to them. Nevertheless a decision was taken that nothing should be touched and Bandholtz was commissioned with securing the museum. Seals were placed on each of the doors. Bandholtz adds: "As the Romanians and all Europeans are fond of rubber-stamp display, and as we had nothing else, we used an American main-censor stamp, with which we marked all the seals." Sure enough, his memoirs reproduce one of the seals duly stamped "Passed as Censored". The statue of Bandholtz was removed from Szabadság tér in 1945. It was kept in the garden of the US ambassador's residence, eventually to reappear in the square in July 1989 just before US President George Bush Sr. visited Budapest.

Another statue which stood in the square from 1949 to 1956 was of an altogether different nature. Entitled *Gratitude*, it depicted in socialist realist manner a stereotypical proletarian family of father, mother and child, and was put up to mark Stalin's 70th birthday. In the same year the first trolley bus ran in Budapest. Inevitably it was given the number 70, and to this day Budapest's trolley bus numbers still range from 70 to 83.

chapter eight

From Markets to Menus

Market Colours

The short street running by the side of the American Embassy in Szabadság tér takes you to Hold utca. Immediately here is the entrance to Market Hall V, one of a number of covered markets built in Budapest in the 1890s. Interestingly, the competition generated by the arrival of large British, French and other supermarket chains one hundred years later in the 1990s, while dealing a severe blow to many small-scale groceries, has not diminished the appeal of the city's traditional fresh fruit, vegetable, fish and meat markets. Indeed, many of these, including the one in Hold utca, have been given a facelift in the past ten years, so that while retaining their colour and life, they have moved beyond their previously rather scruffy state to become a vibrant part of the city's life and an attraction in themselves.

The most impressive of the five Budapest market halls dating from the end of the nineteenth century is the massive, station-like building of the Central Market Hall on Vámház körút, near the Pest end of Liberty Bridge. It was constructed in 1893-6 to plans by Samu Pecz, a professor at the Technical University who ornamented the exterior with glazed terracotta produced at the Zsolnay factory in Pest. The name Zsolnay is known worldwide as one of Hungary's three major producers of finely decorated porcelain (the others being Herend and Hollóháza), and the Zsolnay factory is also renowned in Hungary for its special industrial and building ceramics. The use of coloured tiling and other decorative elements made at the Zsolnay works is a hallmark of many Budapest public buildings, accounting for one of the city's characteristic visual trademarks.

The huge iron framework of the Central Market Hall, which covers more than 100,000 square feet, was originally built for the city's main wholesale market, but for many years the building has been used primarily for retail purposes. Following closure and extensive renovations, the market reopened with its original splendour beautifully restored in 1994. It is well worth a look inside, both for the building and the atmosphere.

On the Buda side the main traditional-style market is at Fény utca, 100 yards from Moszkva tér. This is one of the busiest fruit, vegetable, meat and flower markets in the city. It used to be a traditional open-air market, rather run-down and unsightly, though always crowded. Those premises were pulled down and the municipal architects' office designed an attractive new structure for the market, which opened in 1998. Operating on various levels as before and still with no all-round enclosing walls—though now with a high protective glass roof—much of the colourful atmosphere remains, with a mixture of established traders and elderly peasant women selling their home-grown vegetables.

The range of produce available at the markets has gradually changed over the past fifteen years. It was not the case that there were food shortages prior to 1989-90 (though some items, such as bananas, would only appear irregularly) but rather that choice was more limited and more seasonal, with fewer imports. Yet the seasonal nature of the markets has not completely disappeared, and certainly their "colour" is still much brighter in the spring and summer months. Imports have helped to increase variety, but new home-grown items have also extended what is available. In early summer, for instance, markets are flooded with locally grown asparagus. The sight of an abundance of fresh asparagus, both white and green, surprises Western visitors almost as much as the rock bottom prices.

One sight that has not changed is the row of salami-type sausages hanging above each butcher's stall. Eating the humble sausage (*kolbász*) is an embedded part of the culture of both Budapest and provincial Hungary, though the sausage is rather different from, for example, its popular British counterpart. The traditional Hungarian sausage is a product of the equally traditional pig killing, which takes place in the winter. Parts of the pork are finely ground, liberally seasoned with paprika, garlic and pepper, and then used to fill the pig's cleaned intestines. These are then hung in smoke rooms and when ready can remain as dry sausage for months on end.

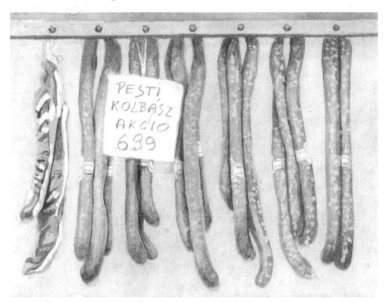

Love and Stuffed Cabbage

An 1896 English-language guidebook, published in Budapest as one of the "Singer and Wolfner's Handbooks for Travellers" series, advised that "the Hungarian cook is making a generous use of lard and of paprika, a Hungarian speciality in the way of spices, as well as of salt, pepper, ginger, etc." It suggested that those "more careful of their health will not do amiss to take a small dose of bicarbonate after indulging in a specifically Magyar dinner," adding by way of conclusion: "It is at all events advisable to try the National Cooking for meals during the day and not for supper."

That rather pointed advice is still partly applicable today, but only partly. While it is true that Hungarian cuisine is traditionally heavy and spicy, or perceived as such, it has been changing and today many restaurants, particularly in Budapest, offer "contemporary" or "modern" Hungarian dishes, meaning on the lighter side.

A common misconception about Hungarian cuisine is that most dishes look red due to the enormous quantity of paprika used in cooking. When properly used, however, paprika is a fine and delicious spice, giving both colour and aroma to reputed dishes such as goulash (*gulyás*), paprika chicken (*paprikás csirke*) and various other stews. Paprika, as can be seen in Budapest markets, involves a wide variety of both sweet and hot peppers in fresh vegetable, dried and powder form. The spice was introduced by the Turks and, according to a 1684 dictionary, its first Hungarian name was "Turkish pepper".

Paprika found a place in refined cookery around the middle of the nineteenth century, a development aided by an invention of the Pálffy brothers of Szeged (the centre of paprika milling today in southern Hungary). Their machine stripped paprika fruits of their hot seeds and ribs. These could then be ground separately from the milder, dried fleshy part. By mixing the two, different strengths of the spice could be obtained.

A curious attribute of paprika, discovered in 1937 by Professor Albert Szent-Györgyi (1893-1986), then of Szeged University and later awarded a Nobel Prize for his work, is that it has five times as much vitamin C as any other fruit. The peasants of the Szeged area had known of the spice's health-promoting properties for centuries and had traditionally used it to ward off malaria, a prevalent disease when the area was very marshy before the River Tisza was regulated.

In addition to Turkish influence, Hungarian cuisine has at different times borrowed from Italian, German, Austrian, Czech, Slovak, Serbian and Croatian tastes and traditions. In the time of King Matthias in the fifteenth century, for instance, gnocchi from Italy was introduced, although transformed into various types and sizes of dumplings to be served with stew or cooked in soups.

In addition to paprika, other characteristic ingredients include onions, sour cream and smoked bacon. It is the way a stew, *pörkölt*, or soups are made from these otherwise basic ingredients that gives them their distinctive taste. The chopped onion is fried in oil or lard and, when lightly brown, paprika is stirred in. Sour cream is either cooked with the food or added at serving.

Hungarians have traditionally consumed an enormous quantity of meat, mainly pork and beef. Today many Budapest restaurants also serve game—venison, wild boar and wild duck being the most popular. Poultry is also popular, as is freshwater fish. Hungary is rich in rivers and lakes, so carp (*ponty*), pike-perch (*fogas*), cat-fish (*harcsa*) and trout (*pisztráng*) are widely available. As for poultry, goose liver (*libamáj*) is a speciality, often roasted or grilled and eaten cold or hot.

Meat dishes are usually served with potatoes prepared in different ways, or rice, though traditionally there are few vegetables unless a side salad is served. Salads differ according to season. In the summer fresh green salads and in the winter a variety of pickles are eaten, though in recent times the variety of salads on offer in the winter has increased.

Hungarian meat specialities include stews prepared of veal, pork or beef (*pörkölt*), pan-fried beef served in various ways (*rostélyos*), pork slices in a mushroom and sour cream sauce (*Bakonyi sertéshús*), served with gnocchi (*nokedli*). Among poultry dishes the most popular is chicken paprika (*paprikás csirke*), similar in the way it is prepared to a *pörkölt*, with sour cream and gnocchi. Hungary's internationally celebrated goulash is available in many of the city's restaurants. *Gulyás*, as it is written in Hungarian, is not a stew as known abroad, but a thick soup of beef and vegetables that can be a meal in itself.

The origins of *gulyás* go back centuries. It is believed that when the Magyars were still nomads they prepared several meals once they had slaughtered an animal. They cut up the meat and cooked it in a heavy cauldron, which was set up over an open fire, until all the juices evaporated. Then they dried the cubes of meat in the sun and stored them. When they wanted to eat they simply added water and other ingredients. Thus *gulyás* is often served in little cauldrons (*bogrács*) in restaurants.

Hungarian cooking has traditionally been a seasonal affair. In winter, heavier, more filling dishes are made, with lots of smoked meat. One of the most popular seasonal dishes readily found in Budapest in the winter is stuffed cabbage (*töltött káposzta*), made of sauerkraut, dumplings of minced pork and smoked sausage, and other smoked meat. Some Hungarian families live on it for days, since it is one of those rare dishes that improves with time. Hence the Hungarian saying: "Love is not like stuffed cabbage, once cold you cannot reheat it." A typical summer dish makes use of tomatoes and fresh paprika in the form of a special type of yellow pepper seen everywhere in the markets at the time. It is called *lecsó*, a Hungarian ratatouille, eaten as it is or added to meat.

Vegetarians can have a hard time in Budapest's meat-eating culture. Yet there are plenty of traditional Hungarian dishes that are meat-free such as *főzelékek* (braised vegetables), mushrooms made in different ways, such as *rántott gomba* (mushrooms coated with breadcrumbs and deep fried), *gombapörkölt* (mushroom stew) and *rántott sajt* (cheese coated in breadcrumbs and deep fried). *Főzelék*, which has always been popular in home cooking and has recently made its way back to restaurant tables, is a Hungarian way of making vegetables whereby chopped, shredded vegetables or pulses are cooked and thickened with roux and/or sour cream.

When in 1988 Eastern Europe's first McDonalds opened in Budapest' s city centre, just off Váci utca, there were long queues, and for some time the outlet enjoyed the highest turnover of any McDonalds in the world. Since then, the company has expanded its presence in Budapest and has been joined by other similarly well-known chains. There is no doubt that this particular "Western invasion" has been popular among the capital's citizens, but now some Hungarian foods seem to be hitting back, and today there are fast-food "*főzelék* bars" in a number of Budapest locations.

chapter nine

MUSIC FUSION

Folk Music Capital

"It's like a living river. You never put your legs in the same water." That is how Márta Sebestyén once described her experience of being a folk singer and part of the Hungarian folk-song community. Sebestyén is probably Hungary's most internationally famous folk singer, a status both reflected and boosted by her evocative and haunting singing which introduced the Oscar-winning film *The English Patient*.

Sebestyén and the group she has frequently performed with, Muzsikás, have been around for over thirty years. The 1970s was a time that witnessed a revival of interest in traditional Hungarian folk music—of different varieties and styles. The Vujicsics Group, for example, was formed in the same period and focussed on southern Slav music, the traces of which remained in parts of Hungary populated by Serbs and their descendants. The group is still performing Balkan music today, and it is not unusual to find Márta Sebestyén on stage with them, so broad is her repertoire.

The popularity of Muzsikás, Vujicsics and other well-established groups such as Méta, Kaláka, Ghymes, Kalamajka and Téka became rooted in what was known as the *Táncház* (literally Dance House) movement, which has been strong, particularly in Budapest, for three decades. A *Táncház* is a folk music event characterized by participatory dancing. A group, either well-known or new to the scene, will perform and then, perhaps with someone giving instructions or experienced dancers showing the way, anyone and everyone is welcome, even encouraged, to join in.

Originally there was a certain political edge to the *Táncház* experience. Traditional folk music, with its national connotations (or connotations that could be interpreted as national), was not banned in post-1945 Hungary; rather, like so many other social phenomena, it was incorporated into the state-managed system. The Hungarian State Folk Ensemble, for instance, founded in 1951 at the height or perhaps depth of Hungary's hard-line Stalinist period, contained excellent musicians and experienced dancers, and served (and still serves) as an attractive spectacle for both domestic and foreign consumption. Yet, as its very name revealed, there was a contradiction between peasant-based and often spontaneous musical events, tied to seasons and the stages of life, and the packaging and presentation of such culture when managed from above and performed on stage for passive, paying audiences in large urban theatres.

Being active in the *Táncház* movement, organized "from below", was widely regarded as a way of goading the authorities, particularly as much of the music played was from Transylvania, the area now in Romania with a large number of ethnic Hungarians, whose interests the then Hungarian government was neglecting—or so it was seen by many. In the words of *Táncház* enthusiast Bob Cohen, "the Dance Houses were meeting places for dissidents, samizdat editors and daring college students." Cohen, an American expatriate, is both a music writer and a performing musician. His Di Naye Kapelye group helped revive the Klezmer tradition (see below) in post-1989 Budapest.

Notwithstanding Cohen's comments, the politics of the movement was not overtly explicit, which is perhaps why *Táncház* events were not banned by the authorities. Nor was its political expression entirely clear or, in retrospect, consistent. The movement's early participants are today just as likely as anyone else to be found applauding excellent "authentic" folk concerts from their expensive seats in large urban halls such as those in Budapest's new showpiece, the Palace of Arts.

The *Táncház* events caught on and almost became part of a generation's youth culture. Over the years "dance houses" specializing in not only Hungarian but also Slovak, Macedonian, Greek, Jewish and even Scottish and Irish folk dance traditions appeared and were organized on a regular basis. The continued existence of such events, spread throughout the city and often taking place in local community centres off the beaten (tourist) track, as well as the large, well-publicized performances in the city's major halls, together make Budapest a Mecca for traditional music enthusiasts. In the words of *World Music: The Rough Guide*, the Hungarian capital is "one of the best places in Europe to hear really good folk music."

The largest event, and arguably a must for anyone even remotely interested in the genre, is the annual *Táncház* Festival that takes place on a weekend near Easter under one roof in Budapest's massive Sports Arena and which has become a one-stop heaven for folk fans far and wide. Throughout the rest of the year enthusiasts and the curious head for the Fonó Budai Zeneház (literally the "spinning music house in Buda") where, in a tradition now reaching back several years, a Hungarian dance house is held every Wednesday evening (with the exception of July and August). In addition there are regular live performances by artists representing different ethnic traditions and different styles from all over the Carpathian Basin.

Cold Outside, Warm Inside

It is a cold winter evening in the middle of January. The crowd at the Fonó is not large, but it is animated and loudly appreciative of the performances on offer. The programme is varied, beginning with the gypsy Latin styles of Robert Bihari's Roma Music World group. A solo flamenco dancer follows, transporting the audience into the world of Spanish sounds. Then comes the main event of the evening: members of the Khamoro Gypsy Dance Association performing a variety of lively songs and dances from north-east Hungary. With fingers and thumbs snapping and feet swiftly tapping to the pounding rhythm, the female dancers, of different ages and not all gypsies, circle the stage and each other, their bright and colourful dresses swirling around as they move. As they noisily and skilfully play their guitars, the musicians add that characteristic gypsy sound—the "hop-hup" notes created just by the throat and the voice (oral or mouth bassing it is sometimes called). It is an engaging evening of gypsy performance, one of a regular series at the Fonó organized by the Khamoro Association, founded in 2001 and which deals not only with performing but also with teaching traditional gypsy performing arts.

The relation of gypsy music to Hungarian folk music has long been a topic of dispute, as has the issue of whether such categories are in themselves useful. Purists like to divide and define, but music, particularly "ethnic" music, often defies strict classification or makes new hybrid categories come into being. A complication of the Hungarian situation is that what has been traditionally regarded as gypsy music, particularly the typical repertoire of gypsy musicians heard in the restaurants of Budapest and elsewhere, is actually based on popular Hungarian melodies from the nineteenth century. A variety of scholars and musicians, from Liszt to Bartók and beyond, have weighed in with their views on the debate. But does it matter?

What certainly matters for gypsy musicians today is that their situation has altered dramatically since 1989-90. In the days of state socialism restaurants were encouraged, if not obliged, to employ gypsy bands, the costs of which were often borne by the large state-owned catering enterprises to which the restaurants belonged. Up to the late 1980s there were hundreds of restaurants with gypsy music in Budapest, which had provided employment for generations of musicians. With privatization and increased competition in the 1990s all that changed. It was no longer automatic that the talented son (and very occasionally the daughter) would follow in the footsteps of the musician father and grandfather. Unemployment among gypsy musicians (up to then regarded by many as the gypsy "elite") now reflected similarly rising unemployment among gypsies throughout the country.

One effect has been a shift in the popular mind, even a rediscovery, of what gypsy music involves. Talented young Roma musicians are now just as likely to attend Budapest's Academy of Music as to gravitate towards restaurant employment as a matter of course. What is emerging is a new generation of Roma musicians, many of whom are reviving their musical traditions and performing both in restaurants and, like the other folk musicians, in the community centres and clubs as well as on larger stages.

The gypsy music revival has been underway for some time, running in parallel with that of Hungarian folk music. Gypsy groups like Andro Drom and Kalyi Jag were performing to enthusiastic audiences well before the turn of 1989-90. Both aimed to reproduce and develop authentic gypsy sounds from the region and indeed beyond. Looking "beyond" was natural, since the roots of gypsy culture can be traced to parts of northern India, the singing and dancing styles brought via the Middle East to Europe where they developed over the centuries in various ways as Roma communities spread across the continent. This historical evolution, ranging from traditional Indian song and dance to Spanish flamenco, is the subject of Tony Gatlif's fascinating 1993 film *Latcho Drom* (Safe Journey), featuring performers from the different countries of the "journey". The group representing Hungary with their "Gypsy Anthem" was Kék Láng, an ensemble from the tiny village of Nyírvasváry in the far east of the country, just a few miles from the Romanian border.

In the 1980s the fame of Andro Drom and Kalyi Jag spread beyond Budapest and even beyond Hungary. The attention they and other groups attracted, and the money they generated for various projects such as the Kalyi Jag Secondary School for Roma, helped to define Budapest as "the gypsy cultural capital of Eastern Europe". The definition probably still holds, if only because of what has been happening in recent years.

In 1998 Romano Drom appeared on the scene. The group was formed by members of Andro Drom, though the latter continues to exist and perform. Around the same time Andro Drom's powerful lead singer Mónika Juhász Miczura, otherwise known as Mitsou, went her own way, building on her solo engagements. Mitsou has been creating a bridge between Hungarian and Rajasthani songs. Depending on which instruments are accompanying, her performance has something of the mixture of gypsy, folk, Indian and jazz. To watch the diminutive figure of Mitsou on stage while she captivates her audience with a piercing voice is unforgettable.

Mixture also characterizes the music of Kálmán Balogh and his Gypsy Cimbalom Band, originally established in the mid-1990s. The cimbalom, sometimes called a dulcimer, is a traditional instrument of Hungarian gypsy bands, though it was also used extensively by the composer Zoltán Kodály in his orchestral suite, *Háry János*. Standing on four legs, the cimbalom has a large number of strings in a horizontal plane. The strings are played by being hit with beaters. The instrument is believed to have developed from the Persian santur, which entered Europe in the Middle Ages and became popular with Romanian gypsy musicians in the nineteenth century. Despite the traditional nature of his instrument, Balogh's work touches on both classical and contemporary music, jazz and folk styles from Hungary, the Balkans and elsewhere.

The Besh o Drom ensemble was founded in 1999 and has since become one of the most popular bands on Budapest's "world music" circuit. Their pounding and rhythmic percussion (described by one critic as a minimum of ten on the Richter scale) with prominent wind instrumentation contains echoes of Balkan, Turkish and gypsy traditions, as well as modern jazz. Slightly older is Djabe ("freedom" in

Ashanti), a jazz group incorporating in their music and instrumentation influences from as far away as East Asia.

Budapest's jazz and gypsy music are now, at least for some musicians and audiences, quite intertwined, which is perhaps not surprising given the ethnic roots, spontaneity, improvisation and lack of formality inherent in both traditions. In 1997 the popular guitarist and composer Gyula Babos, who has been a central figure of Hungarian jazz for years, created the Babos Project, aiming to bring together the musical worlds of Roma and jazz traditions. More recently, pianist Béla Szakcsi Lakatos, a member of the famous Hungarian Lakatos family of gypsy musicians, has launched his New Hungarian Gypsy Jazz group.

What is new? What is Hungarian? What is gypsy? What is jazz? The answers are part of the excitement of the fusion that fuels the "traditional-contemporary" music scene in Budapest today. Some clues are provided by *Gypsy Colours*, a collection produced by Béla and his brother, saxophonist Tony Lakatos, in the summer of 2005. Together with family members Roby Lakatos (violin) and András Lakatos (drums) but also with other accomplished performers such as the internationally renowned Hungarian guitarist Ferenc Snetberger, the tracks on their CD reflect a range of influences and include Indian melodies, Hungarian gypsy folk songs and Hungarian traditional dance music combined with jazz chords, freestyle jazz interpretations of Romanian melodies, a Serbian gypsy folk song, a tribute to Django Reinhart (described as *the* gypsy jazz musician) and a track reflecting connections with Jewish music. That is no isolated phenomenon for, to add to the excitement, into this mixture has been added elements from yet another source—East European Yiddish culture.

In the early 1990s Hungary saw a revival of Jewish culture, including the almost-forgotten culture of Klezmer, a melodic tradition of secular Jewish music dating from the late Middle Ages but with roots reaching back to Biblical times. Much of the repertoire consists of dance songs for weddings and other celebrations. Given its liveliness, spontaneity and instrumentation, which often involves a prominent clarinet, you could be forgiven for thinking you were listening to traditional jazz from New Orleans.

The Budapest Klezmer Band, regarded as Hungary's first Klezmer group of recent times, was formed in 1990. It has since carved out a place for itself not only locally but also world-wide. In its wake have come other groups with captivating Klezmer sounds, such as Di Naye Kapelyc, the Chagall Klezmer Band and Vodhu v Glotku, whose members produce the haunting sounds of "Odessa" Klezmer, echoing sometimes through "hole in the wall" drinking places in the dark streets of Pest, sometimes in the limelight of Budapest's more familiar stages. To add to the intriguing (con)fusion, it is now even possible to hear "gypsy-klezmer" music in Budapest. Opera and Klezmer singer Balázs Fellegi has combined with cimbalom-player Kálmán Balogh to create yet another new mixture, in the form of the Fellegini Klezmer-Gypsy Band.

Ivory and Enamel

No discussion, however brief, of contemporary Hungarian jazz (in so far as it remains a separable, identifiable category) could be complete without a mention of the pianist György Vukán. Arts columnists are fond of writing that a performer divides his or her time between Paris and New York, Berlin and Tokyo, or wherever. György Vukán divides his time between the ivory of the keyboard and the enamel of people's teeth, since he is both a professional musician and a practising dentist. Born in 1941, Vukán has had a distinguished career not only as a jazz performer in Hungary and abroad, but also as the composer of numerous scores for cinema, theatre and radio. An example of his own special brand of fusion can be experienced on his 1994 CDs *Chopin-Vukán* and *Debussy-Vukán*, which, as the titles imply, are his jazz interpretations of these two great composers. The notes accompanying a more recent disc, his 2003 *Gentle Love*, explicitly refer to the "creative development of crossover. An old-new formation, which helps us to express our own ideas, without borders."

British jazz enthusiast Andy Wiggans has been captivated by Vukán's playing, which he has witnessed live on a number of occasions in Budapest. "Vukán often has a very reflective approach, which is sometimes even quite tender. Some distinctive folk rhythms are retained in his music, and his own 'crossover' is there, which makes him different. At the same time, Vukán is clearly a talented composer in his own right and the people he plays with are very gifted musicians."

One of those musicians, playing with Vukán since 1990 and the formation of their Creative Art Trio, is the remarkable drummer Elemér Balázs, who has partly branched out with his own group, adding to the music mix. The Elemér Balázs Group's *Magyar népdalok* (Hungarian Folksongs), released in 2005, features jazz arrangements of traditional Hungarian folk music. In the same year Balázs combined, not for the first time, with acclaimed saxophonist László Dés to produce, with the participation of the Voces4 Ensemble, the intriguingly titled *Contemporary Gregorian*, a mixture involving medieval and Renaissance music and twenty-first-century free jazz.

The art of jazz has been officially taught in Budapest for over forty years, but it is only now on the verge of being officially recognized as a university-level subject by the Academy of Music. Academic status can only boost the already high reputation that the city's jazz musicians enjoy. This reputation can be assessed on a variety of occasions and in a number of locations throughout the year. The summer months, in particular, witness an assortment of even free concerts, for example on the Chain Bridge at weekends, or specifically on 21 June, the European Day of Music. The year 2005 saw the (almost literal) launch, under the auspices of the Hungarian Jazz Musicians Association, of the Columbus Jazz Club—an evening place of entertainment based on a boat moored by the Pest embankment. At the time of writing, it is still one of the best places to turn to for a regular programme of Hungarian jazz, in all its forms of fusion and mixture.

chapter ten
JEWS AND GENTILES

Politics of Inclusion

One of the biggest synagogues in the world stands by the start of Dohány utca in central Pest. It is also one of the most striking buildings in the city and, completed in 1859, it pre-dates many of the other imposing structures on the Pest side of the Hungarian capital such as the Academy of Sciences (1867), the Opera House (1884), the former Supreme Court, today the Museum of Ethnography (1896), parliament (1904), the former Stock Exchange, currently Hungarian TV headquarters (1905), the National Bank (1905), St. Stephen's Basilica (1905), the Fine Arts Museum (1906) and the Academy of Music (1907). The only large building on the Pest side built before this synagogue and still standing is the National Museum (1846).

The size and date of construction of the Dohány utca Synagogue point to something significant. That the Jewry of Pest had this massive, richly decorated temple built in the middle of the nineteenth century reflects the relative stability and wealth of sections of the Jewish community at that time. It also indicates, indirectly, the relative acceptance, or at least tolerance, of Jews by the non-Jewish population.

The land on which the synagogue was built came into Jewish hands soon after the 1848-9 War of Independence against Habsburg rule. As a wall plaque by the synagogue today recalls, many Jews participated in that struggle on the Hungarian side, though they faced a degree of opposition, and it was only radicals like Sándor Petőfi who fully welcomed Jewish involvement. Nevertheless, it was clear that many Jews in mid-nineteenth-century Hungary were eager to be Hungarian patriots, which led many of them to seek full assimilation.

What has been called the politics of inclusion vis-à-vis Jews in Hungary is well illustrated by the fact that legal emancipation, formal recognition of the equality of Jews as citizens, was enacted as early as in 1867. This act further encouraged the self-identification of Jews as Hungarians, even as Hungarian patriots, and this remained a characteristic phenomenon certainly up to the First World War and, for many, even right up to the eve of the Holocaust in Hungary. The reasons behind the inclusive attitude on the part of Hungarian society, or at least most of its elite, can be briefly (and perhaps over-simply) summarized as follows.

In the nineteenth century Hungary was predominantly a peasant, agricultural society. Those with power were, by and large, those who owned the land. They were, with some exceptions, conservative in the sense that they were rooted in non-urban traditions going back centuries. Not from them would come the dynamism and entrepreneurial activity required to fuel the industrial and financial development that boomed particularly in Budapest in the last quarter of the century. The Jews among the German industrialists who came from the West and those Jews with money who came from the East found themselves welcomed as a substitute Hungarian bourgeoisie or newly-developing capitalist class, which occupied itself with the country's economic development.

The integration of the Jews in this group was not restricted to the economic sphere. As William O. McCagg details in his pioneering and remarkable study, *Jewish Nobles and Geniuses in Modern Hungary*, the wealthy Jews of Pest entered Hungarian political life as well. They often did so after being ennobled in recognition of their services to the economy. Nobility no longer involved feudal privileges, but it was a title that still carried psychological and social weight, given that with no well-established bourgeois culture the feudal mentality continued to be significant. McCagg indicates that in the period 1860-1918 there were 338 Jewish noble families, 198 of whom resided in Budapest at the time of ennoblement. Of these just over three-quarters were directly associated with the world of finance, commerce and industry. Not, however, that one had to be a noble to get on. Mór Wahrmann, the grandson of a Pest rabbi, for example, became one of the richest and, as president of the Budapest Chamber of Industry and Commerce, most powerful Jewish figures in the business world. He became the first Jewish MP in the Hungarian parliament, being elected to represent the Lipótváros district in 1869. The building at 23 Andrássy út was constructed for Wahrmann in 1885.

This political integration was an inter-active affair, aided by the Budapest Jews' patriotism (many changed their surnames, adopting a Hungarian form, and many even converted to Christianity). At the same time, the process suited the Hungarian elite for another, not so generous reason. Nineteenth-century Hungary was a country of many nationalities and many ethnic groups. Indeed, the non-Hungarian population—Slovaks, Romanians, Serbs, Croats and others—comprised a slight majority and occasionally displayed rebellious tendencies, particularly in the face of government "Magyarization" policy towards the end of the century. The assimilated Jews' "super-patriotism" was therefore useful in helping to shift the balance of power and influence firmly in the direction of Hungarians.

How and why Hungary's tolerance, acceptance and general "inclusion" of Jews turned, eventually, into a "politics of exclusion" and then destruction is described later. Here, however, a couple of *caveats* are in order. As indicated, in late nineteenth-century Hungary the situation of Jews, particularly that of the urbanized, "cosmopolitan" Jews of Budapest, was relatively more secure and more integrated than elsewhere in Eastern Europe, such as Galicia, Poland, Lithuania or other parts of Tsarist Russia. This did not mean, however, that their situation was unproblematic or that there were no currents of anti-Semitism. There were, as revealed by the notorious Tiszaeszlár affair.

In 1883 members of the local Jewish population in Tiszaeszlár, a tiny village in the far north-east of Hungary, were accused of the ritual murder of a young Christian girl. Although they were eventually acquitted, the moral panic that ensued unveiled the depths of anti-Semitism at that time, even resulting in a self-styled Anti-Semitic Party standing in the parliamentary elections of 1884 and winning 16 seats.

A second, qualifying factor is that in Budapest, not to mention the poorer provincial centres, not all Jews were rich bankers, industrialists and nobles. The majority were not. By 1914 the Jews of Budapest, who constituted 20-25 per cent of the city's population, were to be found in quite different socio-economic groupings. There were very rich Jews, very poor Jews, and others in the middle. This social diversification had an impact on the city, as economic circumstances determined where Jewish communities lived. There was no ghetto as such, nor a single, ghetto-like Jewish area (until 1944). Jews lived where they could afford to live. In the decades prior to 1914 rich Jews lived in the wealthy Lipotváros district, near parliament, or along Andrássy út. Poor Jews, particularly poor immigrants, congregated around Teleki tér, beyond the Great Boulevard. This was a social distinction that continued right through to the 1930s. The atmosphere of both areas has been captured by two works published in English.

Magda Denes begins her memoir, *Castles Burning*, by evoking the lifestyle of a moderately wealthy Jewish family living in a large apartment in Személynök utca (today Balassi Bálint utca), overlooking the Danube to the north of parliament. Her father, an editor, publisher and small-time operetta librettist, would spoil her with trips to the famous Gerbaud café and ply her with cakes and cream. She and her elder brother, Iván, lived in an idyllic world peopled by piano instructors, language teachers, maids and servants. The completely contrasting atmosphere of "Jewish" Teleki tér and its neighbourhood is portrayed later in her book and is also captured in *Homage to the Eighth District*, written by the Pressburger brothers, Giorgio and Nicola. Their work is peopled by sometimes appealing, sometimes obnoxious characters struggling for survival, occasionally helping each other but also fighting among themselves. Their portraits are set in post-war Budapest, but they reflect earlier times as well.

The area to the north of the Dohány utca Synagogue towards Andrássy út, and to the east towards the Great Boulevard, was a third, more middling, predominantly but by no means exclusively, Jewish quarter. This was an older Jewish area. Its roots could be traced back to the early nineteenth century and even beyond. Here could be found a multitude of traders and small-scale businesses—Jewish tailors, barbers, second-hand clothes dealers, bookshops, Jewish printers and publishers, kosher shops, clubs, cafés and soup kitchens frequented by Jews. Before emancipation and entry into the professional associations, business and trading would often be conducted in the cafés. The area also contained several synagogues and prayer rooms.

The historic heart of this district included Király utca. Gyula Krudy, writing in 1930, has left an impression of the street, as he remembered it from his youth:

This narrow street was filled with coaches... huge wagons loaded with enormous quantities of wares... Small carts stood in front of every store loading and unloading all day long... Boxes of oranges, lemons and figs piling up in every courtyard... salesclerks who looked exactly alike, who were all born and raised here, wearing identical

caps... And the trolley bus rode along Király utca in the midst of the
crowd and the seemingly chaotic mess...

There were people shouting, strolling up and down, leading children, "staring at store-windows and shopping as if this was their last day in Király utca." The atmosphere has gone, but you can almost imagine it by walking along Király utca today with your eyes half-closed, trying to ignore the modern-day vehicles and advertising.

Denominations and Differences

The nature of the relation between Jews and Gentiles in the nineteenth century perhaps throws light on some of the historical and physical characteristics of the Dohány utca Synagogue. The plans were made by a non-Jewish architect, Lajos Förster of Vienna. The commissioning body had admired a synagogue he had designed for the Austrian capital. Like his earlier work in Vienna, the style of Förster's Budapest synagogue is Romantic with a mixture of Byzantine and strong Moorish elements, which together make it one of the city's most striking and impressive buildings, both inside and out. Its two minaret-like towers, with their massive bulbous cupolas, echo the two columns before Solomon's Temple in Jerusalem while simultaneously suggesting the twin spires of Christian churches. The basilica form of the interior is also very much like a Christian church, with a nave and two side aisles. Indeed, at the time of its construction locals dubbed it the "Israelite cathedral". Were the Jews of Budapest implying that their place of worship was really not much different from those of their Christian compatriots?

The synagogue is "Neolog", a Hungarian denomination combining elements of both reform and Orthodox Judaism. The *bimah*, for example, where the readings are given, is not in the middle but at one end in front of the Ark, giving the impression of a raised altar area, as in a Christian church. There is a large organ (reform) but separate seating for men and women (Orthodox). Soon after its opening the use of Hungarian replaced Yiddish. Weddings were held inside, and not outside under a *huppah* or wedding canopy, as in an Orthodox synagogue. These details reflected one aspect of differences within the Hungarian Jewish communities; while Orthodoxy and its Hasidic variety were strong in provincial, particularly eastern Hungary, in the capital reform movements held sway.

In the immediate wake of legal emancipation in late 1867 and early 1868 a General Jewish Congress was held to unite all Hungary's Jews and establish representative bodies to consolidate their new legal status vis-à-vis the state. The congress took place in the Pest County Hall on Granadier Gasse (today Városház utca) in the city centre and was addressed by the then Minister of Public Education and Religious Affairs, József Eötvös. In the event, it turned out to be not only the first but also the last general congress of Hungarian Jews. Soon after its opening the Orthodox representatives withdrew and established their own organization. Their Budapest community (much fewer in number than the "Neologs") would eventually have its own synagogue built in Kazinczy utca, not far from Dohány utca. Here the *bimah* is in the middle of the building and there is no organ. The interior decoration (recently restored) is vivid Art Nouveau.

A third group of so-called Status Quo Jews emerged from the congress as a separate entity. Their synagogue was built in 1772 in Rumbach Sebestyén utca, in the same area. Interestingly, it is an early work—and the only one in Hungary—of the Austrian architect Otto Wagner, who later gained fame for his Viennese Secessionist creations. With its Romantic, Moorish-style façade and slim twin towers, also very much like minarets, from a distance you could be forgiven for thinking this was a mosque.

Baron József Eötvös (1813-71), the government minister who addressed the General Jewish Congress, had been instrumental in the drive for Jewish emancipation. He was one of Hungary's leading statesmen and a literary figure of note. He was also a scholar, becoming President of the Academy of Sciences in 1866. In the 1848-9 period he was critical of Lajos Kossuth's politics of confrontation with Austria, though he was actually much more of a radical democrat, being a strong advocate, for example, of peasant emancipation. His Education Act established compulsory elementary schooling in Hungary as early as 1868. His radical Nationalities Bill of the previous year, which would have given a degree of autonomy and language rights to Hungary's large number of non-Magyar citizens, was vehemently opposed and eventually watered down, which only stored up trouble for the future.

In the late 1830s Eötvös had studied social conditions in England and France, returning to Hungary deeply impressed by liberal philanthropy and even, according to some sources, utopian socialism.

Eötvös stood for the social mission of realist literature. His *A falu jegyzője* (The Village Notary, 1845), for example, was a biting satire about old Hungary and its feudal mentality. A statue of Eötvös stands today in the small square in front of the Inter-Continental Hotel, near the Chain Bridge.

Around the Dohány utca Synagogue

Restoration of the Dohány utca Synagogue began in 1989 and was completed in 1996. The costs were covered mainly by the Hungarian state plus donations from a variety of Jewish associations, in particular the American Emmanuel Foundation, whose fund-raising activities were largely spearheaded by film star Tony Curtis, the stage name of Bernard Schwartz, whose father Manuel had been a Hungarian emigrant to the US.

Today the synagogue is one of Budapest's main attractions, its dazzling interior never failing to impress visitors. The entrance ticket also gives access to the neighbouring Jewish Museum, which exhibits both liturgical and non-liturgical items from Jewish history in Hungary. That the history of Jews in what is today Hungary stretches back to well before the arrival of the Magyars is confirmed by a large, more than 2,000-year-old Jewish gravestone dating from the time when the area was part of the Roman Empire.

The Jewish Museum is not a Holocaust museum as such, although in the past it has had a small display dealing with the destruction of Hungarian Jewry. A specific Holocaust museum (more precisely, the Holocaust Documentation and Research Centre) opened in 2004 at 39 Páva utca in District IX. Its permanent exhibition, housed in an adjoining, beautifully restored synagogue dating from 1924, was finally opened in early 2006.

The Jewish Museum in Dohány utca was built in 1931 on the site of a former building that had been the birthplace of Theodore Herzl, the founder of modern Zionism. Herzl (1860-1904) spent his youth in Budapest but then moved to Vienna, with which he is usually associated due to his journalistic and propaganda activities there on behalf of the Zionist cause. Yet partly due to family connections, he never lost touch with Hungary and often visited his native land. What he did not find in Hungary, however, was much enthusiasm for the cause he espoused. Hungarian Jews were too assimilated, too bound up with their patriotism verging on nationalism to be interested in the idea of a separate homeland.

Between the synagogue and the museum building is a symbolic, brick section of the ghetto wall, erected around the local Jewish quarter in 1944. (It is symbolic in that the actual wall was constructed in a hurry from wooden planks.) The ghetto, the last to be established in Europe, enclosed over 60,000 people and existed from November 1944 until the arrival of the Soviet Red Army in January 1945. It was the only European ghetto to be liberated, in the sense that when the Soviets arrived tens of thousands of people were still clinging to life here. A plaque on the symbolic wall commemorates the liberation.

Another plaque with a similar inscription faces Wesselényi utca, behind the museum, marking the site of one of the ghetto gates. The text refers to the ghetto walls being pulled down on 18 January 1945 by the "liberating Soviet army". This is a rare surviving example of such phraseology on a public monument or plaque, though whatever else the Soviets might have brought to the city it was certainly liberation for the city's Jewish population. Between Wesselényi utca and the synagogue are many gravestones. These mark the site of a mass grave for thousands of people who died in the freezing winter of 1944-5 in the ghetto or while crammed inside the synagogue building.

Beyond the gravestones, set sideways to Wesselényi utca, is the Heroes' Temple, built in 1929-31 and named in memory of the Jewish

soldiers and officers who died fighting for Hungary in the First World War. Some of their names are recorded on a large plaque overlooking the graves. The courtyard beyond the Heroes' Temple contains a striking Holocaust Memorial in the form of a weeping willow, which takes the shape of an inverted Jewish *menora* or seven-branched candlestick. The leaves bear the names of families massacred by the Nazis. The metallic monument is the work of one of Hungary's most noted contemporary sculptors, Imre Varga. It appeared here in 1991. An inscription above is from the Bible and reads: "Whose pain can be greater than mine." A broken marble slab in front is inscribed simply with the word "Remember".

A number of marble slabs stand in a circle behind the memorial, bearing the names of "righteous gentiles", non-Jews including both diplomats and ordinary people, who, sometimes at great personal risk, helped save the lives of Jews during the Hungarian Holocaust. On the ground are listed some of the best-known rescuers such as Raoul Wallenberg, Carl Lutz and Angel Sanz Briz (diplomats from Sweden, Switzerland and Spain), Friedrich Born of the International Red Cross, the Papal Nuncio Angelo Rotto, the Catholic nun Margit Schlachta, the Lutheran pastor Gábor Sztehlo and Giorgio Perlasca, the Italian businessman who through bluff and determination assumed the role of a Spanish diplomat and gave protection to many. His dramatic exploits are portrayed in the feature film *Perlasca*, an Italian production filmed in Budapest and released in 2002. The list of "righteous gentiles" inscribed here is not complete. There were actually far more than indicated. At the time of writing, the number of authenticated Hungarian rescuers, whether famous or not, given on the website of the Yad Vashem institute in Jerusalem stands at 658.

The Goldmark Hall is at the far side of the courtyard behind the great synagogue. Built in 1929, it is named after the Jewish composer Károly Goldmark (1830-1913), creator of several renowned works including the opera *The Queen of Sheba*. When the anti-Jewish laws of the late 1930s and early 1940s hindered Jews from appearing on stage, the Goldmark Hall was one of the few places open to them, and thus it preserved the torch of Jewish culture.

Síp utca, a short way along Wesselényi utca, is home to various Jewish organizations. The street has been the focal point of Jewish community activities for decades.

A Tragic Twist

The Hungarian Holocaust represented a peculiarly tragic twist within the overall genocide, coming as it did in the late months of the Second World War and particularly in view of the historical experience of Jews in Hungary, their relative assimilation and their patriotic beliefs. Although many thousands suffered badly and many died in forced labour battalions on the eastern front and elsewhere, Jews in Hungary were relatively safe during the Second World War until the German occupation of the country in March 1944. A terrible exception, however, involved the rounding-up in the summer of 1941 of "alien Jews"—mainly refugees from Poland and other countries, but also Hungarians who could not prove their citizenship—and their deportation from the country. According to Randolph Braham's estimates, over 16,000 were taken to the border and handed over to the SS. They were then transported across eastern Galicia and into occupied Soviet Ukraine, where they were machine-gunned in pits near the village of Kamenets-Podolsk. It was the first five-figure massacre, he says, within the Nazis' Final Solution programme. As a plaque on its wall testifies, the Rumbach Sebestyén Synagogue was one of the holding centres for such Jews rounded up in Budapest

Shortly after the German occupation (Hitler rightly believed that Hungary was a weak and insecure ally, which might change sides), deportations, with the help of the Hungarian political and police authorities, began, first of all in the provinces. In the short space of barely two months around half a million Hungarian Jews (about 95 per cent of the provincial Jewish population) were arrested and sent to Auschwitz and other camps.

Jewish citizens of Budapest were mainly spared that fate, partly due to a decree issued by Miklós Horthy in early July 1944 halting the deportations, although anti-Jewish activities still continued, particularly after mid-October and the Arrow Cross fascist takeover. The reasons for the halt in deportations were mixed; Budapest was being bombed, it was becoming clear that the Allies would soon be victorious, Horthy and others had the idea of pulling out of the alliance with Germany, and international pressure was mounting against the deportations, in particular from neutral countries' diplomats in Budapest and from US President Roosevelt. The assimilation, inter-marriage and often conversion of many Budapest Jews also made it psychologically more

difficult to "cleanse" the city of Jews, as had happened in the provinces.

After the overthrow of Horthy on 15-16 October and the fascist coup, the terror against Jews and anyone who helped them or opposed the new regime intensified terribly. People were simply shot in the street or taken to the riverside and killed. In those weeks the Danube flowed not blue, but red with blood. Of the 35,000 citizens of Budapest who died from whatever cause during the bitter siege of the winter of 1944-5, almost half were Jewish citizens. A movingly simple memorial, consisting of empty shoes, stands on the side of the Danube in memory of those murdered by the Arrow Cross at this spot.

How did all this come about? Why was it that the situation of the Jewish communities of Hungary—whose members for decades had contributed not only to the country's business, industrial and financial development, but also to its artistic and cultural life as prominent architects, sculptors, artists, poets, writers, journalists, playwrights and critics—changed so dramatically, shifting from acceptance and toleration to institutionalized anti-Semitism, hatred and extermination?

From Inclusion to Exclusion

One change began in a formal sense with the passing into law of an act of parliament known as the *Numerus Clausus*, which restricted the rights of Jews to attend university. The act, one of the earliest anti-Semitic laws of twentieth-century Europe, was passed in 1920, a full thirteen years before Hitler came to power in Germany. Although the act was never fully implemented and was even formally repealed in 1928, its appearance on the statute book reflected a major shift in public thinking and discourse. Why did that occur?

The aftermath of the First World War saw chaotic times in Hungary. The collapse of the Austro-Hungarian Dual Monarchy brought independence for the country but also three revolutions of sorts—all within the space of one year. The soldiers' and workers' revolt of October 1918 (mirroring a phenomenon repeated across Europe) brought to power the liberal-radical politician Mihály Károly. His rule, first as premier then as president, quickly gave way in March 1919 to the Bolshevik-inspired Council Republic under Béla Kun and a communist-led leftist coalition. That lasted until August, when Kun's government resigned in the face of encroaching counter-revolutionary forces under the leadership of Miklós Horthy. Meanwhile, the victorious wartime allied powers were putting pressure on Hungary for border revisions, and the country's territory was being invaded by Romanian forces from the east and, to a lesser extent, by Czech and Slovak forces from the north.

Anti-Jewish feeling flourished in these turbulent times. Firstly, there was a tendency to blame Jews for the collapse of the Monarchy, for having been associated with the pre-1914 liberalism that was perceived as having led to its weakness. Secondly and more specifically, since many of the leaders of the Council Republic had been Jews or of Jewish descent, it was easy to conflate anti-communism and anti-Semitism. The Jews could be blamed for what was seen as the catastrophe of the Bolshevik period, even though the "Jewish commissars" were not specifically acting in Jewish interests nor was it the case that most Hungarian Jews supported them. This did not stop atrocities being committed against Jews in 1919-20 as part of the counter-revolution.

Then came Hungary's post-war settlement, the 1920 Trianon Treaty, which dismembered the country as two-thirds of the territory and half the population were lost to neighbouring countries. Ironically, the treaty was signed not by Kun's Bolshevik government but, reluctantly, by representatives of the new Horthy regime, which then devoted the next quarter century to trying to reverse this territorial defeat, leading the country again into a lost war.

One of the consequences of Trianon was that "truncated" Hungary, and Budapest in particular, saw an influx of ethnic Hungarian refugees from the newly created states of Czechoslovakia and Yugoslavia and the enlarged Romania. Some simply did not want to live under a new, non-Hungarian government ruling a non-Hungarian state. Others had been forced to move, having lost their jobs in public administration. As the newcomers struggled to survive in makeshift encampments, sometimes living in railway wagons on the outskirts of Budapest, it was easy for anti-Semites to raise the cry that Jews occupied too many positions of authority—in the municipality, in government and in various offices—and that they ought to give way for "genuine" Hungarians. Another factor was that Hungary, within its new borders, was now almost entirely "mono-ethnic". Magyars constituted the overwhelming majority and thus the Jews, however patriotic, were no longer useful as a counterweight to potentially rebellious minorities.

This was the background to the shift in opinion. Yet despite the "white terror" of 1919-20 and the *Numerus Clausus*, which could be regarded as a temporary phenomenon in a drastic but short interlude, many Hungarian Jews continued to be convinced that their status in the country was secure. There was some justification for this optimism. As noted above, the Goldmark Hall, the Heroes' Temple and the Jewish Museum were all built in Budapest in the middle of the Horthy era. An artist such as the Shakespearian actor Oszkár Beregi, who had fled Hungary in the face of organized protests against him because he was Jewish, felt it was safe to return to Budapest in 1930 and continue his stage career. In the world of sport, Jews continued to excel well into the 1930s. At the infamous 1936 "Nazi Olympics" in Berlin, of the sixteen medals won by Hungary six were gained by Jewish sportsmen. One of them, the wrestler Károly Kárpáti, defeated the German finalist in front of Hitler's very eyes.

Nevertheless, as the 1930s unfolded anti-Semitism increasingly came to the fore. This was partly due to the political influence of Gyula Gömbös, who became Hungarian prime minister in October 1932.

Gömbös clearly had fascist leanings; he was the first foreign statesman to visit Hitler after the latter came to power and he was an admirer of the Italian dictator Benito Mussolini. Furthermore, what drew the Hungarian government and sections of public opinion increasingly towards Nazi Germany was the hope that a strong Germany, and a victorious one in any forthcoming war, would look favourably on Hungary's claims for the return of territories lost in 1920. Even before the war broke out it appeared that this was indeed a fruitful policy, since as Germany apparently grew in strength some of those territories were regained. Meanwhile, important developments were unfolding on the domestic front with regard to Hungary's Jewish citizens.

As if in imitation of Hitler's Germany, between 1938 and 1941 a series of four anti-Jewish laws were enacted, gradually but severely restricting the rights of Hungarian Jews. The first, passed on 28 May 1938, stated that certain professions such as journalism, acting, the law, medicine and engineering could only be practised by members of the relevant professional chamber or association. The number of Jews in each such association could not exceed twenty per cent.

As it was passing through parliament, a public denunciation of the bill was signed by 59 prominent figures, many of them non-Jewish and many in the world of arts. The list of signatories included the composers Béla Bartók and Zoltán Kodály, the writers Zsigmond Móricz and Lajos Zilahy, the painters Károly Kernstok and Tibor Vilt and many others. Their protests were in vain. The bill was passed, with all three heads of the main Christian churches in Hungary, Cardinal Jusztinián Serédi (Roman Catholic), Bishop László Ravasz (Calvinist) and Bishop Sándor Raffay (Lutheran) supporting the legislation in the Upper House and speaking in its support.

For many, like the protestors, the act was already a step too far in the wrong direction. For others it did not go far enough. A second anti-Jewish law was presented to parliament in early 1939. It aimed to exclude Jews from parliament itself and other public bodies, to prohibit Jews from holding certain positions such as newspaper editors, to limit their rights to purchase or hold property and to reduce their proportion in most white-collar professions to six per cent. On 3 February 1939 the Dohány utca Synagogue was the scene of a violent incident when a hand grenade was thrown among people leaving a service. Twenty-two people were injured, some of them mortally. The bill was passed on 5 May.

Yet another anti-Jewish law passed through the Hungarian parliament on 8 August 1941. Its provisions, aiming to "defend the race", prohibited marriage and sexual relations between Jews and non-Jews. "Jewish" was by now defined in strictly racial terms, which this time led to concerns among Christian leaders for those members of their congregations who were former Jews who had converted. The law, it seemed, would now regard them as Jews.

A fourth anti-Jewish law, banning Jews from owning or purchasing land, was adopted on 6 September 1942. By this time the country was at war. Hungary had joined the fighting on Hitler's side soon after the Germans began their invasion of the Soviet Union in early June 1942. As we have seen, while many Jews lost their lives in the forced labour battalions on the eastern front, it was not until the German occupation of Hungary on 19 March 1944 that deportations of Hungarian Jews to extermination camps began. The question remains, however, as to what extent developments in the inter-war period, particularly in the late 1930s, facilitated or made more acceptable those deportations.

Henrik Fisch thought he knew the answer and he issued a book about it after the war. Fisch had been Chief Rabbi of the Kápolnásnyék region, near the south-west end of Lake Balaton. During the war he lost his wife, his mother, his father, his elder sister, her husband and their five children, his younger sister, her husband and their three children, his mother-in-law, two sisters-in-law, another brother-in-law and others. Of twenty-three relatives in all, some died in Hungarian labour battalions, but most perished at Auschwitz, including his only daughter, Judit, aged seven. Fisch's small book, published in 1947, simply reproduced the speeches of the three church leaders in the Upper House during the debates about the first and second anti-Jewish laws of 1938 and 1939. For him their statements represented explanation enough. Parts of their speeches make for shocking reading.

The Jewish Tragedy

The destruction of Hungarian Jewry during the Second World War caused enormous losses to all parts of society. Members of the Weiss, Chorin and Kornfeld families, for example, all major figures in Hungary's economic, industrial and financial world throughout the inter-war period, were either deported or forced to flee the country. National fencing champion Attila Petschauer met a brutal and horrifying death in a forced labour unit. His story forms part of the background to the excellent 1999 English-language film *Sunshine* by award-winning director István Szabó. The film is more than one person's history, tracing the fortunes of three generations of a Budapest Jewish family from the pre-1914 era to the changes of 1989-90. It is a captivating work of art, portraying an essential element of Hungary's twentieth-century history.

Holocaust victims among the prominent personalities of Hungarian literature included Miklós Radnóti and Antal Szerb. The poet Radnóti was born in Budapest on 5 May 1909. Thirty-five years later, on or about 8 November 1944, he was shot in the neck by Hungarian forces near the village of Abda, eighty miles from Budapest, when unable to continue on a forced march from the slave-labour camp established by the copper mines at Bor in Yugoslavia. Twenty months after Radnóti's murder when his body was exhumed from a mass grave containing 22 corpses, a small dirt-soiled notebook was found in the pocket of his raincoat. It contained his last poems. These short but dramatic verses deal with the conditions of captivity and the forced march. "What more do you need for a myth?" asks George Szirtes in an introduction to a dual-language edition of Radnóti's *Camp Notebook*.

Yet as Zsuszanna Ozsváth, Radnóti's passionate and committed biographer shows, his politics, world-view and indeed his fame were not only formed by the terrible experiences of the ultimate stage of his life. Appearing on the scene in the early 1930s, Radnóti who had, she says, an "all-surpassing, at times wondrously sweet, anguished and tragic-heroic voice", was one of those European literary figures who could not but respond to the rise of fascism, even if his own personal circumstances also played a part in his perceptions—his mother and twin brother both died in childbirth.

Like Radnóti, the Budapest-born writer and critic Antal Szerb was a "non-Jewish Jew" from a family who had converted. Nevertheless, Hungary's racial law treated both as Jews. They were both hauled off to labour battalions more than once. Szerb was noted for his literary studies, having authored a popular history of Hungarian literature and a scholarly history of world literature. Though living through the same times as Radnóti, Szerb's own writings are less directly political, in a way lighter with a focus on personal and psychological themes. He was "more in keeping with the eighteenth than the twentieth century," says

Len Rix, translator of Szerb's acclaimed novel set in Italy, *Journey by Moonlight*. His fantasy *The Pendragon Legend* is situated in an English castle and is a parody of a detective-cum-ghost story. Antal Szerb was killed in late January 1945 at the age of 43 while being held prisoner in Balf, a village in western Hungary. Taken in the same transport as Szerb, the literary historian Gábor Halász and the writer György Sárközi also perished there.

Imagining the Holocaust
Like other countries Hungary has its own post-war "Holocaust literature". One of the most moving works in this genre to be found in English is the already-mentioned memoir *Castles Burning* (1998) by Magda Denes. By 1944 Denes was ten years old and living with her brother, mother, aunt and grandparents in Budapest's poor, predominately Jewish Teleki tér, her wealthy father having abandoned the family and fled to America. On 16 October 1944 members of the Arrow Cross fascist movement, which had seized power that day, raided the houses on Teleki tér, dragging the occupants outside and killing anyone who resisted. Magda and her family were living at no. 5, but they were lucky. They lived on the top floor and (with the help of a Christian neighbour) they managed to hide in the attic.

Castles Burning, written fifty years later, is Magda Denes' account of what it was like to be in Budapest during the Second World War and, in particular, during the cruel winter of 1944-5, the most brutal period of the Hungarian Holocaust. It is not often that one book can have so many qualities, but this one is simultaneously moving, humorous, tragic, dramatic, sad, lively, personal, as well as intensely readable. This is a memoir of impoverishment, persecution and survival as seen through the eyes of a young girl, with her thoughts and feelings expressed from the child's point of view. We read of Magda's intimate and loving relationship with her brother, Iván, seven years her senior. He looked like a "real Aryan" and in 1944, as a "runner" for the Jewish underground, was able to undertake the dangerous task of slipping in and out of the ghetto and Jewish safe houses, carrying messages, food and false papers. It is heartbreaking to learn of his fate. We read, too, of the family disputes, the hunger, the passion, the danger and the deaths, all through the eyes, ears and sometimes nose of a ten-year-old. The simple but extremely lucid narrative of the author-child contains numerous gems. As British journalist and war chronicler Phillip Knightley said of the book: "For its insights, passion and the picture it paints of a Jewish family trying to survive, it is unrivalled."

Before the war the poet, playwright and novelist Ernő Szép had been associated with the *Nyugat* circle of writers. In 1944 he was sixty years old. In the wake of the Arrow Cross takeover in mid-October, he and all the other men in his apartment house in Pozsonyi út in Budapest's District XIII were dragged away to forced labour. His *The Smell of Humans*, first published in 1945, is a combination of creative writing and autobiography covering the events following the German occupation of March 1944 and, recounted with both compassion and detachment, his own brief but awful experiences as a prisoner constantly exposed to taunts and possible summary execution.

One of the best-known works of Hungarian Holocaust literature today is undoubtedly *Sorstalanság* (Fateless) by Imre Kertész (although it was written over thirty years ago and barely received any attention in some of the major works assessing literature and cultural history published both before and after 1989-90). The stature of book and author were to change dramatically, however. In 2002, in the year of his 73rd birthday, Kertész was catapulted into international attention after being awarded the Nobel Prize for Literature "for writing that upholds the fragile experience of the individual against the barbaric arbitrariness of history," as the official citation put it. Kertész has written a number of novels, some of which are semi-autobiographical and based on his experiences of surviving Auschwitz and Buchenwald. Those that have been translated into English include his *Kaddish for an Unborn Child* and his *Fateless* (*Fatelessness* in its latest English-language edition). It then became public knowledge that a film version of *Fateless* was in production. The director was to be Lajos Koltai, internationally renowned as a superb Hungarian cameraman who had often worked with the noted director István Szabó and who had also spent time working in America. This was to be his debut as a film director, and it was to be a major (and expensive) production. That news, and the Nobel Prize award, generated a frisson of excitement in the media, and the making of the film was followed with enormous interest. Kertész appeared frequently in the press and on television, new editions of *Fateless* were published and reappraised and the film was eventually premiered with much publicity in 2005. It was Hungary's submission for Best Foreign Language Film for the 2006 Oscar awards.

Kertész has often claimed that his work is not essentially about the Holocaust but about the loss of destiny, how it can be taken away at a moment's notice and about the impact of such loss. Yet in content, at least, the book and film certainly fall within the Holocaust genre. We follow the story of a Jewish boy from Budapest, his experiences of being taken away, of being held in various camps, his interactions with other prisoners, his liberation and his journey home to Budapest and the reception he finds there.

Kertész is the first Hungarian to have been awarded a Nobel Prize for Literature, though he is by no means alone as an award winner. Before him there were already a total of fourteen Hungarian Nobel laureates—a considerable achievement given the number of Hungarians in the world. Interestingly, almost all of those (twelve) received the prize for specialist scientific research in the fields of chemistry, physics or medicine. One, Elie Weisel, in his *Night* had, like Kertész, written about his Holocaust experiences although he was a Nobel Peace Prize laureate. Also interesting is the fact that all bar one were awarded the prize for work they had done abroad, after they had emigrated from Hungary.

Fateless was first published in Hungary in 1975. The previous year had seen the appearance of *Hajtűkanyar* (Hairpin Bend) by Mária Ember, who was ten years old when the war broke out. Mixing documentary writing and fictional prose, Ember told the story of her family's experience of deportation to a labour camp in Austria. It was one of the first full-length autobiographical works about the Holocaust to be published in Hungary since the end of the Second World War thirty years previously—a surprising fact that perhaps needs some explanation.

It might have been assumed that after 1945 the communist authorities in Hungary would have welcomed and supported works about the attempted total destruction of European Jewry at the hands of the German Nazis and their allies in other countries. Not so. In fact, the situation was somewhat reversed in that the experiences of the persecuted Jews and any discussion of "the Jewish question" were ignored and swept under the carpet. The communists tended to view the Second World War primarily through the prism of "fighting fascism", with anti-Semitism and the Holocaust subsumed within a perceived clash of ideologies. There were complications, too, with raising the issue of anti-Semitism. In Moscow the exposure of an alleged, so-called doctors' plot in early January 1953 and the resulting arrests had definite anti-Semitic undertones, as had some of the political show trials elsewhere in Eastern Europe in the early 1950s, particularly in Czechoslovakia.

The man who emerged as Hungary's post-war Stalinist leader, Mátyás Rákosi, was known to be of Jewish descent, as were several of his closest colleagues. It was better not to stir the pot of Hungarian anti-Semitism, which had often been coupled with anti-communism in the past, and the best way to do this, they judged, was to ignore the whole issue. Similarly, it was better to forget that very soon after the war many former rank-and-file Arrow Cross members had joined the Communist Party, including its security apparatus, and had even been encouraged to do so. It was perhaps more than just symbolic that the former Arrow Cross headquarters at 60 Andrássy út was almost immediately taken over after the war by the new organs of state security, the political police.

Those Jews who survived the war in Budapest and those who managed to survive the camps and return home found themselves in a strange situation. There was widespread reluctance to examine where responsibility lay for the fact that around half a million of the country's citizens had not just died in a war, but had deliberately been put to death. It was much easier to put the entire blame on "the Germans" or on "fascism". The tensions and contradictions within such denial still find an echo in today's debates about the Holocaust. Apart from the psychological trauma of returning to a society that had betrayed them, Hungarian Jews returning from the camps also often had to face the shock of finding that their personal property had been stolen and that the apartments where they used to live were now occupied by other people reluctant to give up what they now considered their own. There were even some whispering campaigns against "greedy" Jews returning to cause trouble (again). No wonder that in this almost nightmare scenario many Jews decided to leave as and when they could—for Palestine, for Western Europe, for the United States.

So it was that Holocaust literature only began to emerge in the 1970s, after which there appeared a steady stream of not only

"Holocaust" but also "Jewish" works in Hungary. Few of these are easily available in English, but help is at hand in the form of *Contemporary Jewish Writing in Hungary*, an anthology edited by Susan Rubin Suleiman and Éva Forgács. Published in 2003, it contains extracts from the works of Ernő Szép, Imre Kertész and Mária Ember, and from writings by Béla Zsolt and György Konrád, who are mentioned elsewhere in this book. A total of 24 writers are included, the dates of publication of their extracted works ranging from the post-war era to the late 1990s.

The past decade and a half has seen a revival of Jewish culture and the establishment or re-establishment of Jewish associations, both religious and civic. Today, apart from literary works, there is a spate of pamphlets and books, ranging from tourist brochures to scholarly accounts, about different aspects of Jewish Hungarian history, culture and religious practices. Needless to say, the Dohány utca Synagogue has not been forgotten. Photographed from every angle in all its splendid glory, it is a centrepiece of many a publication dealing with Budapest's rich Jewish heritage.

chapter eleven

ABOVE THE CITY...

Castle Hill

In the summer of 1944, having miraculously avoided deportation to a death camp from the ghetto of Nagyvárad (today Oradea, Romania), the liberal journalist Béla Zsolt returned to war-torn Budapest, which was then the target of Anglo-American bombing. Just outside the Eastern Railway Station his train paused for a while. "From where the train was standing," he later recalled,

> *I could see the Castle District and within it the Royal Palace with its green dome, rising high above the city. For twenty-six years every sort of crime, bluster, villainy and incompetence had spread through the country from this palace. Hovering above the oily cloud, the lead cover of the dome glistened provocatively, as if intent on demonstrating that while the unfortunate city in the valley might be suffocated by smoke and fear, the Castle District up there was still immune... With anger and despondency I gazed at the arrogant Castle District and the dazzling reflection of the sunlight in its hundreds of unbroken windows. Was it conceivable that it would continue to hover over us after the end of the war, because the Anglo-Saxons preferred to see a continental country ruled by an admiral, rather than by the continental people themselves?*

The reference is to Admiral Miklós Horthy, Regent of Hungary, who had been in effect the arch conservative head of state for all but the first twelve months of the twenty-six years that had passed since 1918 and the end of the First World War. Yet Zsolt's presentiment proved unfounded. In October 1944 Horthy was overthrown by a fascist coup after clumsily trying to arrange Hungary's withdrawal from the war. He would never return to power (the rule of the Hungarian fascist Arrow Cross lasted barely four months). Nor did the Royal Palace, Horthy's inter-war seat and residence, escape destruction, though that was due to the winter siege of the capital by the Soviets and the Germans' desperate

189

resistance on Castle Hill rather than to any Anglo-American action. The Royal Palace would never again be either seat or symbol of power. Not that the Castle District had always been the centre of political authority in Hungary. For the first two centuries of the Hungarian state the royal capital had been Esztergom, a town by the Danube up river from Budapest. This was where Hungary's first monarch, Stephen, had been crowned in the year 1000 and this was the location of the royal palace until the mid-thirteenth century, when, following the sacking of the country by invading Mongols and their eventual retreat, King Béla IV had a fortress built on what is now called Castle Hill, a 200-foot-high, mile-long plateau overlooking the Danube. Today nothing remains of either the fortress or its accompanying residence.

During the time of the Angevin kings Charles Robert (ruled 1307-42) and Louis the Great (ruled 1342-82) a new castle was built. Then a large Gothic palace arose under Holy Roman Emperor Sigismund of Luxemburg, who was king of Hungary from 1387 to 1437. A system of fortifications was also built to defend the palace. It is really only from the time of Sigismund that Buda became the permanent royal seat.

The reign of the celebrated King Matthias (1458-90) is regarded as the golden age of the palace and of Buda generally. Matthias had most of the Gothic buildings rebuilt in Italian Renaissance style and had new buildings added. There were marble baptismal fonts, spacious banqueting halls and bed chambers with gilded ceilings. Outside were lawns, gravel paths, fish ponds and fountains. The Royal Palace became a significant European centre of politics, culture and art. A large library was assembled, and scholars, writers, architects, musicians and others flocked to the court, particularly from Italy.

The Italian connection became particularly strong after 1476 and the marriage of Matthias to Beatrix of Aragon, the younger daughter of the King of Naples. With her came Francsesco Bandini, who had entered her father's service after spending years with Marsilio Ficino, the influential Florentine philosopher, theologian, linguist and translator. In Hungary Bandini soon became Matthias' friend and close adviser. Another Italian humanist who promoted Renaissance culture in Buda was Antonio Bonfini, who arrived in the mid-1480s.

Matthias' great Corvina library was renowned throughout Europe as one of the greatest contemporary collections of historical chronicles and philosophical and scientific works. Some sources say that in size it was second only to the Vatican library. In addition to being a sponsor of the arts, Matthias was also a great military strategist and leader. In 1485 he even conquered and for a time ruled from Vienna. Coupled with the traditional view according to which he was also a "just ruler", it is not surprising that many legends grew about him.

In the rear courtyard of the former Royal Palace stands a popular statue composition known as the Matthias Fountain. The work of the renowned sculptor Alajos Stróbl and placed here in 1904, it recalls one of the romantic tales associated with Matthias, who is presented here in hunting garb, holding a crossbow. A stag lies at his feet. A seated figure on the left portrays Galeotto Marzio, an Italian humanist scholar who was a chronicler at the king's court. On the right is Szép Ilonka (Ilonka the Beautiful), immortalized in a romantic ballad of nineteenth-century poet Mihály Vörösmarty. Ilonka falls in love with the king after she meets him by chance hunting in the forest. But later, discovering who he was, she dies of a broken heart, believing her love to be hopeless.

The legend of Matthias the great humanist ruler has lasted over the centuries to this day. Even in the era of state socialism Matthias was put on a pedestal. In a chapter on the history of Hungary, a guidebook published in Budapest in the mid-1950s described him as a great ruler who created a strong national state, built up the country's economy and introduced the art and culture of the Renaissance. But in 2002 a major exhibition at Budapest's National Széchényi Library entitled *Potentates and Corvinas* cast a somewhat different light on the matter. A weighty scholarly volume published simultaneously with the same title examined the question of power and culture in the Renaissance era, arguing that: "While earlier rulers had used the manifestations of culture such as art, architecture, literature or libraries for the purposes of their majestic representation, in the fifteenth century nearly all rulers in Italy faced problems of legitimacy and thus attempted to utilize culture as a tool of legitimation to gain, consolidate or pass on power. Hungary's King Matthias, who himself faced the legitimacy issue both at the beginning and the end of his reign, saw instructive examples and patterns to be followed in the cultural policies of Italian princes and financier-autocrats."

Matthias did not have royal blood in his veins. He came to the throne in defiance of the principle of the right of succession but was rather selected by criteria of suitability, based not on humanist philosophy but on the vested interests of the feudal aristocracy and the lesser nobility. Furthermore, the issue of illegitimate origins arose in connection with his natural son János Corvin, when it became evident that Matthias would have no legitimate successor. Thus, the argument goes, in view of his low lineage and then with regard to the succession, he saw it necessary to support culture, the arts and sciences in an "Italian" manner, not only for purposes of show, but also to justify the legitimacy of his reign and his succession. A rather sharp conclusion is drawn: "What has so far been attributed to his modern education, to his naive admiration for splendour, self-contained patronage of art, to his subtle sense of pomp or perhaps even to his in-born love for books all turn out to be nothing but outward forms of strategies aimed at securing legitimacy. For this, he found the best models in Italian princes."

After Matthias' death in 1490 decline set in, partly and precisely because disputes arose over the succession. A long-term result of political weakness was the Turkish occupation of Buda in 1541, following which there was a period of plunder and destruction. Churches in the Castle District were turned into mosques, most of the wealthy population fled and houses were left to ruin. The palace, however, suffered little structural damage during the period of Ottoman rule, although many of the interior furnishings and the precious library were dispersed. The building was destroyed, however, during the three-month siege of 1686 when a "Western coalition" of Christian armies supported by Pope Innocent XI finally expelled the Turks from Buda.

Victory over the Turks was proclaimed and celebrated all over the Christian world. But the century and a half of Ottoman rule, the destruction caused by the siege and, not least, the ravages carried out by the victorious armies left the castle district with only about 600 inhabitants as against 8,000 in the time of Matthias. Reconstruction began slowly and continued into the following century. Formerly Gothic houses were rebuilt in Baroque style. The traces of reconstruction can be seen today in the many houses with Gothic sedilia in their gateways and Baroque upper floors.

Buda became a royal free borough in 1703, but the former splendour did not return as the Habsburgs maintained their rule from Vienna. Important government offices were situated in Pozsony (today Bratislava). Under Charles III (ruled 1711-40) the ruins of the medieval palace were pulled down and a new, smaller palace was built. Later, during the reign of Maria Theresa in the second half of the eighteenth century, a large palace comprising over 200 rooms was constructed. The university was based here between 1777 and 1784 after it had been moved from Nagyszombat (Trnava, Slovakia). Later the Viennese court assigned the palace to the Palatine, the Habsburg representative in Hungary.

During the 1848-9 War of Independence Buda Castle was occupied by the Hungarians and later recaptured by Habsburg forces. Many dwellings again suffered serious damage and the Royal Palace was burnt down. Following the establishment of the Austro-Hungarian Dual Monarchy in 1867, large-scale extensions were planned for the Royal Palace under the direction of the architect Miklós Ybl. He added a new building looking westwards (today the National Széchényi Library).

With the unification of Buda, Pest and Óbuda in 1873, the Castle District again started to develop, although the municipal authorities were now based in Pest. New government and ministerial offices were built, the Matthias Church was reconstructed and the palace enlarged. After Ybl's death, work was resumed by Alajos Hauszmann in 1893. He more than doubled the length of the buildings overlooking the Danube by adding a replica of the Maria Theresa wing to the north and connecting the two wings by a central block topped by a dome. This symmetrical neo-Baroque palace was completed in 1905.

The Second World War brought a further wave of destruction when in the winter of 1944-5 German troops entrenched on Castle Hill attempted to hold out in face of the besieging Red Army. By the time Budapest was finally liberated on 13 February not a single habitable house remained in the residential area in the northern part of the Castle District. Painstaking reconstruction took place over the following forty years. The war-time destruction had revealed earlier Gothic, Baroque and some Renaissance elements that had been built over. Where possible, these were reincorporated into the reconstructed houses and other buildings, almost every one of which is today a listed monument. The streets of the Castle District are hence a product of post-1945 rebuilding, but in view of the way in which that was carried out, the area has a certain "medieval" atmosphere.

As for the Royal Palace, all that remained at the end of the war was a burnt-out shell. During the course of reconstruction, which started in 1950, excavations revealed remnants of the former medieval palace. Hauszmann's large block was rebuilt, though with a simpler roof and a neo-Classical dome. The interior was reconstructed for museums, work being finally completed only in the 1980s. Today the former Royal Palace, which dominates the Buda skyline as seen from the Pest embankment, is home to two major museums: the Hungarian National Gallery and the Budapest History Museum.

The National Gallery

Unlike the National Gallery in London, the Hungarian National Gallery (Magyar Nemzeti Galéria) in Budapest actually *is* "national" in that, with very few exceptions, only Hungarian paintings and other works of art can be found here (the country's main collection of non-Hungarian works is housed in the Museum of Fine Arts in Heroes' Square). The contents of the National Gallery owe much to the nature of its origins, which stem from the national reform movements of the first half of the nineteenth century. A founding society of the National Picture Gallery was set up in 1845 to embrace the cause of Hungarian artists, its first exhibition opening the following year. The National Picture Gallery was fully established in 1851 and this can be regarded as the precursor of today's National Gallery.

When it opened in 1906, the Museum of Fine Arts took over the holdings, which had been greatly enhanced by the acquisition of the Esterházy family's collection in 1870. Later, a separate New Hungarian Picture Gallery opened in 1928 in the building which is today the Academy of Fine Arts on Andrássy út. In 1953 works belonging to the municipality of Budapest were incorporated and the resulting collection constituted the core of the National Gallery. In 1957 the Hungarian National Gallery was established as an independent museum in the building of what is today the Museum of Ethnography in Kossuth tér. It moved to the reconstructed Royal Palace in 1975. The first large painting at the rear of the landing at the top of the first flight of stairs is Peter Krafft's huge *Zrínyi's Sortie* (1825), portraying a major national event of Hungarian history—Miklós Zrínyi's attack against Ottoman forces at Szigetvár in 1566. Paintings of the nineteenth century like this with a strongly national theme are well represented in the gallery as a major element of the permanent exhibition. Prominent, for example, are two large canvases by Gyula Benczúr. His *The Baptism of Vajk* (1875) depicts King (St.) Stephen (ruled 1000-38), whose pagan name was Vajk. His conversion to Christianity, and that of the Magyars, signified a major step in the integration of Hungary into European culture and politics. Benczúr's *Recapture of Buda Castle* (1896) is another work based on a national theme, the end of 150 years of Ottoman rule. The portrayal here of Karl of Lotharingia and Eugene of Savoy indicate, however, that the end of one empire meant the start of another, that of the Habsburgs. The picture pointedly highlights one of the many triumphs-cum-tragedies in the twists and turns of Hungary's history. Further examples of "national historical" painting include *The Mourning of László Hunyadi* (1859) by Viktor Madarász. Hunyadi was beheaded by the Habsburg Ladislas V in 1457, but the allusion to the execution of many Hungarians following the failed 1848-9 War of Independence was clear to all. Hungary's tragic fate, depicted here, is also reflected in many of the other paintings in the gallery.

Considerable space is devoted to works of Mihály Munkácsy. Munkácsy, as we have seen in Chapter Four, was one of the very few nineteenth-century Hungarian painters to gain international recognition, partly because he spent most of his time in Munich and later Paris. He is noted for his genre paintings and rather romantic representation of ordinary characters, as exemplified here by his *Last Day in the Condemned Cell* (1870), but he also produced images of the better-off, as with his *Greyhound* (1882). Some of his landscapes have a definite "Turneresque" quality. Nineteenth-century trends departing from the national theme are represented by a number of artists including Pál Szinyei Merse, the "founder of Hungarian Impressionism". His *Picnic in May* (1873) is one of his most noted productions, but also on display are his *Lovers* (1870) and his bright *Meadow with Poppies* (1902).

All the schools of twentieth-century Hungarian painting up to 1945 are represented in the National Gallery, including the *plein-air* painters of the influential Nagybánya colony (Károly Ferenczy, Simon Hollósy *et al.*) and the "Pre-Raphaelite" artists based in the town of Gödöllő (Sándor Nagy, Aladár Körösfői Kriesch *et al.*). Although most are unknown outside Hungary, it can be seen that the trends that unfolded throughout Europe (post-Impressionism, Art Nouveau, Fauvism, Cubism, Constructivism, etc.) are reflected in many of the works exhibited here.

One who did not neatly fit any trend or category was Tivadar Csontváry Kosztka (1853-1919). His strange fusion of Expressionism and Symbolism is shown in the large *Ruins of the Greek Theatre at Taormina* (1905), hanging on the landing between the first and second floors of the gallery. Two of his other works are on either side. Csontváry's massive, colourful post-Impressionist canvases were virtually unknown in Hungary during the artist's lifetime. It is only in recent decades that his work has become appreciated both at home and abroad. On seeing his paintings at an exhibition in Paris in the 1940s, Pablo Picasso is alleged to have commented: "I did not know that there was another great painter in our century besides me."

Among the other exhibitions in the National Gallery one deserves particular mention—a group of late fifteenth- and sixteenth-century winged altarpieces in the former grand throne room of the Royal Palace. This striking collection is somewhat special in Central Europe. The majority of altarpieces and panel pictures on display come from churches in the former Upper Hungary (today Slovakia). Hungarian late Gothic painting reached its pinnacle in the early sixteenth century in the art of Master MS, as he is known, whose work is represented here by *The Visitation.*

A small Habsburg Crypt can be found in the basement of the former Royal Palace. Access is via the National Gallery, though it can be visited only at set times with a guide. Here are several tombs of members of the Habsburg family associated with Hungary, notably Palatine Archduke Joseph (1776-1847). The Habsburg palatines (imperial representatives) resided in the Royal Palace from the late eighteenth century to 1849.

Visitors entering or leaving the National Gallery via its main entrance on the Danube side may care to pause and admire the magnificent neo-Baroque equestrian statue of Prince Eugene of Savoy, who led the "Christian coalition" that drove the Turks out of Hungary, his victory at the battle of Zenta in 1697 sealing the fate of Ottoman rule over the country. The statue is considered to be the finest work of sculptor József Róna, a self-made man from a poor background who had only three years of schooling but managed to obtain a scholarship to study at the Academy in Vienna. The statue was originally commissioned by the town of Zenta (today in Serbia) for the 200th anniversary of the battle, but in the event Emperor Francis Joseph bought it and ordered that it be erected in the Castle District. Róna is reported as saying that it was placed in "one of the most beautiful spots in the world". Certainly, on a fine day the view from the terrace here, overlooking the Danube and Pest, is magnificent.

Yet there is something rather curious about this wonderful statue being placed and remaining in such a prominent position above the city. Eugene's victory, which involved considerable destruction, not only signalled the end of a century and a half of Ottoman rule, but also heralded the much longer period of Habsburg domination over the whole of Hungary. To use the terminology of, and to draw a parallel with 1945, the driving out of foreign forces by other foreign forces in 1697 was simultaneously liberation and occupation. Could one imagine a large statue of, say, Soviet Marshal Voroshilov being erected in a similar place and still standing today?

Minus a Century

The Budapest History Museum is situated in the southernmost wing of the former Royal Palace, access being via the Lion Courtyard at the rear. The permanent exhibitions range from pre-historic, ancient, Roman and pre-Magyar times to the nineteenth century The displays are rather sketchy, which is understandable for some periods (local medieval culture, for example, having been almost literally swept away during the 150 years of Turkish rule) and for some periods are peculiarly non-existent (Budapest's twentieth century seems to have "disappeared" entirely).

The museum's exhibition of Gothic statues from the Royal Palace contains items found unexpectedly in 1974 during excavations undertaken in parallel with the long-term reconstruction of the Palace following the damage of 1944-5. These late fourteenth- and early fifteenth-century statues are mainly of secular figures and are believed to be the product of a Buda workshop where French influence was strong. Below ground are reconstructed parts of the medieval palace. Visitors are invited to weave through a series of passages, galleries, reconstructed halls, courtyards and gardens. Another fairly large permanent exhibition of the museum, Budapest in Modern Times, is lively, with texts in English, though it skips through quite a lot, sometimes with minimal presentation. Nineteenth-century themes predominate.

The large wing attached to the History Museum and forming the rear, western wing of the former palace complex today houses the National Széchényi Library, Hungary's main "deposit" library, on a par in terms of national standing with the Library of Congress in Washington and the (still-named) Lenin Library in Moscow. The collection was begun in 1802 on the initiative of Count Ferenc Széchényi (1754-1820), father of István, the noted nineteenth-century Hungarian reformer. Széchényi searched the entire country and, at his own expense, amassed a collection of books, which he donated to the nation. At the start the main home of the library was the National Museum in Pest, which opened in 1846. The Széchényi Library was officially declared the National Library in 1949.

The Church on the Hill

Can a pope be excommunicated by ordinary members of his Church? An attempt to do just that was made in Buda in 1302 after the death of András III, the last monarch of the Magyar Árpád dynasty, when citizens and clergy "excommunicated" Pope Boniface VIII for supporting Charles Robert of Anjou's claim to the throne in opposition to their favoured candidate, King Wenceslas of Bohemia. The scene of this extraordinary event was the Church of Our Lady on Castle Hill, commonly known today as the Matthias Church. In the event, the resistance of Buda crumbled after a few years and Charles Robert was crowned in the church in 1309. Apart from this occasion the church was not used for coronations in the Middle Ages, Hungarian kings usually being crowned in Székesfehérvár, a town some forty miles to the south-west.

Tradition has it that in 1015 King Stephen built a small church to Mary here, but that was destroyed during the Mongol invasion of

1241-2. The present church was founded by Béla IV following the invasion. It was originally a basilica comparable in style with the northern French Gothic architecture of the period. It became the parish church of the Germans who had recently settled in Buda, the poorer Hungarians, who were mostly farmers, vinegrowers and craftsmen, having to make do with the less grandiose Church of Mary Magdalene at the northern end of the Castle District.

At the turn of the fourteenth century the Church of Our Lady was remodelled into a hall church in high Gothic. A royal oratory was built during the reign of King Matthias Corvinus (1458-90) and the tower, which had collapsed in 1384, was rebuilt. The church became the scene of ceremonies and political events. Matthias' two marriage ceremonies (with Catherine Podebrad and Beatrice of Aragon) both took place here amidst great splendour.

Following the Ottoman victory over the Hungarians at the battle of Mohács in 1526, the ecclesiastical treasures of the church were transferred to Pozsony (today Bratislava). The Turks occupied Buda in 1541 and converted the church into the city's main mosque. The medieval furnishings were destroyed, as were the wall decorations. Two ornamental chandeliers above the high altar were taken to Constantinople, where they still hang in St. Sophia's. With the 1686 recapture of Buda, the church was given first to the Franciscans and later to the Jesuits, who restored the building, decorating its interior in a rich Baroque style. The church regained some of its former importance only in the second half of the nineteenth century. In 1867, following the founding of the Dual Monarchy, the splendid coronation of Emperor Francis Joseph as king of Hungary took place here to the music of Liszt's Coronation Mass, which had been specially composed for the occasion.

Deterioration, however, necessitated reconstruction of the church, and this took place under the direction of the architect Frigyes Schulek between 1873 and 1896. Where possible original structural and decorative elements were preserved, but Schulek designed new elements of his own with the result that only parts of the main walls, the square bottom part of the southern tower, the interior pillars and some parts of the Mary Portal on the south façade are genuinely medieval. The last king of Hungary, Charles IV, was crowned here in 1916 during the First World War. During the 1944-5 siege of Budapest the church was badly damaged, post-war restoration work not being completed until 1970. Today the Matthias Church, along with the Hungarian parliament and the Chain Bridge, is one of the emblematic buildings of Budapest and is a prime focus of interest for visitors to the city. In one sense, this puts the church on a par with Vienna's Stephansdom and the Cathedral of St. Vitus in Prague, though it is by no means as grand. A striking peculiarity of the interior is the decorative painting on the walls and pillars, designed by Bertalan Székely at the end of the nineteenth century and consisting of floral and geometrical motifs, partly medieval and partly Art Nouveau in character. The overall effect gives the church a rather Byzantine feel in contrast to the overall structure, which is neo-Gothic.

Part of the attraction of the Matthias Church is its location on Castle Hill and the view over the city obtained from the Fishermen's Bastion to its rear. The neo-Romanesque Bastion was also designed by Frigyes Schulek and built at the turn of the twentieth century as part of the reconstruction of the church and its surroundings. Tradition has it that this stretch of the medieval ramparts used to be defended by the fishermen's guild, though the name might also derive from a nearby former fish market. The panorama from here is superb, though the view from the less-frequented Citadel at the top of Gellért Hill, which is much higher than Castle Hill, gives a much more rounded, overall perspective of the city.

A large equestrian statue of King (St.) Stephen stands between the Matthias Church and the Fishermen's Bastion. Stephen (István), Hungary's first monarch, is depicted here wearing the Hungarian crown and the coronation mantle. Stephen's significance is manifold. He ended by force the squabbling of the Magyar tribes, thus unifying the country and establishing the Hungarian state. He was also instrumental in the conversion of the pagan Magyars to Christianity, thus "Westernizing" the country. During the celebrations of 2000, marking the 1000th anniversary of his coronation, it sometimes seemed from the propaganda that Stephen was the precursor to Hungary joining the European Union.

The statue was designed by Alajos Stróbl and completed in 1906, its altar-like, neo-Romanesque limestone plinth the work of Frigyes Schulek. The relief at the rear modestly shows Schulek as a bearded figure kneeling before King Stephen holding a model of the Matthias

Church. This historical mix-up is complemented by the fact that the crown on Stephen's head could not have existed in Stephen's time (see Chapter Seven). Nevertheless, the entire work well suited the pompous nationalism of the time of its creation.

Most visitors to the Castle District tend to restrict themselves to the area between the former Royal Palace and the Matthias Church. Relatively few venture into the tranquil streets to the north of the church, even though there are a number attractions here such as the Music History Museum, the Museum of Catering and Commerce, the large Military History Museum, the Telephone Museum and the Castle Cave, which gives access to part of an extensive network of underground passages dating from the Middle Ages.

chapter twelve

...AND BELOW

With a Pure Heart: Attila József

Gát utca is a narrow, not-too-clean and unremarkable street in Budapest's District IX, on the Pest side of the Danube. The entrance marked no. 3 leads to a small courtyard with several doors, beside one of which a marble plaque proclaims: "Hey, bourgeois! Hey proletarian! Here I come—Attila József." A tiny one-room-and-kitchen flat here was indeed the place where, on 11 April 1905, Attila József, one of the greatest of modern Hungarian poets, first came into the world.

A century ago Gát utca was in the heart of the working-class district known as Outer Francis Town. You could not get much farther away, at least in atmosphere and spirit, from the Castle District and the Royal Palace above the city, and you can still feel the contrast today, as no. 3 now contains the small Attila József Memorial Museum, and so a visit allows a view of a two-room dwelling and courtyard in a classically poorer part of Pest.

József's father, a Romanian whose original name was Áron Josifu, worked in a soap factory on Soroksári út, a long thoroughfare running parallel with the Danube through southern Pest. Some of the old factory buildings in this formerly exclusively industrial area are still standing. Josifu abandoned his family when the young Attila was just three years old. His mother, who worked as a washerwoman, struggled on next to nothing to bring up Attila and his two older sisters. After being farmed out for periods to live with foster parents, Attila was taken under the wing of his guardian, Ödön Makai, a lawyer who married his elder sister, Jolán, in 1918. Recognizing the boy's talent, Makai helped him enter grammar school and then university in the southern town of Szeged, at the time the largest provincial centre in Hungary. In 1924, however, now aged 19, he was forced to leave the university, in effect expelled after an uproar following the local publication of his poem *Tiszta szívvel* (With a Pure Heart). It opened with lines declaring that the poet had no father and no mother, no country and no god, later continuing with the assertion that "with a pure heart" he would burn and loot, and, if necessary, even shoot. Such rebellious sentiments did not go down well in the early years of the conservative Horthy regime. He was told in no uncertain terms by the university's professor of linguistics, Antal Horger, that it would be impossible for the writer of such lines ever be able to find a teaching post and have influence over young minds.

This was not the first time that Attila József's poetry had landed him in trouble. Earlier in 1924 he had been accused of blasphemy due to his *Lázadó Krisztus* (Rebelling Christ). The case had gone all the way to the High Court before being dismissed.

In the mid-1920s József travelled abroad, spending time in Vienna and later Paris. In both cities, apart from studying, he mixed with Hungarian emigrés as well as with local anarchist, socialist and avant-garde circles. Back in Budapest, although already a member of the (legal) Social Democratic Party he joined the (illegal) Communist Party. In addition to producing "political" poetry, he occasionally led what today would be called writers' workshops for factory workers. Around 1933, however, in circumstances that are still unclarified, he was edged out of the Communist Party. Whatever the specific reason or reasons, József was arguably too much of a libertarian individualist and too interested in the wider, socio-psychological aspects of politics to fit neatly into the communist orthodoxies of the early 1930s.

This political estrangement, together with personal problems caused by repeatedly falling in love without finding real happiness, occasional skirmishes with the authorities caused by his poems, as well as financial difficulties (though he gained the support and the sponsorship of members of the wealthy Hatvany family) all contributed to depression and schizophrenic tendencies. He was only 32 when he committed suicide under the wheels of a train near Lake Balaton in December 1937. It was his eighth attempt to kill himself since the age of nine.

A number of themes overlap within Attila József's vast poetic output. He can be considered a poet of urban and industrial Pest. Verses such as his 1932 *Külvárosi éj* (Night in the Slums) talk of factories, textile plants, steel mills, cement works and power plants. The subject matter might be proletarian, but the approach was not forced in a Soviet-style "heroic" manner. Here the workplaces are like "family crypts" guarding the secret of a "mournful resurrection". Though highly political, language and style raise these works well above mere propaganda. Also with an urban connection, but not its industrial base, is József's classic *A Dunánál* (By the Danube), written in 1936. His biographer and a translator of his works, Thomas Kabdebo, calls this "the most majestic poem ever written on the theme of the river". (See Chapter One)

Love is another inescapable theme of József's poetry. It is a theme closely tied to his responses to individual women who burst into and sometimes equally quickly left his life at different times, yet reaching beyond the specifics of individuals. One of his most famous love poems is his 1933 *Óda* (Ode), a poem of heated passion which helped cause the attempted suicide of his then partner of three years standing, Judit Szántó, when she realized—on József's own admission—that it was intended for another woman. Commentators are fond of asserting that the woman he was really looking for, in his life and in his poetry, was his mother. "I love you like a child his mother" is one line of *Ode*, and a number of separate poems were written about his actual mother.

Rebellion was never far away from Attila József's thinking. The youthful despair and revolt of his 1924 *With a Pure Heart* was something spontaneous and predated his mixing with politically conscious activists in Vienna and Paris. (Read in a certain way and with a literal translation—"I have no father, I have no mother; I have no country, I have no god"—it could be concluded that Attila József was the world's first rap poet!) His direct political involvement in Vienna, Paris and later Budapest has tended to be interpreted in terms of a Marxist orientation, particularly in view of his attraction to the Communist Party. His anarchist connections and thinking have been somewhat overlooked, which tended to suit his Marxist promoters in post-1945 Hungary (by which time he had been "rehabilitated" and accepted into the then officially perceived canon of Hungarian literature). Such connections have also been overlooked by his anti-Marxist or non-Marxist promoters post-1989.

Yet there is something entirely different and entirely modern in József's anarchistic orientation, which arguably speaks to today's world of youthful rebellion much more than is usually acknowledged. As he wrote to one of his sisters from Paris in April 1927, instead of the "free competition of shopkeepers" he saw "the dictatorship of banks and great industrial trusts". With this, he continued, "goes the militarization of both state and public life, and… with the division of global territory and the colonization of small states by the great powers, we are living in the age of world wars," such that "it becomes obvious we can't even speak of 'freedom'."

There is also much, often desperate, self-analysis in his verses. "Sitting on a branch of nothingness" was how he once described himself in a poem. Kabdebo quotes an interview he made in 1964 with the Hungarian writer Tibor Déry, who recalled the young Attila József as having had "a chip on his shoulder from being a working-class lad among middle-class intellectuals, for which he overcompensated by being cocky almost all of the time." József was not only the object of psychoanalysis and psychotherapy in his last years, but was also an interested student of their theories and an advocate of fusing the nascent traditions of Freudian insights with left-wing political thinking. (In this he was perhaps also ahead of his time, though he was not alone, even in his own era. George Orwell in Britain—see the relatively unknown second half of his famous *Road to Wigan Pier*—and Wilhelm Reich in Germany—see his *What is Class Consciousness?*—were two other inter-war figures grappling with the problems of the mass psychology of politics against the background of the rise of fascism. Like József, they were creative, individualistic, libertarian figures who ran up against the political orthodoxies, both left and right, of their day.)

Inevitably, perhaps, overall interpretations of Attila József have varied greatly. The changing reception has partly reflected changing times, both during his lifetime and since his death, though, importantly, his underlying popularity has remained intact throughout. József even anticipated such changes of taste. The poet's name, "if he has one," he once wrote in a verse, "is just a trade-mark." Thomas Kabdebo discusses who was closest to Attila József among his European contemporaries. He finds parallels, among others, with Brecht, Mayakovsky, Aragon and Lorca, though he emphasizes that "he was his own man with experiences unique to him," hence difficult to compare with others.

For years 11 April, the date of József's birth, has been Hungary's "day of poetry". In 2005, coinciding with nationwide celebrations in Hungary of his centenary, UNESCO declared that the "world poetry day" would that year be an "Attila József Day". That the rise of someone born into poverty in 1905 in Gát utca in Pest, who received little formal education, studied at universities but obtained no degree, and who became a poet of Budapest, should be acknowledged both nationally and internationally can only be described as remarkable.

On the Margin: Lajos Kassák

Lajos Kassák was another unusual, creative and provocative figure of twentieth-century Hungarian arts, whose perspective, like that of Attila József, was also far removed from the worldview of those who ruled from Castle Hill. He was born in 1887, eighteen years before József, in Érsekújvár (then in Hungary, today the sleepy town of Nové Zámky in Slovakia, fifteen miles from the present Hungarian border).

The son of a Slovak pharmacist's assistant and a Hungarian washerwoman, Kassák failed his primary school exams and became a fitter's apprentice. He worked in Győr and Budapest as a metal-worker, occasionally becoming involved in the organization of strikes. In 1909 he embarked on a European journey, much of it on foot, which would take him through Austria, Germany, Belgium and France. After his return to Hungary he wrote about his experiences of life at the bottom. In 1915 Kassák launched a journal called *A Tett* (The Deed), which aimed to be a forum for the avant-garde. It was also anti-war and in October of that year it was banned by the authorities. Almost immediately Kassák began publication of another journal on the same lines called *Ma* (Today). It also had a chequered but somewhat longer career, involving literary programmes, concerts and exhibitions aimed at inducing social change.

Both politically and artistically Kassák was always a radical internationalist; a contributor to the 1991 work by Mansbach *et al.*, *Standing in the Tempest*, calls him "one of the most outstanding advocates of international modernism in the twentieth century"—so it was perhaps inevitable that he had clashes both with established cultural circles and with orthodox left-wing political leaders.

Although at odds with its dogmatism, Kassák was an active supporter of the 1919 Council Republic, participating in the work of the cultural commissariat. Yet in a famous exchange Béla Kun, the communist leader of the time, once denounced Kassák's journal as representing "bourgeois decadence". Kassák wrote a critical article in reply, "Letter to Béla Kun in the Name of Art", which he also issued as a pamphlet. György Borsányi, in his biography of Kun, published in English in 1993, comments that later generations may well wonder: "in which Communist country could a writer attack the top man of the 'party-state' in a pamphlet published legally by himself, yet retain his office even after that?" The episode proves, he concludes, that "the ethics and norms of the Communists in 1919 were rather different from their ethics after 1945." That may be true in many respects, but Borsányi fails to add that shortly after Kassák's response, his journal, *Ma*, was banned.

After the dissolution of the Council Republic Kassák spent some time in prison and then left for Vienna, where he restarted the publication of *Ma*. Among his works of this period was a joint production with László Moholy-Nagy (of Weimar Bauhaus fame) of *Buch neuer Künstler* (Book of New Artists), which appeared in 1922 (republished in English in 1992). Kassák returned to Hungary in 1926 and continued his publishing activities. His output in this period included *Angyalföld*, the novel's title referring to the name of a working-class district in Budapest. What many regard as his major achievement is his *Egy ember élete* (Life of a Man), a work of biographical literature that appeared in several volumes in the late 1920s and 1930s.

In the same period he was involved in a leftist political-cultural journal and movement called *Munka* (Work), concerned with the cultural and political education of young workers and students. Kassák's attitude was critical of both orthodox communism and social democracy, but from a left-wing perspective. This intriguing position probably explains the lack of attention given to his politics in works of literary and cultural history published both before and after 1989-90. For example, Tibor Klaniczay's *History of Hungarian Literature*, published in 1983, hints that Kassák dropped out of revolutionary politics, meaning rather that he was estranged from the Communist Party. László Kósa's cultural history of the past two centuries, which appeared in 2000, tends to ignore Kassák's politics.

For a while in the post-1945 period Kassák occupied a prominent post, being appointed vice-president of the Hungarian Arts Council, in which position and as an editor he contributed to the development of post-war cultural life. After 1949 and the rise of local Stalinism his anti-authoritarian unorthodoxy inevitably led to a period of "internal exile", during which it was difficult for him to be published. Unlike some of his colleagues, however, he never renounced the radical Constructivism of his earlier period, and in the post-1956 era of "reconciliation" he even received a certain amount of official recognition, being the recipient of the state Kossuth Prize in 1965.

Lajos Kassák died in 1967, aged eighty. He is buried in the "resting place of writers", the large Farkasrét Cemetery in Buda. A small museum in Budapest is devoted to his life and work. It can be found in a wing of the eighteenth-century former Zichy Mansion in Óbuda, the entrance to which is at 1 Fő tér. The exhibition includes examples of Kassák's Constructivist designs, montages, book jackets and paintings.

The Spirit of Joseph Town

Born in 1878, the son of a middle-class Jewish doctor, Ferenc Molnár, was brought up in circumstances quite different to those of both Lajos Kassák and Attila József. Yet he, too, in his most famous work, *A Pál utcai fiúk* (The Paul Street Boys), wrote of the city and its everyday life. The novel, written in 1906, has been translated into many languages and is still one of the most popular books in Hungary today. Set in Pest in the turn-of-the-century environment of Pál utca or Paul Street (still there, running between Mária utca and the Great Boulevard in District VIII), the work revolves around two groups of schoolboys who fight for control of a derelict building site. This simple story, which has captured the imagination of different generations, is in part an allegory about the causes of violence and war, though on the surface it can be read simply as an amusing and captivating tale of young lads in Pest, whose exploits range from playing marbles by the wall of the National Museum to having fun in the Botanical Gardens. A film version of *The Paul Street Boys*, directed by Zoltán Fábri, was made as a Hungarian-American co-production in 1968.

Molnár spent the last years of his life in the US. His international fame rests not only on his well-known novel. He was the author of the play *Lilliom*, better known in its 1945 musical version, *Carousel*, by Rodgers and Hammerstein. His *The Play's the Thing* was adapted by P. G. Wodehouse for the English stage and, according to Mátyás Sárközi, Molnár's grandson and biographer, had "the misfortune to be ruined" by a later, "over-ambitious adaptation" by Tom Stoppard under the title *Rough Crossing*.

Paul Street is part of the Józsefváros (Joseph Town) district of Pest, for years a mixed though predominantly poor area of central Budapest. Six decades after the appearance of Molnár's *The Paul Street Boys*, the writer Endre Fejes based his *Rozsdatemető* (Scrapyard) largely in the same neighbourhood. Published in 1962 and considered one of the greatest books of its time, it tells the story of the Hábetler family, working people whose main concern is to live a decent life, no matter what happens around them—be it wars, liberation or the introduction of a new social system. Whatever happens in the outside world, the family continues to celebrate birthdays and namedays with fried fish and special wine. Writing to this author about the book in early 1985, Eszter Timár, a keen observer of the Budapest cultural scene, remarked: "Perhaps it was the first time we read about this section of society, people who are unaware of the changes around them. The novel was a kind of sociological proof that however wonderful our socialism might be, it just does not reach a very considerable layer." One reason for its success, she offered, is the book's "very simple and very effective style, presenting every 'great' historical event from the point of view of whether fried fish was or was not available at the time."

Zsuzsa Koncz, consistently one of Hungary's most popular singers of the past four decades, has also evoked the spirit of Joseph Town. One of her most enduring songs, *A Kárpátiék lánya* (The Kárpátis' Daughter), opens with the line: "In the depths of Joseph Town, where the lights are dark, a blond girl was brought up in the 1950s." It tells the story of this young woman who eventually leaves for America and ends up successfully married, with two sons, a house and car in New Jersey. Yet she constantly dreams of home and one day returns, sentimentally ordering cakes from the old patisserie in the Joseph Town district she remembers so well.

Koncz was born in 1946 in the small village of Pély on the Hungarian Great Plain. She shot to fame while still a teenager after being one partner of a winning duo in a 1962 TV talent contest. She performed with several big-name pop and rock bands of the 1960s and 1970s including Illés, Metró and Fonográf, but became mostly known for her poignant and moving solo performances of songs written by her colleague of many years, János Bródy. One of those songs, *Ha én rozsa volnék* (If I Were a Rose) almost became an anthem for change in the 1980s:

If I were a rose, I would bloom not only once
I would blossom four times every year...

If I were a gate, I would always be open;
I would let anyone in, wherever they came from...

If I were a window, I would be so large
that the whole world would be visible...

If I were a street, I would always be clean...
And should tanks happen to tread on me
the earth would collapse underneath, crying.

The political message was not lost on anyone, and when it came to this number in her concerts the audience would light up candles, hold them aloft, and sway back and forth, singing along with her.

Zsuzsa Koncz continues to attract a large following. She is still performing in front of enthusiastic audiences, as well as making discs. In 2005, as if in acknowledgement of an affinity with the poet who reached out to people below the level of official power structures, she recorded her sung versions of a number of Attila József's poems, the centenary of whose birth was celebrated that year.

Penetrating the Language Barrier
It is not easy to walk into a bookshop in Western Europe or the US and find an array of translations into English of Hungarian literature from the "liberalized" Kádár era, even less so from the post-Kádár, post-1989 years, let alone even earlier periods. Some Hungarian publishers do issue English translations of modern and contemporary poems and novels, but international distribution and marketing difficulties, not to mention lack of foreign demand due to lack of knowledge of the Hungarian literary scene (itself partly a reflection of the distribution and marketing predicament, but also due to the peculiarly isolated nature of the Hungarian language) mean that these translations do not reach as wide an audience as potentially possible. At the same time, this explanation is not as clear cut as might be implied, since a perusal of the range of contemporary Hungarian literature published in German reveals a more positive picture. Perhaps the inward-looking nature of the Anglo-Saxon mentality also plays a part—as does distance, since clearly the average Austrian or German has a better idea of where Budapest and Hungary are.

Nevertheless, all is not negative. People with access to academic or well-funded public libraries may be able to find copies of *The Hungarian Quarterly*, a journal which traces its roots to the 1930s and the desire, sometimes blowing officially or semi-officially hot and sometimes cold, to present Hungarian culture to the English-speaking world. The journal has consistently published an array of selected fiction and poetry, as well as articles about Hungarian history, society and the arts in general. The standard has been invariably high, although the style of the analytical pieces is generally somewhat over-academic and dry.

Even more accessible insights into contemporary literature became available in 2004 with the publication of *An Island of Sound: Hungarian Poetry and Fiction before and beyond the Iron Curtain*. The introductory essay by George Szirtes is very readable, understandable and informative. It touches with insight on some of the perennial themes of Hungarian letters—the issues of anxiety, isolation of language and geography, melancholy and withdrawal, displacement and flight (sometimes inner, sometimes as emigration) and it does so with a certain amount of humour. "The deep myth of Hungarian history is that of defeat snatched from the jaws of victory, of centuries of misery following on days of joy," writes Szirtes. Nor does he fail to acknowledge and locate historically the essentially political nature of much Hungarian literature. Hence the attraction of this collection, since it revolves around the political turning points of 1956 and 1989. Presented here are selections from the works of some writers (relatively) well-known outside Hungary, such as György Konrád and Péter Esterházy, as well as some lesser-known figures who have emerged on the scene in the past decade or so, though as Szirtes pointedly notes: "It is too early to generalize about the new generation."

George Szirtes was born in Budapest in 1948 and arrived in England as a refugee in 1956. He is prolific both as a literary translator and as a writer and poet and is thus admirably suited to perform the role of mediator between Hungarian literature and the English-speaking world. In this sense, Szirtes partly follows in the footsteps of Professor George Cushing, who up to the time of his death in 1996 could rightly be described as the doyen of a very rare breed, in that he was a British, but non-Hungarian, specialist in and translator of Hungarian literature. Cushing first learned Hungarian during the Second World War after he had been called up during his studies at

Cambridge to serve in the secretive SOE, or Special Operations Executive. As a member of a small unit he was going to be parachuted into Hungary, but the operation was eventually abandoned. He pursued his Hungarian studies after the war, applying for a scholarship and being admitted to Budapest's prestigious Eötvös College. In 1949, however, he was expelled as a suspected British agent, a victim of the emerging Cold War hysteria (all other Western graduate students were also asked to leave). From his 1952 PhD thesis, *Széchenyi, Kossuth and National Classicism in Hungarian Literature* to the time of his death, Cushing wrote profusely and enthusiastically on Hungarian themes, often for specialist journals. In 2000 the Budapest publisher Corvina Books issued a collection of his writings under the title *The Passionate Outsider*. The book contains a selection of his essays, both on diverse themes of Hungarian literature and on some of its great writers, including Sándor Petőfi, Imre Madách, Endre Ady, Mihály Babits, Dezső Kosztolányi and Zsigmond Móricz.

Expatriates and Bank Robbers

What of the post-Kádár era in terms of everyday experience? What was life in Budapest like after the political changes of 1989-90? The answer depends on who you ask and what they remember, or on what you read. One writer who has apparently left us an image of Budapest in the early 1990s is Arthur Phillips, who spent two years in the city at that time. His well-received debut novel is set in Budapest and revolves around the attitudes and mini-adventures of a small group of North American expatriates. Paradoxically, the title of the work is *Prague* and on the front cover of the first edition there was an atmospheric image of the Czech capital's famous Charles Bridge.

"The novel is named not for a city, but for an emotional disorder," the author explains in an interview reproduced on the book's website. The disorder, he continues, leads people to think that "if only I were over there, or with her, or doing that, or born fifty years earlier, then I would be where the action is. So for some expatriates living in Budapest, Prague felt like the place to be. Had those same people been in Prague, Budapest would have seemed like their paradise misplaced."

Nevertheless, because of its setting the book certainly captures, or is believed by many to capture, something of the atmosphere of early 1990s Budapest, albeit through expatriate eyes. But is it real? In so far as the characters in the book come across, in varying degrees and combinations, as pretentious, often rich, often shallow, ignorant of their surroundings and dreaming of things that are not there, then it is real—given that many, though by no means all, of the North American expatriates who flooded to Budapest after 1989 in search of fortune and adventure were, indeed, some or all of these things.

Prague received a wave of extremely positive publicity, as can be seen from the book's website, which, at the time of writing, includes extracts from well over fifty reviews. The praise is generous: "Ingenious debut novel... haunting poignancy" (*New York Times*); "devastating emotional accuracy" (*Christian Science Monitor*); "rich meditation on post-ideological ennui" (*The New Yorker*). Most of the comments highlight what might be called the book's psychological or sociological dimensions, though some comment on the author's "grasp of history" and his "sense of place" (*The Baltimore Sun*).

Phillips himself says that while his main characters are "entirely fictional", Budapest's geography in his book—streets, metro lines and parks—are "as close to accurate as I could recall." That is a fair assessment; though what of the book's grasp of history? A large section of the work deals with over a century of Hungarian history through the fate of the fictional Horváth family publishing house. It is a bold and laudable attempt and is to a large extent, as the author claims, historically "accurate-ish". Yet it is disappointing that by the time the story gets to the post-1918 period the freer-flowing format gives way to a schematic list of historical "points", presented in the novel in the form of a questionnaire concerning how to keep a business afloat during difficult times. It is here that, unfortunately, some historical mix-ups and misunderstandings occur. The German occupation of March 1944, for example, is confused with the Arrow Cross coup of seven months later. However, Phillips has been quite honest: "As for research, I did a little background reading in standard Hungarian histories, and lied whenever I couldn't find the details I wanted. It would be very foolish to treat anything in *Prague* as trustworthy history. It's a novel, and I was therefore free to fudge and fiddle whenever I liked the sound of something better than the truth."

Anyone turning from *Prague* to another highly-praised work, set mainly in 1990s Budapest and also written as the first book by a young American author, might be forgiven for being initially sceptical, since the author, journalist Julian Rubinstein, spent only eight months in Hungary and Transylvania. Rubinstein's *Ballad of the Whiskey Robber*, as suggested by its intriguing sub-title, "A True Story of Bank Heists, Ice Hockey, Transylvanian Pelt Smuggling, Moonlighting Detectives, and Broken Hearts", is not a work of fiction, although it reads like a thriller. Fact is often stranger than fiction, and this account of the adventures of a real-life, whiskey-swigging Budapest bank robber, the Hungarian Transylvanian and ice hockey fanatic from an underprivileged background, Attila Ambrus, often seems unbelievable.

Not unlike some Western expatriates, Ambrus made his way to the Hungarian capital (in his case illegally) to seek his fortune and make a name for himself. He did both eventually, but not by realizing his aim of becoming a (rather inconsistent) goalie for Budapest's renowned Újpest ice hockey team. His fame and fortune came from robbing post offices and banks, and running rings around the Budapest police. Between January 1993 and October 1999 Ambrus planned and executed, sometimes alone, sometimes with a partner, 29 robberies, netting, as Rubinstein calculates, over 195 million forints in total (US$840,000 at the 1999 exchange rate). Not that the money was prudently invested—after each robbery it was frittered away on fast cars, fast women, casino gambling and expensive holidays in exotic locations.

As *Ballad* relates, the media attention in Hungary given to Attila Ambrus' bank-robbing exploits and the difficulties the police had in tracking him down generated a certain mythical status for this obviously bright and energetic criminal. The fact that his robberies were essentially non-violent (he only fired his gun occasionally into the air, and many of his female bank employee victims remembered him as being rather polite when he demanded the cash—he even brought flowers on one occasion) contributed to a "gentleman bandit" image, allowing comparison with Robin Hood and Sándor Rózsa, a romanticized Hungarian highwayman of the nineteenth century.

Rubinstein's account of the robberies, the mistakes of the police and the emotional roller-coaster of Ambrus' personal life make for a good read by themselves, but what adds to the spice is the inclusion, through anecdotal and factual evidence, of a picture of the social setting within which this small-time criminal sprang to national prominence. *Ballad of the Whiskey Robber* undermines the widely held (Western) myth according to which the 1989-90 political and economic changes in Budapest and elsewhere in Eastern Europe, which "brought democracy and the free market", were obviously and of necessity "a good thing". True, many people benefited from these changes, but many did not, at least not in the initial period, as is reflected by some striking data.

Between 1989 and 1993 Hungary's GDP actually fell—by more than twenty per cent. It recovered in the second half of the 1990s, but that meant it was still only around the level of a decade before. Those on low incomes were particularly hard hit, as revealed by the level of inflation relating to consumer goods and services, which peaked in 1991 at an annual rate of 35 per cent. The rate abated, but it was still just under 25 per cent in 1994. Registered unemployment was only 0.6 per cent in early 1990. Four years later it had jumped to over 12 per cent.

These "economic shock" statistics should be viewed in a regional context. As noted right at the start of this book, Budapest is not Hungary and the capital managed to avoid the most serious effects of the economic downturn. In the worst hit regions, the far east and north-east of the country, unemployment was more than double that of Budapest, in some areas even approaching forty per cent. Furthermore, the murky rules of the privatization process, whereby state-owned enterprises were sold—often for a song—allowed for shady deals and corrupt practices, or practices perceived as such. People accused of political and financial wheeler-dealing, making billions in the process, often got away with it. The new emerging elites were often the old elites articulating a new jargon. No wonder a "nobody" like the whiskey-drinking Attila Ambrus appearing on the scene, grabbing his share of the loot without harming anyone, while thumbing his nose at the authorities, could assume almost heroic status.

Julian Rubinstein may have only spent eight months in the region, but he says he spent three years on his book, interviewing with the help of interpreters over one hundred people, many of them several times. He has also used documentary material from both the media and the police/legal/prison establishment(s). (Ambrus was eventually caught and sentenced, but to relate how and why here would be to spoil a potentially good read for many.) We can, in good faith, therefore, assume that what *Ballad* says is true. That assumption, however, is undermined somewhat by a number of factual mistakes in the book, which really should not be there. Some of them are rather curious, such as the reference to Csepel Island, "in the middle of the Danube River as it enters Budapest from the south." Csepel is, indeed, at the southern end of the city, but the Danube flows into Budapest from the north! Hungary famously opening its border with Austria to allow fleeing East Germans to cross to the West *en masse* took place in September 1989, not as given in the book in May of that year. "Most of the street names were Russian," Rubinstein writes of Budapest in 1988, giving a certain, perhaps "expected" flavour to the city of that time. However, what he writes is simply not true.

Nevertheless, *Ballad of the Whiskey Robber* can certainly count among English-language works worth reading for an insight into aspects of Budapest in the 1990s, and it has been noted as such. Rubinstein's website, like that of *Prague*, includes a number of glowing recommendations, with one from an authoritative source. According to the respected Hungarian publication *Élet és Irodalom* (Life and Literature), *Ballad of the Whiskey Robber* is "one of the best books ever written about post-1989 Hungary".

Attila Ambrus, Rubinstein tells us, was often troubled by animosity and name-calling due to his Transylvanian origins. Here another myth (though not specifically a Western one) is undermined. The idea that Hungarians in Hungary have a natural sympathy for their ethnic brothers and sisters from neighbouring countries is not as close to reality as might be expected from the habitual pronouncements of Hungarian nationalists. It is one thing to express strong feelings on behalf of Transylvanian Hungarians "over there"—it is quite another when the recipients of such empathy might end up "here".

Nothing seemed to show the limits of ethnic solidarity more clearly than a virtual test of the matter, which took place on 5 December 2004 in the form of a referendum, the first of its kind on the issue in Hungary. The question concerned whether Hungarians living in neighbouring countries might gain Hungarian citizenship. It produced a bitter conflict and generated much argument. The question was: "Do you think parliament should pass a law allowing Hungarian citizenship with preferential naturalization to be granted to those, at their request, who claim to have Hungarian nationality, do not live in Hungary and are not Hungarian citizens, and who prove their Hungarian nationality by means of a 'Hungarian Identity Card' issued pursuant to article 19 of Act LXII/2001 or in another way to be determined by the law which is to be passed?"

It was not a simple question, and many of those who argued for a "no" vote stressed the lack of clarity, particularly with reference to the final phrase. There were also arguments about what it would mean if passed, whether there would be an influx of immigration to Hungary, whether the country could cope financially with the potential extra claims on services like education, health care and pensions, and whether such new citizens remaining abroad might be able to vote in Hungarian elections. In the event, just under 19 per cent of the electorate voted "yes" to this question, while just under 18 per cent voted "no". The referendum could not be declared valid since for it to be so at least 25 per cent of the electorate had to vote one way or the other. Furthermore, the overall turn-out was low, an uncommon event in post-1989 Hungary where earlier referenda on NATO and EU membership both produced turn-outs of over fifty per cent and where in the last general election before the "citizenship" referendum, in 2002, the turn-out was over seventy per cent.

The issue touched on historical and emotional questions stemming from the break up of the Austro-Hungarian Dual Monarchy after the First World War and the 1920 Treaty of Trianon, under which large numbers of ethnic Hungarians found themselves "stranded" in neighbouring countries. The treatment and status of these minorities and how the Hungarian state should relate to them has been a prominent theme ever since. Part of the campaign for a "yes" vote in the referendum involved the claim that it would help heal the wounds of the past. Nevertheless, the fact that over eighty per cent of the electorate either did not think the issue was worth turning up to vote about or actually voted "no" surely says something. Discovering what exactly that is still probably depends on who you talk to.

A Clothes Hanger Perspective
A third American writer who has put pen to paper, or fingers to keyboard, to record something of the atmosphere of Budapest in the 1990s is Michael Blumenthal, who lived in the city for four years from 1992, working as a visiting university professor. Blumenthal's *When History Enters the House* is a collection of essays he wrote during his stay,

mainly for the locally published *Budapest Week* and *The Budapest Sun*, two "expatriate" newspapers of varying quality, though always benefiting from the inclusion of one of his pieces.

Blumenthal's style is both readable and poetic, which is not surprising since he is a published poet. It is also humorous, often in a self-deprecating way, as with his hilarious account of struggling with a weirdly designed clothes hanger he once encountered in the locker room of the university's swimming bath. With his treatment—a whole essay is devoted to it—the hanger somehow becomes a metaphor for Central Europe.

Blumenthal was certainly enraptured by many aspects of the city others would be glad to see the back of. In that sense, it reflects a certain nostalgia for times past, or rather in danger of passing. There is a short elegy, for example, for *lángos*, that popular fried batter still available at markets and some street stalls, though quickly giving way to American "fast food". Blumenthal also manages to find praise for the battered look of the city and even its car-parking chaos (in his time you could park for free anywhere, often on the pavement, a practice encouraged by street signs showing a parked car mounted on the kerb). The practice and the signs, curious to Western visitors, continue, but now one must pay for the privilege of parking throughout the city centre, which, along with the construction of both above-ground and underground car parks, has eased somewhat the earlier chaos of non-stop searching for non-existent parking places.

When History Enters the House is a cry of anguish against many aspects of post-1989 Hungary. Blumenthal was not happy to see Budapest flooded with mobile phones and one thousand and one varieties of soap powder. For him "real life" (read humanity) was/is elsewhere, to be found, partly at least, among the elderly men and women he lovingly portrays. It is also to be found among society's critical thinkers, and in this regard his collection includes sympathetic appreciations of Árpád Göncz, Hungary's president throughout the 1990s, and the internationally renowned writer György Konrád, clearly one of Blumenthal's favourites.

Michael Blumenthal counts himself as "a writer of relatively unread, unavailable, unadvertised and undistributed books", a self-defined reputation clearly undeserved, though unfortunately probably true. His nostalgia for certain "old" practices and "old" social phenomena is shared by many Hungarians who view the Kádár era in a rather benign way. Does this explain the fact that of the five general elections to have taken place in Hungary between 1990 and 2006 three produced winning results for the Hungarian Socialist Party, successor to the former ruling party of the Kádár era? Perhaps, but jumping to conclusions should be avoided; the party is quite different, for example in its free-market economic policies, from its predecessor.

Again, Budapest itself has been different from elsewhere. Though a Socialist Party stronghold, the mayor, consistently re-elected throughout the period 1990-2006 (another election is due as this book is appearing) has been Gábor Demszky, a prominent founding member of the liberal Alliance of Free Democrats, which emerged in the late 1980s from Hungary's underground opposition movement.

Traditions and discontinuities, progress and paradoxes—these are the characteristcs of Hungary and, often in complicated and diverse ways, of its capital, Budapest.

FURTHER READING

History

Andrási, Gábor *et al.*, *The History of Hungarian Art in the Twentieth Century.*
Budapest: Corvina, 1999. An illustrated account, period by period.
Bender, Thomas & Schorske, Carl E., *Budapest and New York. Studies in
Metropolitan Transformation, 1870-1930.* New York: Russell Sage
Foundation, 1994. Scholarly, readable studies of contrasting urban,
political, social and artistic development.
Braham, Randolph, I.., *The Politics of Genocide. The Holocaust in Hungary.*
Detroit: Wayne State University Press, 2000.
Buzinkay, Géza, *An Illustrated History of Budapest.* Budapest: Corvina, 1998.
Detailed, very readable large-format book, with fine illustrations.
Cunningham, John, *Hungarian Cinema: From Coffee House to Multiplex.*
London: Wallflower Press, 2004. A very good history, including social
and political aspects.
Dent, Bob, *Budapest 1956—Locations of Drama.* Budapest: Európa, 2006. An
account of the 1956 uprising in Budapest, examining what happened at
different locations.
Frigyesi, Judit, *Béla Bartók and Turn-of-the-Century Budapest.* Berkeley, CA:
University of California Press, 1998. In addition to Bartók, includes
much on Ady.
Gerő, András, *Modern Hungarian Society in the Making: The Unfinished
Experience.* Budapest: CEU Press, 1995. A critical look at issues of social
consciousness and popular cults in the era of the Austro-Hungarian Dual
Monarchy.
Gluck, Mary, *Georg Lukács and his Generation, 1900-1918.* Cambridge, Mass:
Harvard University Press, 1985. The story of an influential group of
Budapest thinkers and artists.
Jalsovszky, Katalin & Balog Stemler, Ilona (eds.), *History Written in Light: A
Photo Chronicle of Hungary, 1845-2000.* Budapest: Helikon, 2001.
Excellent pictures on political and social themes with informative
captions.
Lendvai, Paul, *The Hungarians: One Thousand Years of Victory in Defeat.*
London: C. Hurst & Co., 2003. Perhaps the most readable and
enjoyable work in English on the complicated history of the Hungarians.

Hajdu, Tibor, *The Hungarian Soviet Republic*. Budapest: Akadémiai Kiadó, 1979. Includes a chapter on the cultural politics of the 1919 Council Republic.

Hanák, Péter, *The Garden and the Workshop: Essays on the Cultural history of Vienna and Budapest*. Princeton, NJ: Princeton University Press, 1998. Themes include urbanization, images of Germans and Jews, the cultural role of operetta and social marginality and cultural creativity.

Király, Béla & Bozóki, András (eds.), *Lawful Revolution in Hungary, 1989-94*. Highland Lakes, NJ: Atlantic Research & Publications, 1995. How Hungary's peaceful political changes came about.

Komoróczy, Géza (ed.), *Jewish Budapest: Monuments, Rites, History*. Budapest: CEU Press, 1999. A detailed illustrated guide to Budapest's rich Jewish history and heritage.

Litván, György (ed.), *The Hungarian Revolution of 1956*. London: Longman, 1996. One of the best all-round accounts; includes discussion of different interpretations.

Kósa, László (ed.), *A Cultural History of Hungary in the 19th and 20th Centuries*. Budapest: Corvina/Osiris, 2000. Up-to-date scholarship covering intellectual life and social history. Full of facts, but sometimes rather dry.

Lukács, John, *Budapest 1900: A Historical Portrait of a City and its Culture*. New York: Grove Weidenfeld, 1988. A celebrated work revolving around some key events of 1900 but which takes in the whole pre-1914 era.

Mansbach, S. A. *et al.*, *Standing in the Tempest: Painters of the Hungarian Avant-garde, 1908-1930*. Cambridge, Mass: MIT Press, 1991. On the Hungarian contribution to early twentieth-century modernist aesthetics. Includes the role of artists during the 1919 revolutionary upheaval.

McCagg, William O., *Jewish Nobles and Geniuses in Modern Hungary*. Boulder, CO: East European Monographs, 1972. A pioneering work on the role of influential Jews in Budapest up to 1918.

Mitchell, David, *1919: Red Mirage*. London: Jonathan Cape, 1970. Covers the political upheavals that erupted across Europe and elsewhere following the First World War. Includes eyewitness accounts and discussion of events in Budapest.

Ranki, Vera, *The Politics of Inclusion and Exclusion*. New York: Holmes & Meier, 1999. A clear account of the changing relationship of Jews and nationalism in Hungary.

Romsics, Ignác, *Hungary in the Twentieth Century*. Budapest: Corvina, 1999. Covers economic, social, political and cultural developments.

Török, Gyöngyvér (ed.), *The Széchenyi Chain Bridge and Adam Clark.*
Budapest: City Hall, 1999. Essays on the history of Budapest's most
famous bridge and the people who created it.
Völgyes, Iván (ed.), *Hungary in Revolution, 1918-1919: Nine Essays.* Lincoln,
NE: University of Nebraska Press, 1971. Includes Frank Eckelt's "The
Internal Policies of the Hungarian Soviet Republic".

Other Non-fiction

Bart, István, *Hungary and the Hungarians: The Keywords. A Concise Dictionary
of Facts and Beliefs, Customs, Usage and Myths.* Budapest: Corvina, 1999.
A well-written and often humorous insight into things Hungarian.
Bartók, Béla, *Letters.* Budapest: Corvina, 1971. A selection edited by János
Demény.
Bátki, John (ed.), *Krúdy's Chronicles: Turn-of-the-Century Hungary in Gyula
Krúdy's Journalism.* Budapest: CEU Press, 2000. Selections from the keen
observer of Budapest life.
Blumenthal, Michael, *When History Enters the House: Essays from Central
Europe.* Port Angeles, WA: Pleasure Boat Studio, 1998. Insightful
observations and reflections of an American who spent time in Budapest
in the early 1990s.
Bojár, Iván András (ed.), *Contemporary Architecture in Hungary.* Budapest:
Vertigo, 2002. A large section is devoted to individual buildings in
Budapest. Includes explanatory texts.
Denes, Magda, *Castles Burning.* London: Anchor, 1998. An outstanding
memoir of life in Budapest before, during and after the Second World
War, as seen through the eyes of a ten-year-old Jewish girl
Dent, Bob, *Blue Guide Budapest.* London: A&C Black, 2001.
Eősze, László, *Zoltán Kodály. His Life in Pictures and Documents.* Budapest:
Corvina, 1982.
Éri, Gyöngyi and Jobbágyi, Zsuzsa (eds.), *A Golden Age. Art and Society in
Hungary 1896-1914.* Budapest: Corvina/Lund Humphries 1990. An
excellent collection of illustrated essays.
Ernyey, Gyula (ed.), *Britain and Hungary. Contacts in Architecture and Design
during the 19th and 20th Centuries.* Budapest: Hungarian University of
Craft and Design, 1999.
Fekete, Éva & Karádi, Éva, *György Lukács: His Life in Pictures and Documents.*
Budapest: Corvina, 1981.

Gerő, András, *Heroes' Square Budapest: Hungary's History in Stone and Bronze*. Budapest: Corvina, 1990.

Heathcote, Edwin, *Budapest: a Guide to 20th Century Architecture*. London: Ellipsis, 1997. A pocket guide, district by district, concentrating on modernism.

Kenedi, János, *Do It Yourself: Hungary's Hidden Economy*. London: Pluto Press, n.d. An amusing and revealing tale of how a private house was built in the late Kádár era.

Keserü, Katalin. *Women's Art in Hungary 1960-2000*. Budapest: Ernst Museum, 2000.

Kürti, László, *Youth and State in Hungary. Capitalism, Communism and Class*. London: Pluto Press, 2002. A cultural history, focusing on Csepel, historically one of Budapest's main industrial districts.

Legány, Dezső, *Liszt and his Country, 1869-1873*. Budapest: Corvina, 1983.

Konrád, György, *Anti-Politics*. London: Quartet, 1984. Arguments from a prominent writer for change from "within" and from "below".

Konrád, György, *The Melancholy of Rebirth: Essays from Post-Communist Central Europe, 1989-1994*. San Diego/New York/London: Harcourt Brace & Co., 1995. An assessment of the situation created by political changes.

Lőrinczi, Zsuzsa (ed.), *Budapest in Detail*. Budapest: 6Bt, 1999. A very impressive, lavishly illustrated publication on the architectural details of the city—including cast iron, carved wood, ceramics and stained glass.

Lőrinczi, Zsuzsa and Vargha, Mihály (eds.), *Architectural Guide. Architecture in Budapest from the Turn of the Century to the Present*. Budapest: 6Bt, 1997. Almost 300 buildings, with illustrations and maps. Includes a historical survey by András Ferkai.

Márai, Sándor, *Memoir of Hungary, 1944-1948*. Budapest: Corvina/CEU Press, 1996. A celebrated writer records his experiences of post-war Budapest.

Moravánszky, Ákos, *Competing Visions: Aesthetic Invention and Social Imagination in Central European Architecture, 1867-1918*. Cambridge, Mass: MIT Press, 1998. Architecture of the Austro-Hungarian Empire, with comparisons of Budapest, Vienna and Prague set against the cultural and political background.

Pogány, István, *The Roma Café: Human Rights and the Plight of the Romani People*. London: Pluto Press, 2004. Not exclusively about Budapest or even Hungary, but a very absorbing account of the situation of gypsy communities.

Prohászka, László, *Equestrian Statues*. Budapest: City Hall, 1997. One of a pocket-book series entitled "Our Budapest", mainly including works on the city's different architectural styles and monuments.

Rév, István, *Retroactive Justice: Prehistory of Post-Communism*. Stanford, CA: Stanford University Press, 2005. Published in a series entitled "Cultural Memory in the Present", this work examines some of the ideological battlegrounds that have occupied Budapest intellectuals in recent times.

Rubinstein, Julian, *Ballad of the Whiskey Robber*. New York: Little, Brown & Co., 2004. A real life tale of crime and society, reflecting elements of Budapest life in the 1990s.

Szép, Ernő, *The Smell of Humans*. Budapest: CEU Press, 1994. A memoir of the Holocaust by one of the prominent voices of twentieth-century Hungarian literature.

The Hungarian Quarterly (formerly New Hungarian Quarterly) has consistently been a rich source of information in English about Hungarian history, literature, arts and society. The standard is invariably high, though somewhat over-academic. Published in Budapest, but should be available in major libraries world-wide. Some parts available on the internet.

Zsolt, Béla, *Nine Suitcases*. London: Jonathan Cape, 2004. A liberal publicist describes how he got caught up in, but finally managed to avoid, the deportations of Jews from Hungary in 1944.

Literature and Literary History/Biography

Aczel, Tamas & Meray, Tibor, *The Revolt of the Mind. A Case History of Intellectual Resistance behind the Iron Curtain*. New York: Praeger, 1959. Recounts the tense development of relations between writers and the political authorities in the years leading up to the 1956 uprising.

Ady, Endre, *The Explosive Country: A Selection of Articles and Studies, 1898-1916*. Budapest: Corvina, 1977. Writings from one of the "great voices" of early twentieth-century literary life. Introductory essay, translation and annotation by G. F. Cushing.

Ady, Endre, *Neighbours of the Night*. Budapest: Corvina, 1994. A collection of his short stories.

An Island of Sound. Hungarian Poetry and Fiction before and beyond the Iron Curtain. Introduction by George Szirtes. London: Harvill, 2004. A useful collection with much recent material and an informative introduction.

By the Danube: Selected Poems of Attila József. Budapest: Corvina, 2002. A bilingual edition of works by the great twentieth-century Budapest poet, translated by John Bátki.

Cushing, George F., *The Passionate Outsider: Studies on Hungarian Literature.* Budapest: Corvina, 2000. Selected essays by the late British doyen of Hungarian literary studies.

Czigány, Lóránt, *The Oxford History of Hungarian Literature.* Oxford: Oxford University Press, 1984. An excellent guide to a subject often regarded, due to language difficulties, as impenetrable to non-Hungarians.

Dalos, György, *The Circumcision.* Rose Bay, NSW: Brandl & Schlesinger, 1990. Set in Budapest in the post-1945 years, the novel portrays a slowly vanishing Jewish world through the eyes of a boy.

Esterházy, Péter, *The Glance of Countess Hahn-Hahn.* London: Weidenfeld & Nicolson, 1994. A trip down the Danube, which, according to the jacket, is "not quite a novel, not quite a travel book".

Fischer, Tibor, *Under the Frog.* London/New York: Picador, 2001. The improbable adventures of two Hungarian basketball players in the period 1945-56.

Foamy Sky: The Major Poems of Miklós Radnóti. Budapest: Corvina, 2000. A bilingual edition, selected and translated by Zsuzsanna Ozsváth and Frederick Turner.

Garrison, Paul, *Concrete Statues.* Budapest: Kassák, 2001. A story of two brothers set against the background of Budapest 1956.

Gömöri, George & Atlas, James (eds.), *Attila József: Selected Poems and Texts.* Cheadle Hulme: Carcanet Press, 1973. Translated by John Bátki.

Kaffka, Margit, *Colours and Years.* Budapest: Corvina, 1999. Originally published in 1912. Kaffka was one of the few prominent women in the *Nyugat* circle. An informative introduction by Charlotte Franklin gives an insight into Kaffka and her times.

Kabdebo, Thomas, *Attila József: "Can You Take on This Awesome Life?"* Budapest: Argumentum Kiadó, 1992. A first-rate biographical portrait of the renowned poet who emerged from the slums of Budapest.

Kertész, Imre, *Fatelessness.* London: Harvill, 2005. Currently Hungary's best-known "Holocaust" novel.

Klaniczay, Tibor (ed.), *A History of Hungarian Literature.* Budapest: Corvina, 1983.

Kosztolányi, Dezső, *Anna Édes*. London: Quartet, 1991. Set at the tail end of the 1919 Council Republic, revolves around the mistreatment of a servant girl. Translated and introduced by George Szirtes.

Krúdy, Gyula, *Sunflower*. Budapest: Corvina, 1997. Originally published in 1918, a novel about male-female relationships, partly set in turn-of-the-century Budapest.

Lengyel, József, *The Bridgebuilders*. Budapest: Corvina, 1979. A fictionalized documentary about the construction of Budapest's most famous bridge.

Madách, Imre, *The Tragedy of Man*. Budapest: Corvina, 1988. Hungary's most internationally famous drama. Translated by George Szirtes and with an introduction by George Cushing.

Makkai, Adam (ed.), *In Quest of the Miracle Stag: The Poetry of Hungary*. Chicago: Atlantic-Centaur, 1996. An extensive anthology in English translation, ranging from the thirteenth century to present times.

Marcus, Judith, *Georg Lukács and Thomas Mann. A Study in the Sociology of Literature*. Amherst, Mass: University of Massachusetts Press, 1987.

Molnár, Ferenc, *The Paul Street Boys*. Budapest: Corvina, 1994. First published in 1907, one of the most enduring of stories set in Budapest.

Móricz, Zsigmond, *Seven Pennies and Other Short Stories*. Budapest: Corvina, 1988. An easily digestible selection from a Hungarian master of realistic story-telling.

Nyiri, János, *Battlefields and Playgrounds*. London: Macmillan, 1989. The story of a Jewish boy growing up in Budapest during the Second World War.

Ozsváth, Zsuzsanna, *In the Footsteps of Orpheus: The Life and Times of Miklós Radnóti*. Bloomington, IN: Indiana University Press, 2000.

Phillips, Arthur, *Prague*. New York: Random House, 2002. Despite the title, this over-hyped novel is actually set in Budapest.

Pressburger, Giogio & Nicola, *Homage to the Eighth District: Tales from Budapest*. London: Readers International, 1990.

Suleiman, Susan R. & Forgács, Éva (eds.), *Contemporary Jewish Writing in Hungary*. Lincoln NE: University of Nebraska Press, 2003. An anthology of works from the post-Holocaust era. Includes poetry, short stories and extracts from memoirs and novels.

Szirtes, George, *The Budapest File*. Newcastle upon Tyne: Bloodaxe Books, 2000. A collection of his "Hungarian" poems.

Sárközi, Mátyás, *The Play's the Thing: The Life of Ferenc Molnár*. London, White Raven Press, 2004. Short biography of the author of *The Paul Street Boys*.

FURTHER BROWSING

The following are all in English or have English-language pages:
www.budapestinfo.hu
> Official website of the Tourism Office of Budapest.

www.festivalcity.hu
> Budapest's spring and autumn festivals, plus other cultural events throughout the year.

www.fono.hu
> Information about and events listings (folk/ethnic music) for the Fonó Budai Zeneház.

www.hung-art.hu
> Excellent guide to Hungarian painters and their works of art.

www.majazz.hu
> Website of the Hungarian Jazz Musicians' Association; includes events.

www.mupa.hu
> Details and programmes of Budapest's Palace of Arts.

www.museum.hu
> Not quite the comprehensive guide to museums it claims to be, but nevertheless very useful, giving information about over 100 museums in Budapest, with some details of temporary exhibitions.

www.opera.hu
> For the Opera House programme.

Index of Historical, Literary and Artistic Names

INDEX OF PLACES AND LANDMARKS